Ski Pointers by the Experts

SKI POINTERS
by the Experts

BY THE EDITORS OF *SKI LIFE* MAGAZINE

Illustrated

Harper & Brothers · New York

SKI POINTERS BY THE EXPERTS
*Copyright © 1958, 1959, 1960, 1961
by Universal Publishing and
Distributing Corporation.*

*Printed in the United States of America
All rights reserved.*

*No part of the book may be used or reproduced in any manner whatsoever without written permission except in the case of brief quotations embodied in critical articles and reviews. For information address
Harper & Brothers,
49 East 33rd Street, New York 16, N.Y.*

Library of Congress catalog card number: 61–10233

796.93
5628

CONTENTS

INTRODUCTION   ix

I. THE BASICS   1

    Step Turn   2
    Falling and Rising from a Fall   4
    Kick Turn   6
    Edging   8
    Fall Line   9
    Side Step   10
    Herringbone   12
    Diagonal Side Step   13
    Straight Running   14
    Snow Plow   15
    Snow-Plow Turn   16

  Ski Pointers on the Basics   18

    Important Basic Steps BY WALTER PRAGER   18
    Proper Downhill Position BY ALLEN C. WILLMAN   20
    Rising After a Fall BY ALLEN C. WILLMAN   22
    Improving the Snow Plow BY HANS GARGER   24
    Key to Snow-Plow Turns BY STUART A. ATWELL   26

  Basic Problems: Causes and Cures   28

    Snow Plow, Snow-Plow Turn   28

  Ski Life Extra: Quick Tips for Riding Lifts   32

II. INTERMEDIATE STEPS   37

    Traversing   38
    Weight Shifting   40
    Sideslipping   42
    Christie-into-the-Hill   44
    Snow-Plow Christie   46
    Stem Christie   48

v

Ski Pointers for Intermediates   50

      Traversing and Its Importance BY NEIL ROBINSON   50
      Weighting the Downhill Ski BY DON LARSH   52
      Edge Control BY DON POWERS   54
      Skiing Without Poles BY JOHN H. HENDERSON   56
      Short Cut to a Stem Christie BY WALTER PRAGER   58
      Turning Made Easier BY JOHN CHURCH   60
      When Unweighting Should Vary BY MERLIN BINGHAM   62
      Ski from the Hips Down BY DICK FINLAY   64
      Learning by Exaggeration BY DON POWERS   66
      Pole Action on Turns BY PHILIP S. MILLER   68
      Controlling Length of Turn BY JOHN WHEELER   70
      Strengthening Weak Side Turns BY BOB BOURDON   72
      Improving Balance BY BOB BECK   74
      Skating on Skis BY CLIFTON TAYLOR   76
      Breathe—and Ski Better BY JOHN CHURCH   78

Intermediate Problems: Causes and Cures   80

      Traverse, Sideslip, Uphill Christie, Stem Christie   80

Ski Life Extra: The Fine Art of Falling BY DOUG PFEIFFER   88

III.   ADVANCED TECHNIQUE   91

      Parallel Turn   92
      Hop Down the Fall Line   94
      Transition from Hop to Wedeln   94
      Wedeln   96

Ski Pointers on Advanced Technique   98

      Break the Stem Habit BY DON SCHWARTZ   98
      Use More Knee Action BY ROBERT W. CRAIG   100
      Practicing Knee Action BY PIERRE CHAUVIN   102
      Unweighting the Skis BY JOHN YONKOW   104
      Controlling Speed by Edge Set BY K. SMITH, JR.   106
      Learn to Bank Your Turns BY CLIFTON TAYLOR   108
      Exercise for Wedeln BY ALEX PETRIE   110
      Stem Approach to Wedeln BY WALTER BLAESI   112
      Parallel Approach to Wedeln BY LUTZ AYNEDTER   114

Tips on Schussing BY JOHN CHURCH   116
Exercise for "Off Days" BY K. SMITH, JR.   118

Advanced Technique Problems: Causes and Cures   120

Parallel Christie, Wedeln   120

Ski Life Extra: Emphasis on Poles BY WILLY SCHAEFFLER   124

IV. THE FINER POINTS OF SKIING   127

Variety Is the Spice of Skiing BY ERNIE MC CULLOCH   128

Ski Pointers for Refining Your Technique   134

Using Two Techniques in One Turn
    BY FRED LONSDORF   134
Jumping and Pre-Jumping BY LUTZ AYNEDTER   136
"Bunny Hop" off Bumps BY JIM SNOBBLE   138
Gazelle Turn BY MAX GOOD   140
Royal Christie BY JACK MOREHEAD   142

Ski Life Extra: The Secret of Championship Form
    BY CHARLES BOZON   144

V. TEACHING CHILDREN TO SKI   147

Ski Pointers for Teaching Children   148

Advice to Skiing Parents BY PAULA VALAR   148
Teaching Children BY MARTHA MILLER   150

Ski Life Extra: Pablum in My Rucksack
    BY MERRILL POLLACK   152

VI. DIFFICULT SNOW CONDITIONS AND TERRAIN   159

How to Ski Ice and Like It BY JIMMY JOHNSTON   160
The Key to Skiing Deep Powder BY SIGI ENGL   165
Skiing in Heavy Spring Snow BY ALF ENGEN   170
Don't Let Moguls Throw You BY OLAF RODEGARD   174

Ski Pointers on Difficult Conditions and Terrain   175

Battle of the Boiler Plate BY NEIL ROBINSON   176
Skiing Deep Powder BY ED LYNCH   178
Skiing in Flat Light BY MANFRED PARKER   180
Planning Your Run BY JERRY WESSLEN   182
Adapt Technique to Conditions BY TOM HALL   184

       Handling Spring Conditions BY RICK SHAMBROOM   186
       Downhill Running on Rutted Tracks BY LEE QUINN   188
       Traversing Moguls BY DUNCAN GRANDIN   190
       Picking Your Turns on Moguls BY JACQUES LEGRAS   192
       Hopping Moguls BY PAUL BROWN   194

VII. CHOOSING PROPER EQUIPMENT   197

       How to Select Boots   198
       How to Select Skis   201
       How to Select Bindings   204
       How to Select Poles   205

Ski Pointers on Equipment   206

       Proper Way to Lace Boots BY NEIL JACOBS   206
       Proper Care of Boots BY JOHN H. HENDERSON   208
       Ski Care between Trips BY HANS GARGER   209
       Sharpening Edges BY BOB BOURDON   210
       Conditioning Skis to Temperature BY WALT HAEFLI   212
       Applying the Proper Wax BY OTTO OST   213
       Where to Mount Bindings BY ERNIE MC CULLOCH   215
       Proper Weight of Poles BY BOB BOURDON   216
       Strengthening Ski Poles BY GRAHAM WHITE   218
       Repairing Broken Poles BY JERRY MIKACICH   220
       Quick Tips for Comfort BY GEORGE BURGESS   222
       How to Keep Goggles from Fogging
           BY ADDISON AUGUSTA   223

Ski Life Extra: Getting Your Equipment in Shape
           BY BILL BECK   224

VIII. PRE-SEASON CONDITIONING   229

       Coach Yourself into Shape BY TAP GOODENOUGH   230

Ski Pointers on Conditioning   236

       Warm-up Exercises BY RUDY KUERSTEINER   236
       First Run of the Day BY RICK SHAMBROOM   238

Ski Life Extra: Confessions of an October Backslider
           BY MERRILL POLLACK   240

GLOSSARY OF SKIING TERMS   249

INTRODUCTION

No one can really put his finger on the exact number of people who ski in this country although a figure as high as five million has been used. This may surprise some, but the fact is that it has become a cliché to say that skiing has "boomed" since the end of the Second World War.

It is not a sport that one can usually perform without a great amount of effort expended in getting to where one can practice it, yet the ski industry ranks with golf in sales of equipment, clothing, and allied accessories. More and more people are skiing; areas are mushrooming at the rate of at least a dozen a year.

This brings us to the question of why so many have taken up the sport. There are varied answers which have to do with leisure time, more money to spend, the atavistic desire, perhaps, to fling one's radiator-bound self against nature. A six-year-old of our acquaintance says she likes to ski "because it's slippery." Another youngster, veteran Otto Schniebs, calls skiing "a way of life."

The average person who skis, when pressed, might say he is in constant pursuit of an ideal—that blinding flash of accomplishment which comes on a crystal-like day when the sun, unburdened by clouds, hangs high over the mountains. The snow is superb and the skier knows that everything is right and the whole world is on his side. This, in the end, is what skiing is all about.

Golfers, among other sporting types, have such moments of glory. Skiers, in their own way, are as driven as golfers, constantly seeking perfection of form. In the case of the skier, the ultimate is grace and control under all terrain and snow conditions.

Perfection being what it is, the person who skis for recreation may achieve it occasionally, or may never achieve it. But he doesn't stop trying. He is always eager to find out from those who can perform the sport without blemish how to handle himself as well as they do.

And that is what this book attempts. More than sixty experts have given the readers of *Ski Life* (now combined with *Ski Magazine*) during the past few years the benefit of what would probably add up to a century of teaching. In this book their experience is pooled to give the skier tips to help him ski better than he is skiing now.

The careful reader may find contradictions. This is explainable; *Ski Pointers by the Experts* is not intended as a syllabus for step-by-step learning, but as an adjunct to that best of all methods for learning how to ski—instruction by a certified professional. While the end result is the same (that ultimate ideal of formful control), and the basic system for achieving it may be the same, every pro has certain unique tricks that he imparts to his pupils. Years of experimentation have taught him that they work. Here, for the first time, they have been compiled by learning stages. Within one set of covers, they are finally available to the person who skis for fun, for challenge, or because he is a follower of the Schniebs dictum.

New York City, 1961

THE EDITORS

Ski Pointers by the Experts

I. *The Basics*

Like a child, who must learn to walk properly before he can run, a skier must learn the basic steps well before he can become a dazzling technician of this highly complex sport. Walking, edging, climbing, downhill running, braking, and turning—get these fundamentals right in the beginning and advancement will come as a matter of course.

Step Turn

The step turn gives you a complete change of direction without moving away from the spot. Practice it on packed snow on flat terrain.

With the poles lifted off the snow, raise the tip of one ski off the ground and move the raised tip away from the other ski, keeping its tail in the snow.

Set the tip down and shift your weight to the ski you've just moved.

Raise the tip of the other ski and move it toward the first ski. Set the ski down and shift your weight onto it. Repeat this several times to face in the opposite direction.

Falling and Rising from a Fall

If a fall is inevitable, fall backward and to one side, using one hip as a shock absorber. Keep the knees as close together as possible.

Start to get up immediately after a fall. Swing the skis horizontally across the slope below the body. Draw the feet up close to the hips.

Use both poles together as one pole, one hand on the baskets and the other on the handles. Thrust them into the snow near the hips.

Push down hard on the poles, pushing yourself up onto your feet.

Kick Turn

The kick turn is a method of changing direction quickly while remaining in the same spot. Practice standing with your weight on one ski, swinging the unweighted ski forward and backward like a pendulum. When swinging the ski forward, lift the tip of the ski as high as possible off the snow.

Place right pole forward, left pole to the rear, both poles close to the skis. Now swing the left ski forward and upward, resting the tail on the snow close to the other ski.

Keeping its tail on the snow, swing the tip of the left ski around and down, parallel to the right ski, but pointing in the opposite direction.

Shift your weight to the left ski.

Lift the right ski around and set it down parallel to the left ski. Pole follows.

Edging

Edging prevents skis from sideslipping down the hill.

Transfer most of your weight to the uphill edges of the skis with an uphill roll of the ankles. The uphill edges will cut into the snow, pushing against it so you cannot slip sideways down the hill.

Fall Line

The fall line is the line of least resistance down the hill. From wherever you are on the slope there is a fall line, and you should learn to know where it is automatically. You will want to use it whenever you ski, taking advantage of its descent to gain speed and its ascent to check speed.

Skiing down the fall line (indicated by dotted lines) to gain speed.

Skiing across the fall line (dotted lines) to check speed.

Side Step

The side step is the easiest way for beginners to climb a slope. It is also the most efficient way for all skiers to climb a narrow, rather steep trail. Side-step up the fall line—in other words—with skis horizontal to the slope or perpendicular to the fall line.

Place skis horizontally across the slope, slightly edged on soft snow (as shown), well-edged on hard-packed snow, with feet close together.

Step uphill with the uphill ski, edging it into the snow. Uphill pole moves up with the uphill ski.

Shifting your weight to the uphill ski, bring the downhill ski up close to it. Downhill pole moves up with the downhill ski.

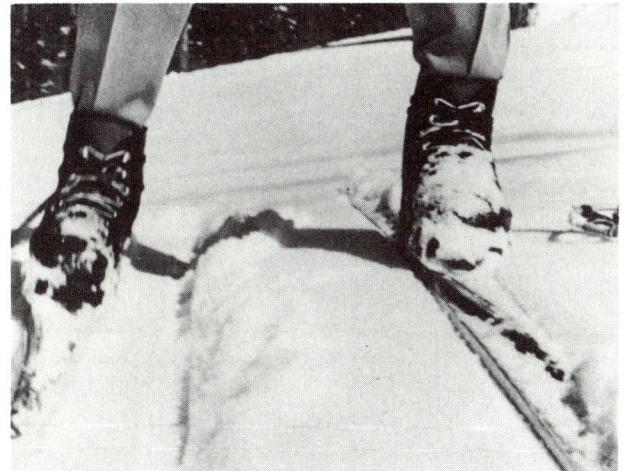
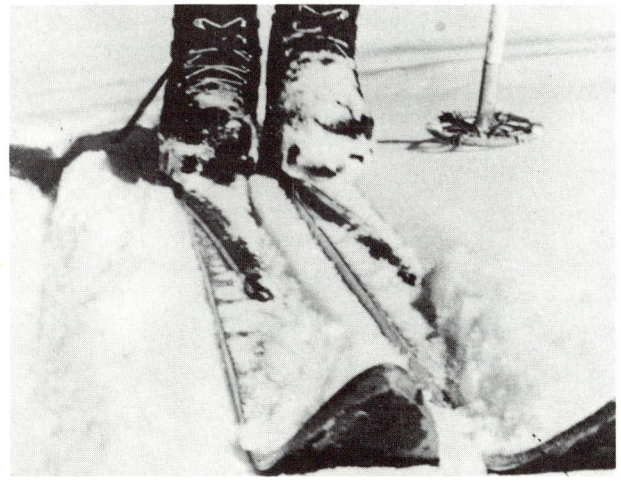

Herringbone

The herringbone is an efficient way to climb a short, direct ascent. Practice it first on flat ground, then on a steeper slope. On steep slopes, place your hands over the tops of your pole grips so that you will have better support.

With skis in a V, edge inside edges. Lift right ski forward, keeping its tip pointing outward, and edge it into the snow. Move left pole forward, while pushing yourself forward with right pole.

Shift your weight to the right ski. Repeat the procedure, moving the left ski and the right pole forward in the same manner while pushing yourself forward with the left pole.

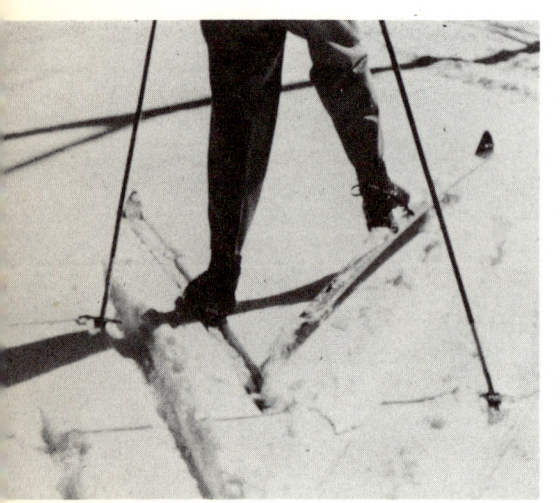 

Diagonal Side Step

The diagonal side step is an efficient way to climb an open slope or a wide trail. It combines the walking step with the side step. Since each step will take you upward and forward, you will be climbing up and across the slope.

From a position with skis horizontally across the slope, move uphill ski simultaneously forward and upward, edging it well into the snow.

Uphill or downhill poles are used with opposite skis, except on steeper slopes where the uphill pole is used with the uphill ski.

Shifting your weight to the uphill ski, bring the downhill ski up close to and slightly ahead of the uphill ski. Now shift your weight to the well-edged downhill ski, bringing the uphill ski forward and up again.

Straight Running

A supple, relaxed body is the first requisite of straight downhill running. Keep your body centered over both skis at all times. Practice on gentle slopes and ski straight down the fall line.

Skis are parallel, one ski slightly advanced. Knees are slightly bent, your weight somewhat forward on the balls of the feet. Arms are curved as shown. Hands are forward and low. Points of poles are safely to the rear.

Now practice some knee action—raising and lowering the body by flexing your knees as you ski. Knee action helps maintain balance over uneven terrain.

Snow Plow

The snow plow is a safe, easy braking maneuver. It will let you stop or check your speed at will when skiing down a slope or trail of any considerable length. To increase the braking effect, or to stop completely, increase the angle of snow plow and increase edging.

Tails of the skis are apart. Ankles are directly above the inside edges of the skis. Weight is on the balls of the feet and distributed equally on both skis. Knees and ankles are slightly bent. Hands are forward and low. Points of poles are to the rear.

Snow-plow exercise—start down the slope in the straight running position. Snow plow by lowering the body and pushing the tails of your skis apart into the snow-plow position. Be sure to edge the skis. Return to the straight running position. Repeat this exercise several times during the same run down the slope.

Snow-Plow Turn

The snow-plow turn enables you to change direction while moving on your skis. To link snow-plow turns, start to turn in the opposite direction as soon as the first turn is completed by shifting your weight to the outside ski. Continue to shift your weight at the end of each turn to begin the next turn.

Start with a snow plow directly down the fall line. Keep your body centered over your skis, with knees equally bent, weight evenly distributed on both skis.

Shift your weight to the outside ski and begin the turn with a steering action of your foot and knee.

Keep your weight out over the outside ski as you make the turn.

As you reach your new direction, resume the same position as in the straight snow plow, with your body again centered over your skis.

SKI POINTERS ON THE BASICS

Important Basic Steps
by Walter Prager, Certified Instructor, USEASA

Invariably, my advice to beginners is to take lessons from a certified instructor. However, if this is impossible for you, start out on your own in the following manner: devote the entire first day to familiarizing yourself with your skis. They are long, heavy, and not easily managed at first. It is most important to walk and climb until they begin to feel an integral part of you. To walk, from a standing position, slide your right foot forward and, at the same time, place your left ski pole in the snow halfway between binding and ski tip. Now repeat this same motion with the left ski and right pole. Relax and keep repeating, shifting weight from ski to ski. After a short distance, you will want to turn around. However, before you attempt to turn, it is wise to practice first this simple side-stepping exercise. Lift the right ski and pole simultaneously, place them to the side, approximately one foot from their original positions. Now bring your left ski and pole parallel to the right ski. Continue, moving to the right for a short distance, then side-step to the left and return to the starting point. *Turning around is accomplished by lifting tips of skis and pivoting around in a circle until the desired direction is reached.* Here again, ski and pole on the same side are moved simultaneously, tails stay together on the snow. All these exercises should be performed over and over again, before any attempt is made to ski downhill. They will strengthen muscles unaccustomed to skis and, while tedious and boring at first, will pay big dividends later on in relaxed and sure-footed skiing on more advanced runs.

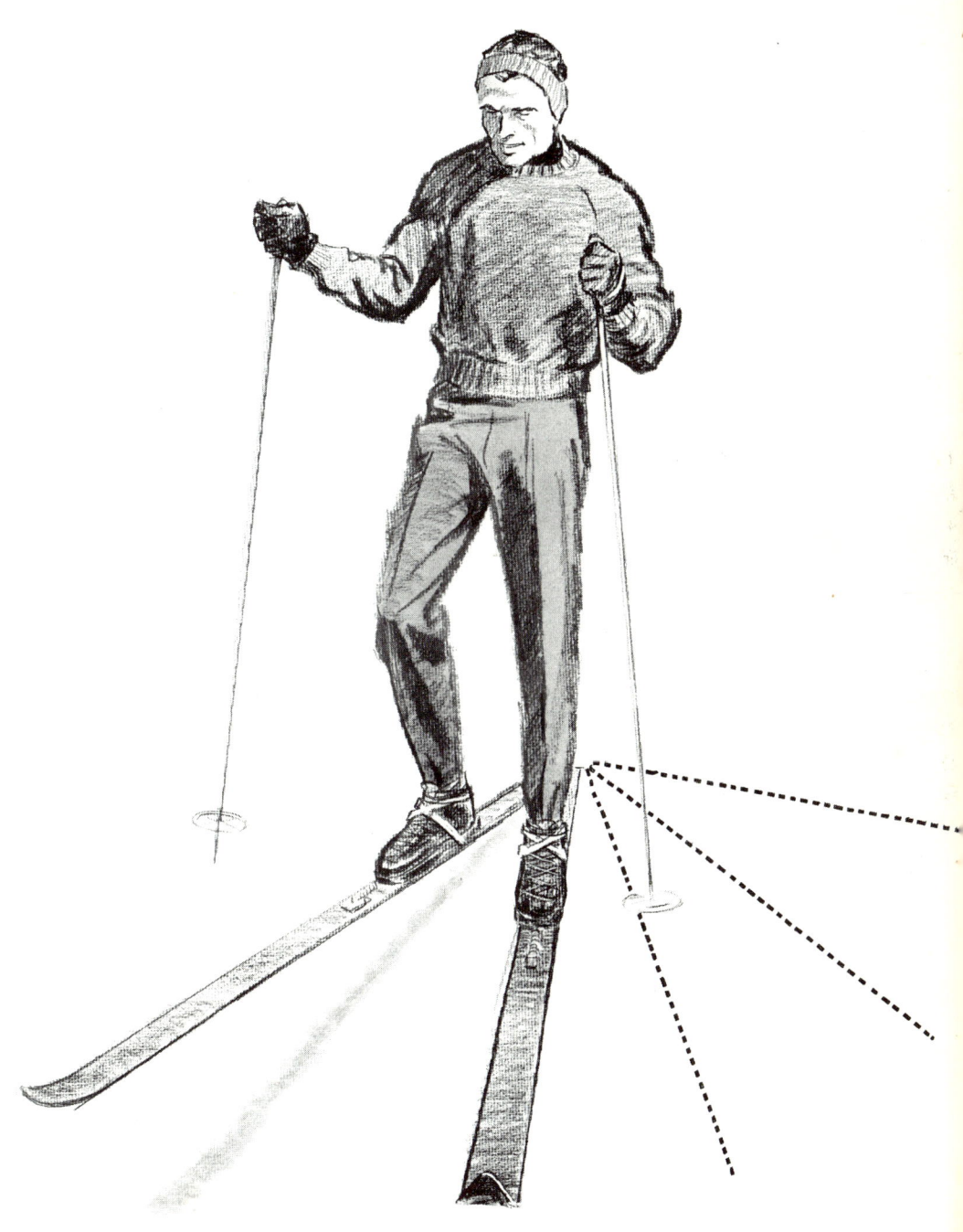

Proper Downhill Position

by Allen C. Willman, Director, Mont du Lac Ski School, Duluth, Minn.

The downhill running position is one of the most important phases of skiing for both beginner and expert. To assume the proper position, stand naturally and relaxed over your skis, feet about one or two inches apart. Now shift one ski forward about five or six inches, and place your weight evenly on the balls of both feet. Bend your knees until they are in a line with, and over, your toes. Bring your shoulders forward until they too are in line with both knees and toes. (*If you were to put a ski pole in the snow directly in front of you, it should touch your toes, knees and shoulders all at the same time.*)

Keep your back straight and your derrière in. Your head and eyes should look forward, not at your skis. Let your arms hang naturally from shoulder to elbow (in a relaxed position, not tight against your body). Place your hands in front of you at waist level, and hold your ski poles so they form a V in back of you. Now flex your knees up and down a few times and, as you flex them, try to keep your derrière in and your weight evenly distributed on the balls of both feet.

Practice this position on the flat first, then on a gentle slope with a good runout. Be sure to bend forward from the ankles, not the waist, so that your body will be perpendicular to the slope. The steeper the slope, the more you will lean forward. Make sure you are in the proper position, then let your skis begin to slide downhill.

Rising After a Fall

by Allen C. Willman, Director, Mont du Lac Ski School, Duluth, Minn.

Many skiers, and not just beginners, don't know how to get up properly after a fall. Here is the easy, quick way.

After a fall, first check to see that you are all in one piece, then check to see if any part of you or your equipment is stuck in the snow. Now roll over on your back with your feet in the air. Get your skis parallel, close together, and pointing in the same direction. Now roll over on your side, so that your head is uphill, and swing your skis downhill. Make sure that the skis are at right angles to the hill, even pointed just slightly uphill. Draw your feet and skis as close to your body as possible, with knees bent to the maximum. *When drawing up your feet, make sure they are drawn up under your seat, not in front or behind.* If your feet are too far forward or behind, your skis will shoot out from under you as you attempt to rise.

Once the skis are properly drawn up under your seat, remove the wrist straps of both poles from your wrists. Place both poles together and grasp them near the hand grip with your downhill hand (the hand that is farthest from the snow). Place your other hand near the baskets of the poles and plant the poles in the snow on a line with your head and fairly close to you on the uphill side. *Now push down hard on the poles, pushing yourself up and away from the hill.* If you are pushing and not pulling, it should require very little effort to get up on your skis again.

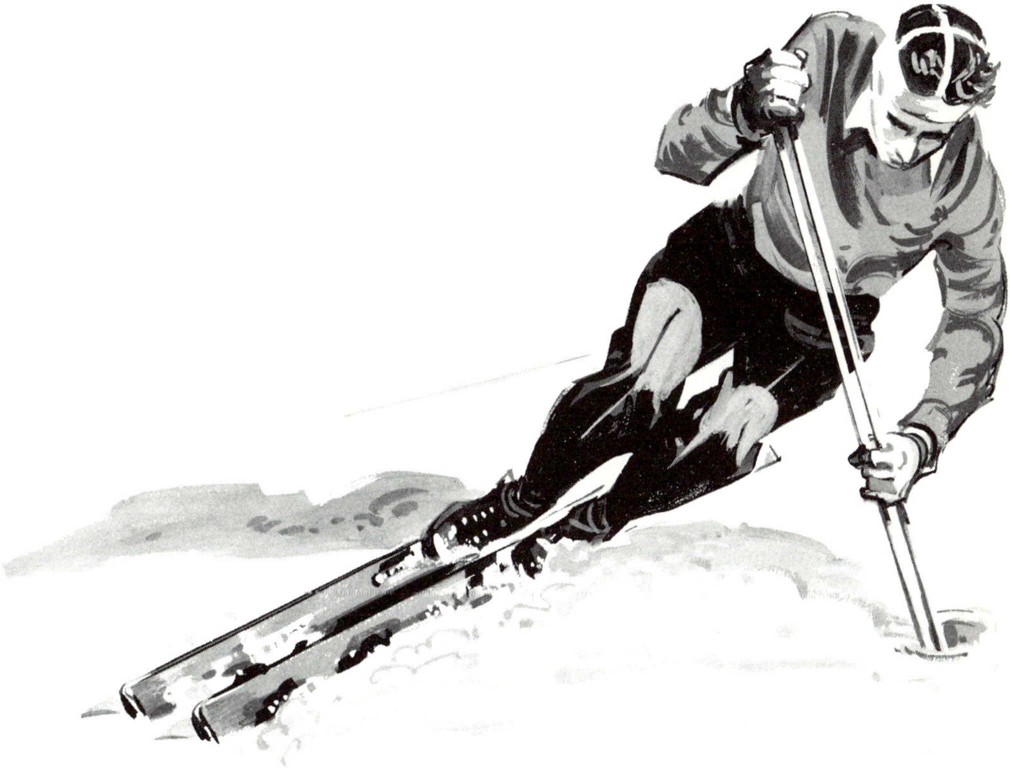

Improving the Snow Plow

by Hans Garger, Certified Instructor, SRMSA, Loveland Basin Ski School, Georgetown, Colo.

Two frequently made mistakes when learning the snow plow are raising the hands and poles skyward (as if to seek help from above!) and trying to control speed or to stop by poking around with the poles in front of the ski tips. Actually, though your hands and poles must be in the proper position, they have nothing otherwise to do with the effectiveness of a snow plow.

In order to eliminate these panicky hand actions and to improve body position, try this temporary aid. When ready to take off in snow-plow position, twist both wrists slightly outward and *tuck your poles under your armpits, keeping your hands comfortably ahead of your body. Then, upon taking off and gaining proper momentum, rather than staying in a locked or frozen position, start a smooth down-up-down motion with your knees and ankles. Sink, lift and sink, applying short but firm and equal heel push onto both skis each time you sink down.* This will increase and decrease the width of the snow plow, thus giving you better control of edging, body position, and speed. At the end of each run, sink down, applying equal and firm heel push, and snow plow to a complete stop. As you apply heel thrust to each ski on the down motion, press your knees forward and slightly inward, making your edges work for you. As soon as you feel that you are able to maintain a good, controlled snow plow, move your hands and poles back to their original and proper position.

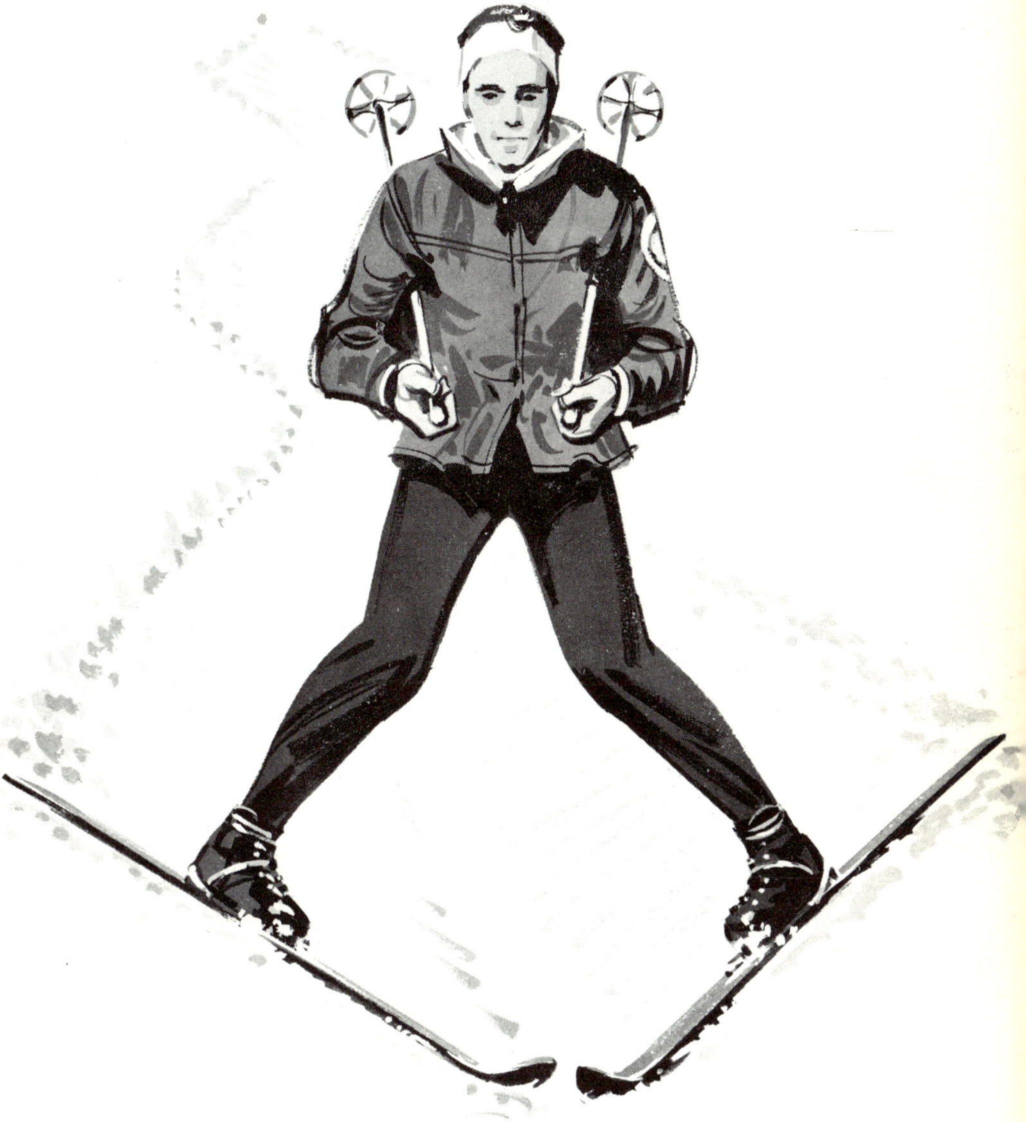

Key to Snow-Plow Turns

by Stuart A. Atwell, Certified Instructor, CUSSA, Dryden Ski School, Dryden, Mich.

Invariably, in the minds of beginners at the time they reach the snow-plow turning stage, there is much confusion as to which ski must be weighted in order to make the skis turn.

I find the easiest and quickest way to explain the snow-plow turn is to say that, with your skis in the snow-plow position, you should *press your weight down on the ski that is pointing in the direction you desire to turn.* The most effective way to press the weight down on this ski is to bend your knee. This will help to eliminate the stiff downhill knee tendencies that most beginners have.

This is not only the easiest way to describe a snow-plow turn, but it is also the easiest way for a beginner to remember the turn correctly.

Remember too that, once that downhill knee is properly bent, your weight should be centered directly over it, with the downhill shoulder, hip and knee in a line above the downhill boot.

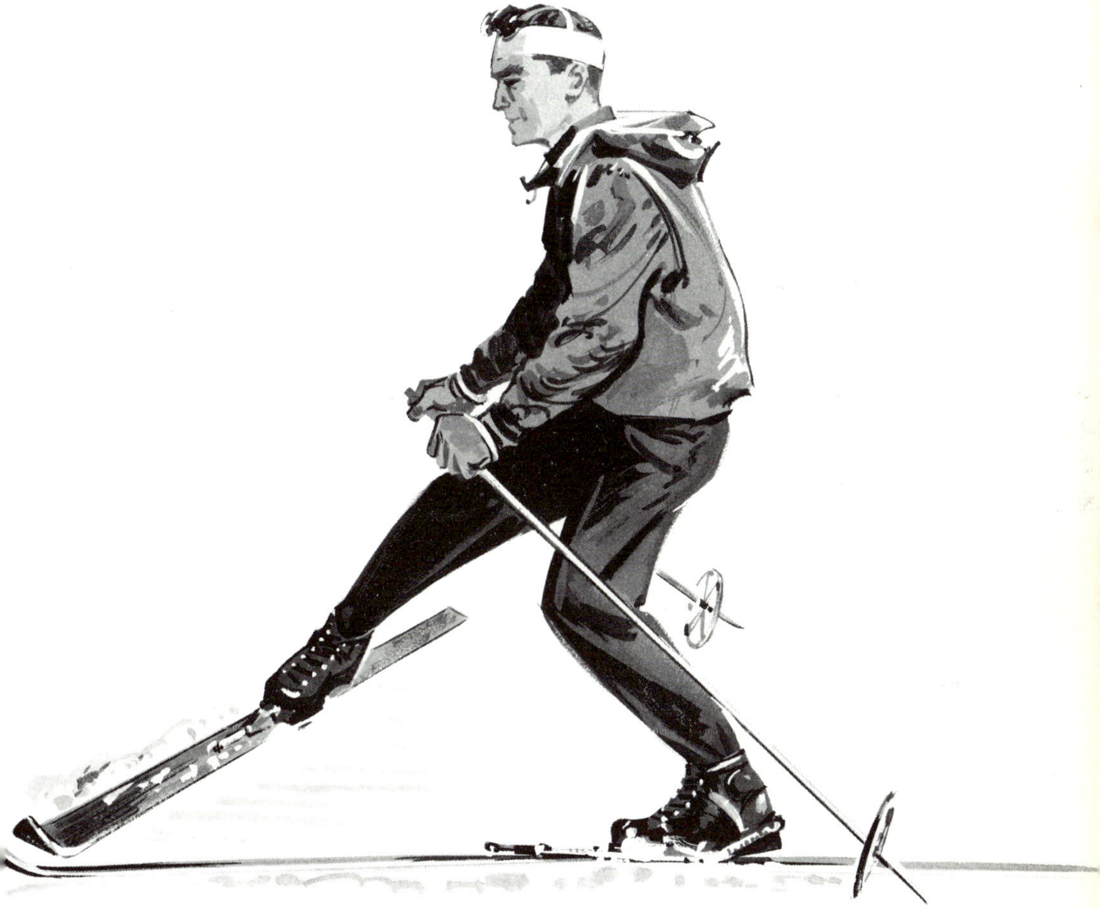

BASIC PROBLEMS: CAUSES AND CURES

Snow Plow

PROBLEMS	CAUSES	CURES
Too fast, can't slow down or stop	Insufficient edging	Press knees forward and in, roll ankles in
	Insufficient snow plow	Increase angle of snow plow
Skis wander or cross	Unequal edging	Press knees forward and in equally, roll ankles in equally
	Unequal weighting	Center weight squarely over each ski with equal knee bend
Skis separate, can't maintain snow plow	Improper weighting; sitting back, stiff knees or standing up	Center weight equally over each ski, bend knees and press forward and in. Push heels out, keep tips together
Inside edges catch	Overedging or knock-kneed position	Roll ankles out, press knees forward
Outside edges catch	Insufficient edging or bow-legged position	Press knees forward and in, roll ankles in
	Loose boots	Tighten, or have boots refitted by ski shop
Can't control edges	Stiff knees	Bounce to loosen up. Press knees forward and in
	Loose boots	Tighten, or have boots refitted by ski shop
Can't hold direction	Unequal weighting	Center weight equally over each ski with equal knee bend
	Rotation of upper body	Keep hips and shoulders facing in direction of snow plow
	Unequal edging	Press knees forward and in equally, roll ankles in equally

PROBLEMS	CAUSES	CURES
Forward fall	Extreme bending at waist	Straighten upper body, press knees forward
	Extreme forward lean	Keep weight on balls of feet
	Loose bindings	Have bindings adjusted by ski shop
Backward fall; skis slip forward	Standing up, stiff knees	Flex knees and press them forward
	Bending at waist	Straighten upper body, press knees forward
	Sitting back on skis	Flex knees and press them forward
Instability, poor balance	Standing up, stiff knees	Flex knees and press them forward
	Upper body or arms tense	Relax. Keep hands low

Snow-Plow Turn

PROBLEMS	CAUSES	CURES
Can't turn	Weight on inside ski	Line up outside knee, hip and shoulder over outside foot
		Press outside knee forward
	Outside ski overedged	Roll outside ankle out
	Stiff knees	Flex knees, press them forward
Can't start turn. (*See* "Can't turn," above)	Outside ski too flat	Roll outside ankle in
	Upper body leading turn	Keep hips and shoulders perpendicular to skis; don't rotate, but let waist break slightly
Uneven turn	Incomplete weight shift	(*See* cures for "Can't turn," above)
	Outside ski too far ahead	Inside ski is overedged. Flatten it and unweight it
	Overrotation	Keep hips and shoulders perpendicular to skis. Don't let hands lead turn
Can't complete turn	Faulty weight shift	Keep weight on outside ski. Press knee forward
	Stiff knees, standing up	Flex knees and press them forward
	Overrotation	Keep hips and shoulders perpendicular to skis. Don't let hands lead turn
Turn in wrong direction	Weight on wrong ski	Line up outside knee, hip, and shoulder over outside foot. Press outside knee forward
Skis cross or wander	Sitting back	Move weight forward, press knees forward
	Faulty or incomplete weight shift	Keep weight on outside ski. Press knee forward
	Overedging, faulty edging	Flatten skis by rolling ankles out
	Lead ski too far forward	Inside ski overedged—flatten it

PROBLEMS	CAUSES	CURES
One ski runs straight	Stiff knee	Flex knee and press it forward
	Ski overedged	Flatten ski by rolling ankle out
	Faulty weighting	Weight the outside ski (*see* above)
Inside edges catch	Skis overedged	Flatten skis by rolling ankles out
Downhill fall	Faulty edging	Roll both ankles in, toward each other. Don't roll outside ankle out
Uphill fall	Weight on wrong ski	Keep outside hip and shoulder directly over outside ski
	Sitting back	Press knees forward

SKI LIFE EXTRA

Quick Tips for Riding Lifts

HOW TO RIDE A ROPE TOW Slip the straps of both poles over the wrist of the outside hand. Side-step into tow line, placing both skis in tracks a few inches apart. Grasp rope gently with inside hand, letting it slip through fingers freely. When ready, gradually tighten grip until speed is attained. Keep knees flexed. For support, place outside hand behind back and grasp rope from underneath as shown.

HOW TO RIDE A T-BAR LIFT Hold poles in outside hand, away from bar. With partner, step into track, skis parallel and pointing uphill. Watch bar over inside shoulder and grasp it with inside hand, pulling it down gently and letting it catch against back of thighs. Don't sit on bar. Let it pull you up slope. While riding, lean against bar but don't sit. Keep knees flexed to absorb terrain variations and let skis run in track with inside ski next to partner's inside ski. Relax; avoid pushing against partner's ski.

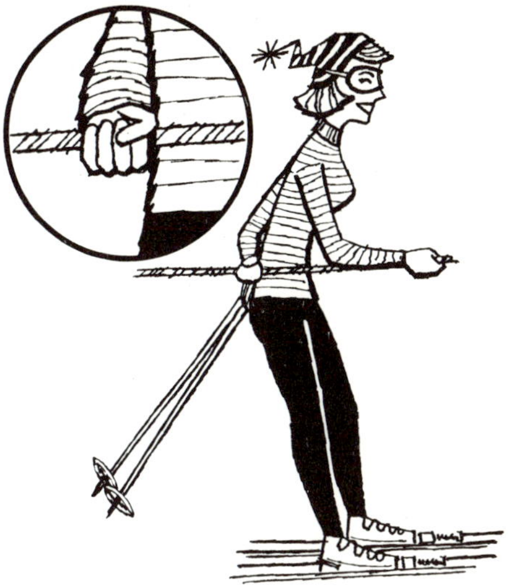

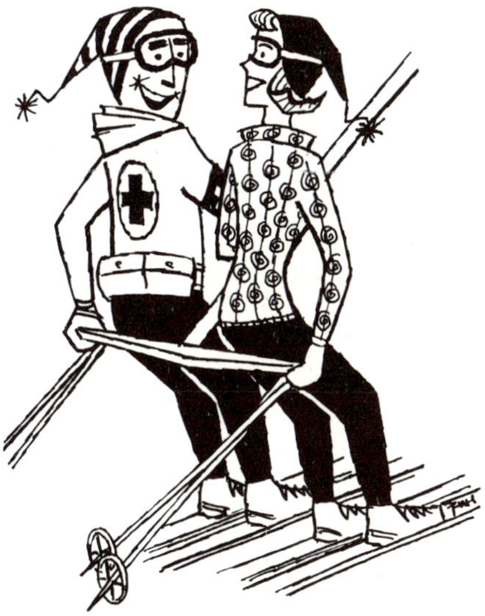

HOW TO RIDE A POMALIFT Hang both poles over one wrist. Step into lift track and place both skis parallel pointing uphill. When attendant offers bar, pull down on it and place it between your legs, letting the disc take hold from behind.

When ready, attendant will hook bar onto cable. A slight downward pull on bar with both hands will condition against initial jerks. Keep knees flexed and always avoid sitting on the disc. Let it pull you.

Once comfortably under way, bar can be held with one hand. Relax and, keeping knees flexed to absorb minor terrain changes, look ahead for bumps or hollows which may occur in path. Keep skis parallel.

HOW TO RIDE A CHAIRLIFT Loading double bar—step quickly into position indicated by markers or by the attendant. Hold poles in inside hand and watch for oncoming chair over outside shoulder. As chair approaches, grasp bar with outside hand and sit down gently.

Loading single bar—step quickly into indicated position as above. Hold poles in outside hand and watch for chair over inside shoulder. As chair approaches, grasp bar with inside hand, sit down gently as chair catches you behind knees.

II. *Intermediate Steps*

The transition from beginner to advanced skier is not merely a matter of one giant leap. Rather, it is a build-up of gradual steps starting with traversing and sideslipping for control, to a series of turns that begin and end with skis parallel. While the basis of the snow-plow turn was a steering action; in the faster christies, a skidding action is the important link with advanced skiing.

Traversing

Traversing is like straight running, except that you will be skiing down and *across* the slope, descending it diagonally. Uphill ski is always slightly advanced. Knees should be forward and locked together, pressed slightly toward the slope. Holding your downhill hip slightly back and into the hill will force your weight onto the downhill ski. It will also cause a natural lowering of the downhill shoulder. When traversing a steep hill, this position will give a faint reverse-shoulder look, as shown. However, when traversing gentle slopes, the shoulders should look more square to the skis.

Normal traverse position on a fairly steep slope. Notice the slight "reverse-shoulder" position.

Traverse position on a more gentle slope.

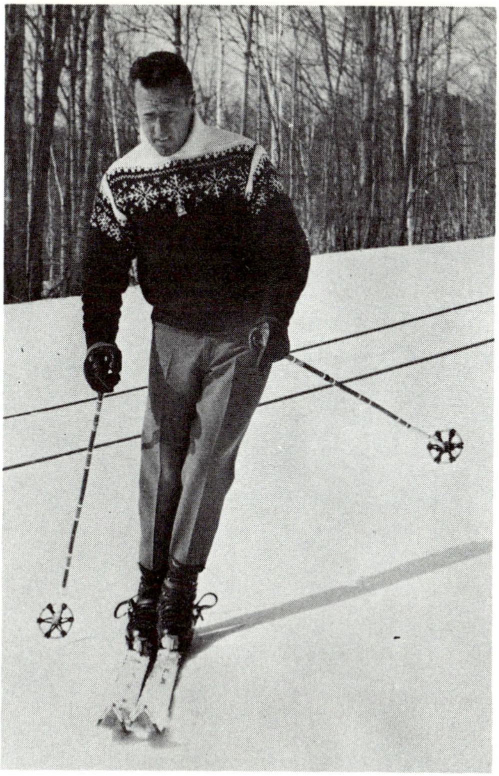

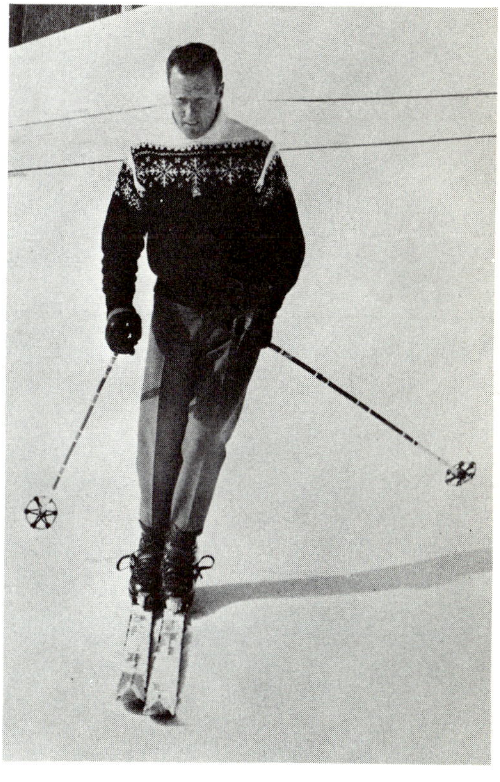

Weight Shifting

This exercise shows the transfer of weight from ski to ski. It should be done several times while traversing, then repeated while skiing down the fall line on a very gentle slope, alternating left and right skis.

Start in traverse position with your weight on downhill ski.

Lift your uphill ski and place it in semi-snow-plow position. Shift your weight to this uphill ski.

Now transfer your weight back to the downhill ski.

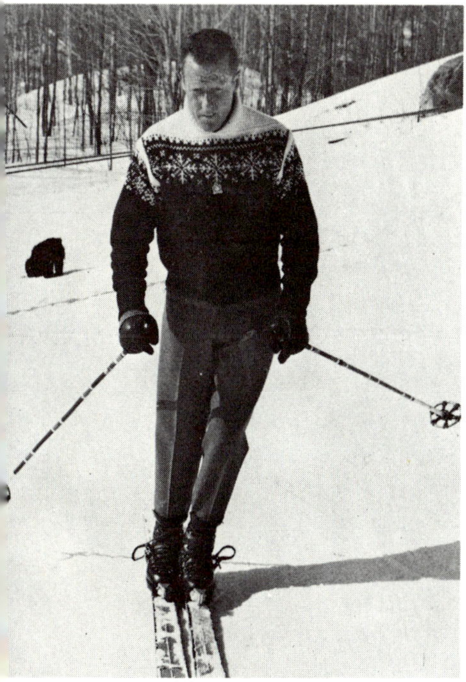

Sideslipping

Sideslipping is a link between slow speed, steered turns, and the faster turns such as stem christies and parallel christies. Before learning these faster turns, you must learn how to sideslip deliberately, controlling direction, speed, and duration of the sideslip.

To sideslip, release the edges of both skis by rolling the ankles and knees outward.

To bring the sideslip to a stop, the skis are edged into the hill by rolling the knees and ankles in toward the hill.

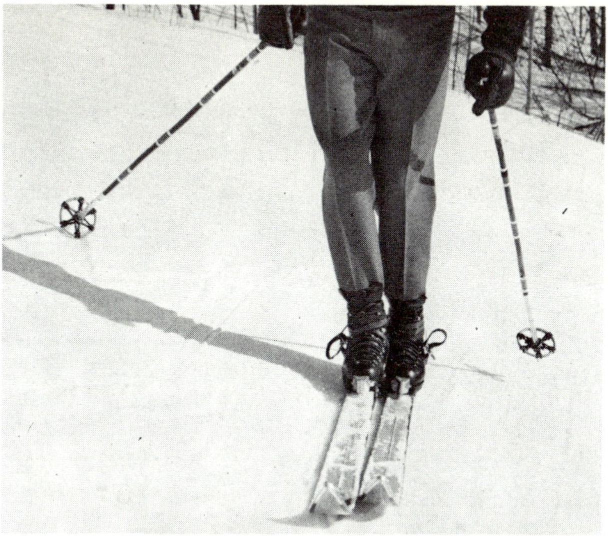

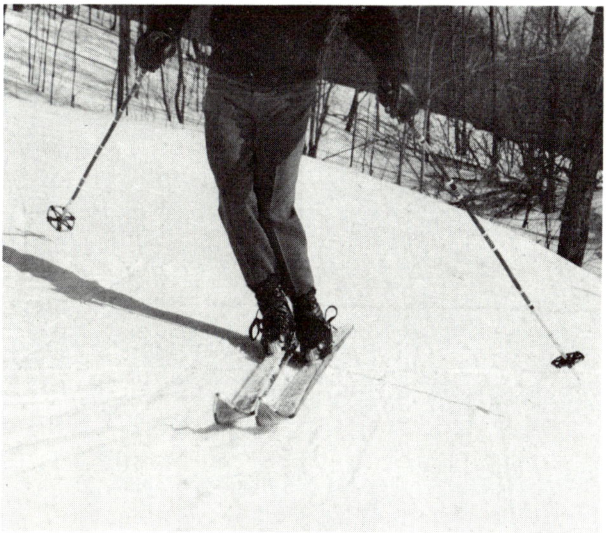

Christie-into-the-Hill

A christie-into-the-hill is a smooth, gradual turn which depends on smooth body co-ordination. It is important because it is, in fact, the last half of a christie turn.

Start in a traverse position.

Draw the uphill arm and pole forward, planting the pole in the snow. Simultaneously, lower your body from the knees and hips.

Now rise from the knees. At the same time, release the edges of your skis and let the skis begin to skid forward.

With a steering action of your knees and feet, the skis will begin to turn into the hill. Now a slight follow-through will bring your shoulders square to your skis.

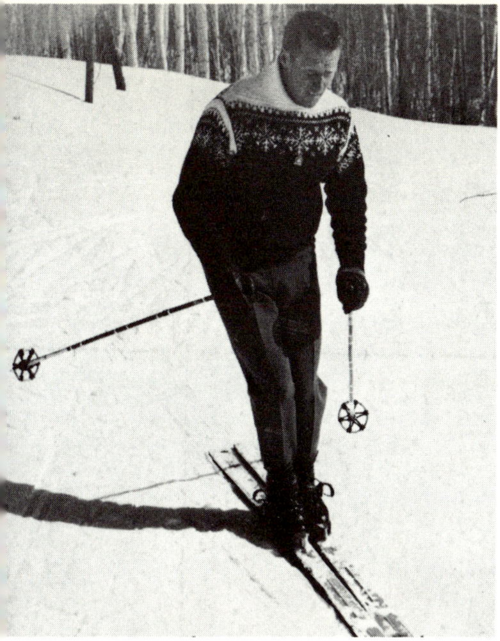
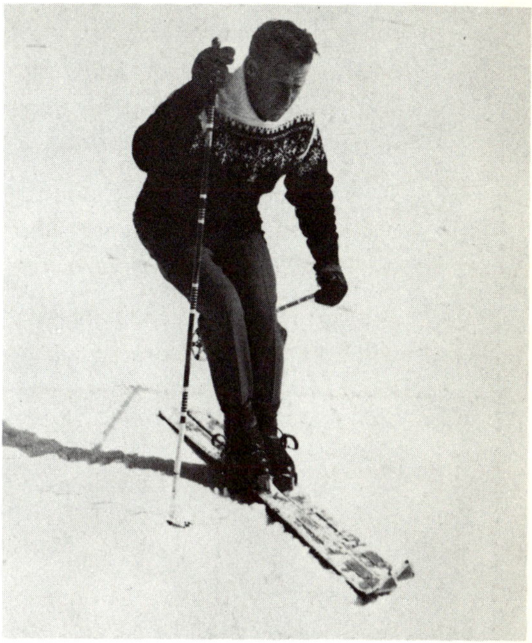
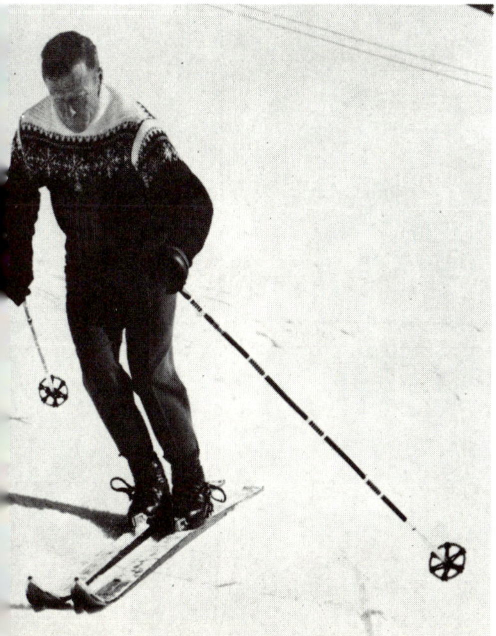
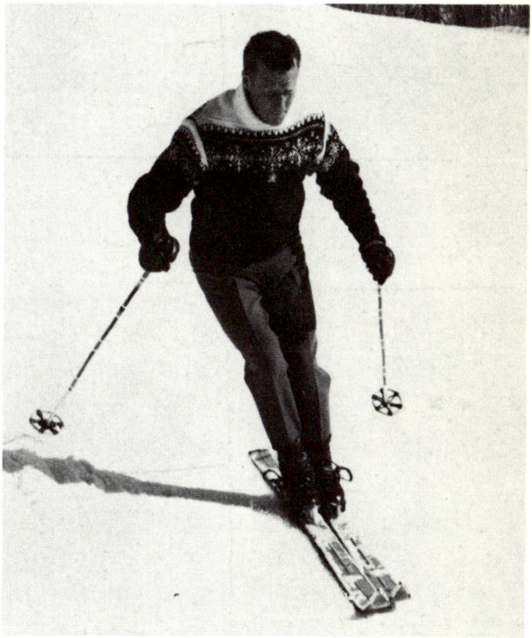

Snow-Plow Christie

Start in a straight running position.

Now assume a narrow snow plow, at the same time counterrotating with your inside arm and pole. Place the pole in the snow, close to the tip of the ski.

With a smooth, rising motion, transfer your weight to the outside ski, bringing the inside ski parallel to it. The lifting motion and transfer of weight will cause your skis to begin to skid.

Pressure on the outside ski, plus a steering action of the legs and feet, will start your skis turning.

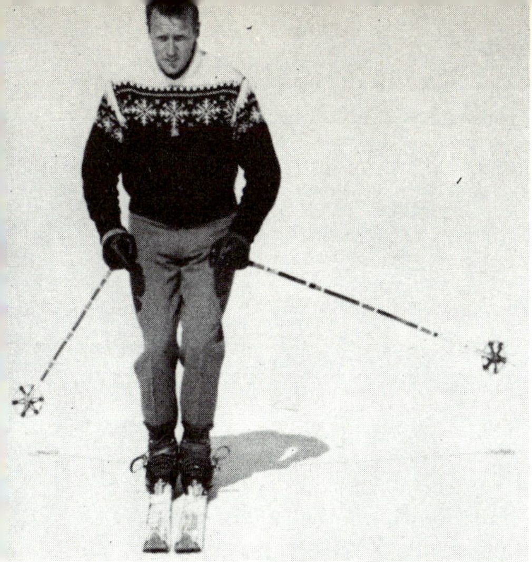

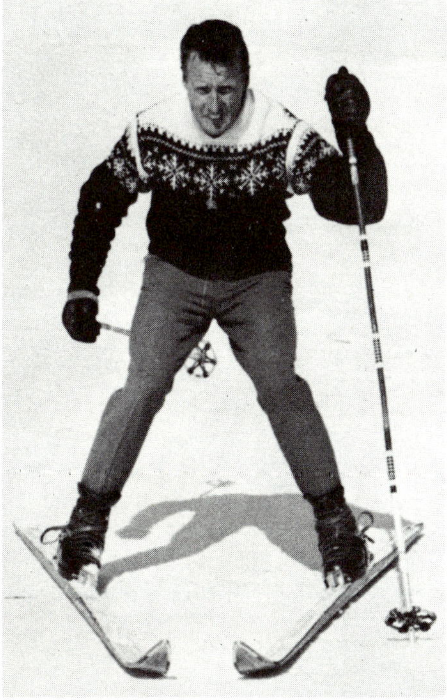

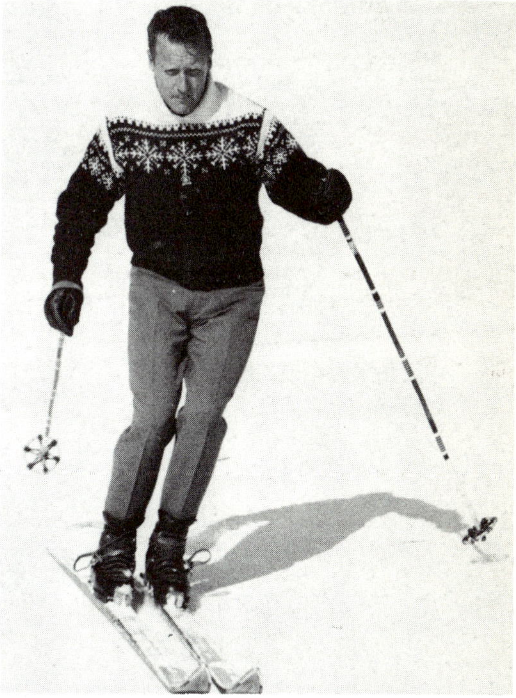

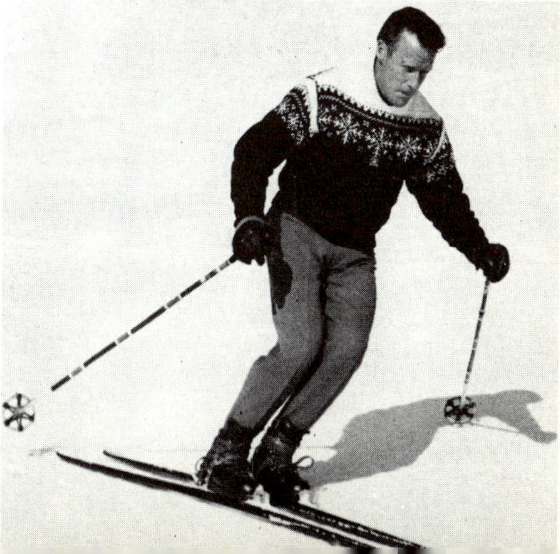

Stem Christie

Start out in a traverse position.

Stem the uphill ski (in this instance, the right ski) and, at the same time, begin a downward motion of your knees. As your left pole touches the snow, rise up from the knees and transfer your weight to the right ski.

By a steering action of your legs and feet, your skis will begin turning toward the fall line. Because the turn is initiated by the lower body, your upper body will have a faint reverse-shoulder look.

A slight follow-through will complete your turn. This follow-through of your upper body will bring your shoulders square to the skis.

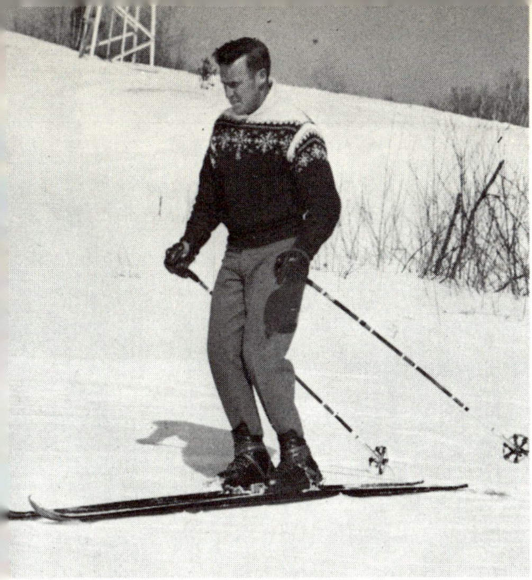
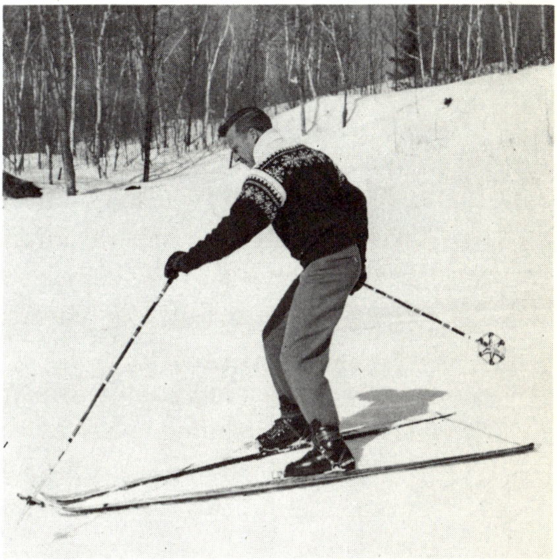
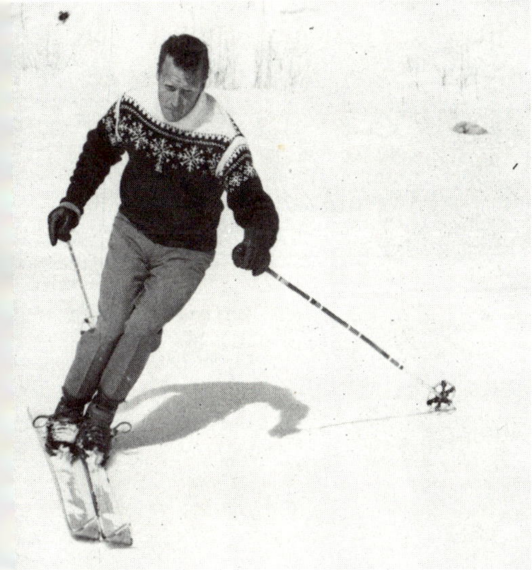
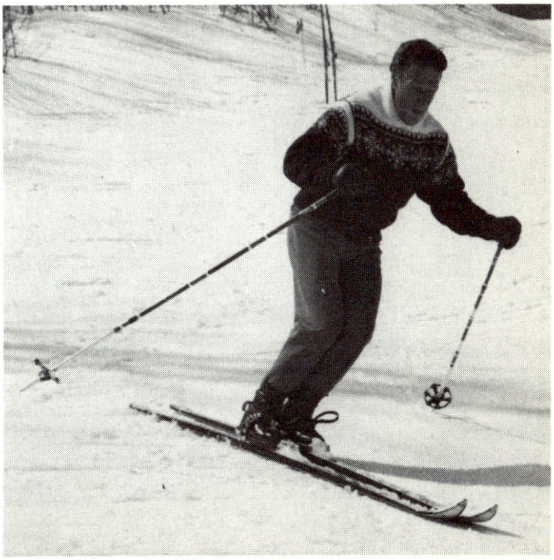

SKI POINTERS FOR INTERMEDIATES

Traversing and Its Importance
by Neil Robinson, Director, Bromley Ski School, Manchester, Vt.

The traverse running position is essential to skiing. There are times when icy conditions demand making long traverses between runs. Also, without the correct traverse position, it would be impossible to do a controlled sideslip (which is little more than releasing the edges of the skis). Finally, and most important, the traverse position is not only the beginning but also the completion of all parallel turns. Therefore it is necessary to perfect your traverse position in order to advance in your skiing ability.

To practice the proper position, start with your skis across the slope, knees bent, uphill ski, hip and shoulder slightly advanced. Hands are held relaxed at your sides, with the uphill hand slightly forward. Your weight should be on your downhill ski with knee and ankle flexed forward. This is of great importance. To have good edge control, the knees must be pressed in toward the slope slightly. *At the same time, by leaning your upper body slightly downhill, more weight will be forced onto the downhill ski.*

Now that you have the correct position, start your traverse. Choose a flat run rather than a steep crossing. Practice on a firm surface, where edging is necessary. The few hours you spend practicing the traverse running position will be more than rewarded by the satisfaction you will get out of controlled, confident skiing.

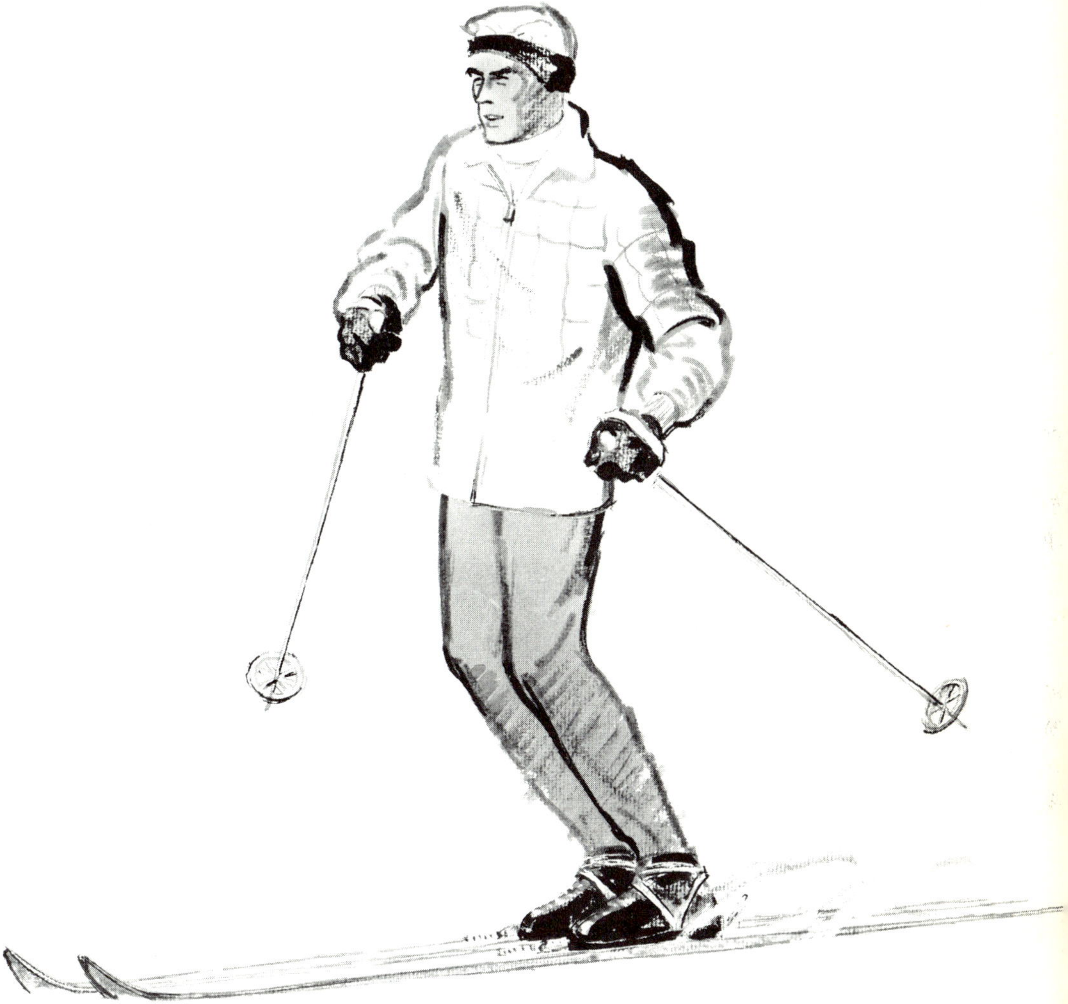

Weighting the Downhill Ski

by Don Larsh, Director, Ski Program, Climax, Colo.

The correct weighting of the downhill ski is the basis of all known techniques. It is also the answer to that age-old question: "How do I keep my skis parallel?" If there is no weight on the uphill ski, the ski can be placed anywhere.

Try this simple exercise. Traverse a gentle slope in snow-plow position, lifting your uphill ski. Repeat this maneuver in both directions, lifting the uphill ski each time. If you have not become too dependent on the uphill ski, this maneuver should be simple.

Now ski straight down a gentle slope, in a snow plow, shifting your weight from ski to ski and raising the unweighted ski. Try a snow-plow turn, raising your uphill ski at the bottom arc (or end) of the turn. Link snow-plow turns, raising your uphill ski at the bottom arc of each turn and keeping it raised until you start the next turn.

Once you have mastered the exercises above, go back to your original snow-plow traverse. *Snow plow across a gentle slope, raise your uphill ski and tuck it over close to your downhill ski.* Again, try the snow plow down the slope. Transfer your weight from ski to ski, lifting the unweighted ski each time and tucking it close to the weighted ski. Be sure to keep your unweighted (uphill) ski about four inches ahead of the weighted (downhill) ski. This will prevent your ski tips from crossing.

Now try two linked turns. Snow plow into the fall line, then transfer your weight to the downhill ski, raising and tucking your uphill ski close to the downhill one. Snow plow again into the fall line, and repeat the exercise. You'll quickly learn why expert skiers look as though they are skiing on only one ski. They are—on the downhill one!

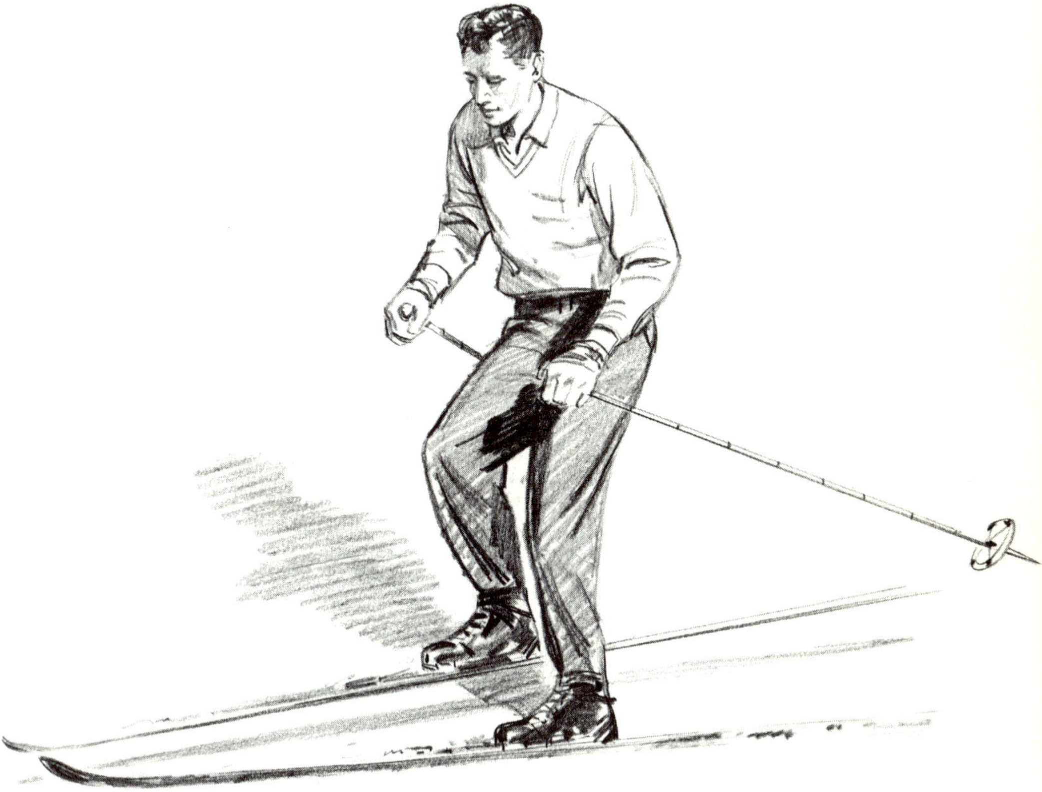

Edge Control

by Don Powers, Certified Instructor, USEASA, Whiteface Mountain Ski School, Wilmington, N.Y.

Edge control is one of the basic principles of skiing, and it is the one and only principle that controls your speed and direction. To be specific, edge control is the amount of sideways tilt or tip applied to a ski when you are sliding sideways. The amount of edge is determined by speed, terrain, and snow conditions. To control speed, you must vary the amount of edge—more to slow down, less to speed up. The slower you ski, the more critical edge control becomes. Terrain affects the amount of edge since the steeper the slope, the more edge you need to maintain a constant speed, up to a point of overedging. Snow conditions offer a slightly more complicated effect on edging, but basically, on a very hard surface, you need more edge than on a softer surface to maintain constant speed.

One of the best exercises I know for learning edge control was demonstrated to me by a past master at it, Othmar Schneider. He was making long swinging turns and, in each individual turn, there were what appeared to be a multitude of little wiggly turns. I thought he had a bad case of the shakes until he skied over and said, "That was a wedeln inside a wedeln." Actually, what he was doing was releasing and catching his edges continually throughout each long turn. *This exercise can be best practiced in a sideslip traverse by releasing and increasing your edges all the way through the traverse.* Start out with a moderate rhythm until you have the feel of the edges, then increase the rhythm. Once you get the feel of edge control, you will have a great deal more confidence in your skiing ability.

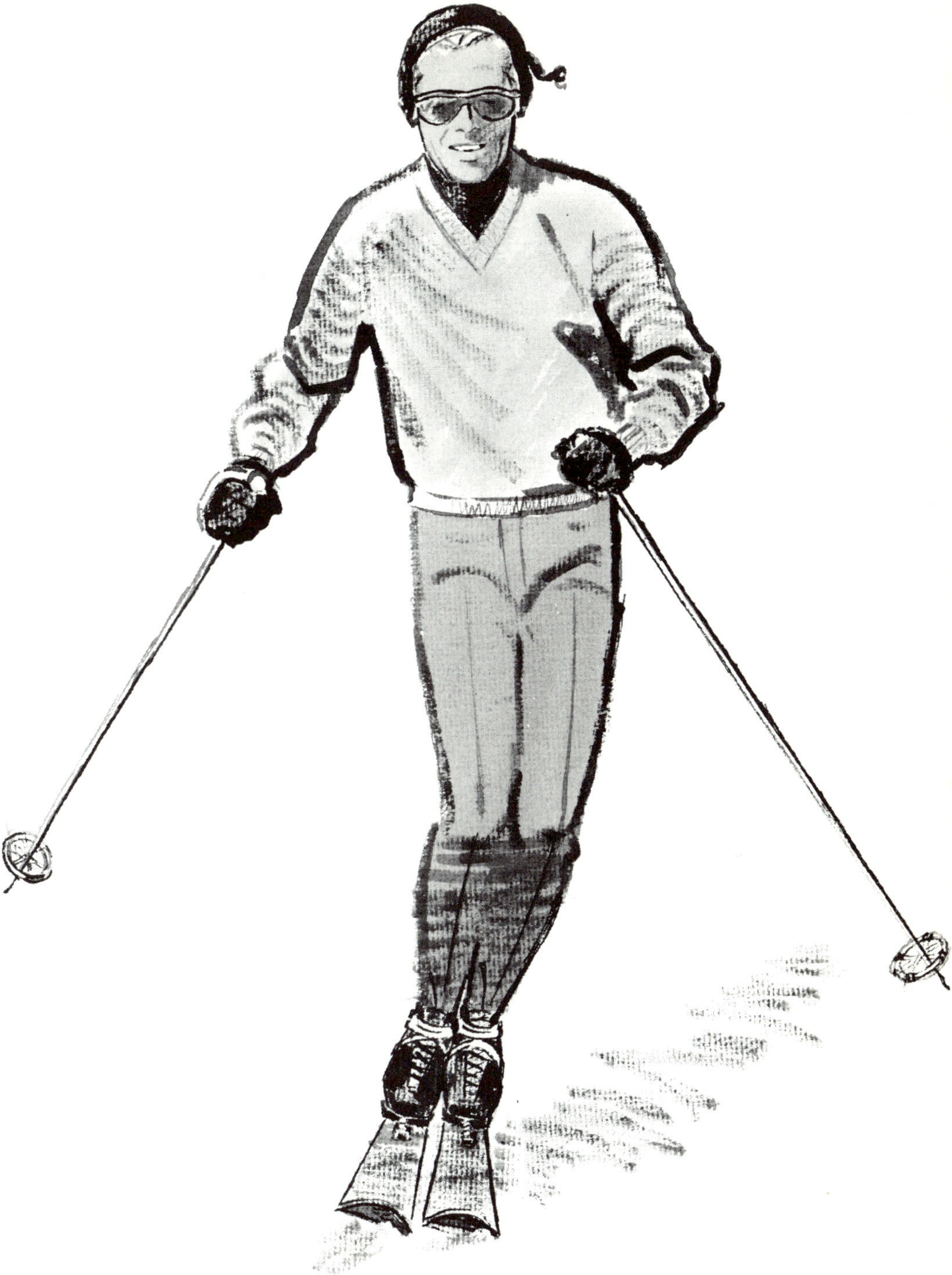

Skiing Without Poles

by John H. Henderson, Director, Jiminy Peak Ski School, Hancock, Mass.

Most novice and intermediate skiers tend to magnify the importance of their ski poles. They depend too much on poles for stopping, balancing, and actual support of body weight. Unfortunately, these instinctive reactions are sometimes dangerous and impede progress toward the development of a safe, enjoyable skiing technique.

There are several common faults in the use of ski poles which skiers can correct by themselves. For instance, the neophyte bravely attempts the herringbone climb by thrusting his feet uphill, arching his back, and leaning 90 per cent of his weight backward onto the poles.

The simple solution is to leave the ski poles at the bottom of the slope and practice climbing without them. I tell my pupils to get lazy when they climb. Use the law of gravity to advantage by "falling up the hill." Let the hands lead and the skis *follow after* the body. Use the poles only for balance in setting up a slow, steady climbing rhythm, not for support. This rule applies to any climbing maneuver as well as to walking on the level.

A more serious fault of many skiers is their attempt to slow down or to stop by thrusting the ski poles into the snow in front of the body. If a skier finds himself doing this, it would be much wiser to leave the poles at the bottom of the slope until some other method of stopping is learned.

The traverse running position is most important in any skiing technique. Yet many intermediates attempt to learn high-speed turns before they master this basic maneuver. The comfortable feel of ski poles dragging underhand for support is no help to the skier who should be striving for more forward lean in order to do his skid turns properly. *A few long traverses on a hard-packed slope can be very revealing—when done without poles.*

Likewise, confidence in a sideslip may not be acquired until it is practiced without poles. What skier can say he doesn't put an occasional "lean" on his uphill pole, when doing a sideslip? However, the skier who finds himself *depending* on that uphill pole for constant support should try the sideslip with ski poles tucked under his arms.

In general, depending too heavily on ski poles is not only dangerous for a beginner, but it can also hinder the skier later on, when he is striving for that first feeling of free flight in a well-done skid turn. One run a day without ski poles can give a good indication of what a skier should practice to improve his technique.

Short Cut to a Stem Christie

by Walter Prager, Certified Instructor, USEASA

When you are attempting to learn a stem christie, these simple pointers will aid you.

The faster you ski, the easier it will be to turn. For your first try, select a smooth practice slope with a good grade. Approach the spot of turning in a traverse position, relaxed with uphill ski slightly advanced and more weight on the downhill ski. Just before you start your turn, allow your ski tips to drift toward the fall line. Stem your uphill ski and plant your lower (downhill) pole in the snow near the tip of the downhill ski. *By reaching forward and planting the pole in the snow, you will automatically assume a counterrotation position.* Now, with the same motion (and you must not hesitate), push from your downhill pole, shifting your weight to the stemmed uphill ski. With a decided rotation of your body toward the new direction, the stemmed ski will be forced around, and, with the weight now on this ski, the new inside ski will easily slide over the snow to rest parallel to the stemmed ski. Thus you will finish the turn with skis parallel. Your pole, which you have removed from the snow as soon as your feet have passed around it, is now brought forward to its original position and you are ready to traverse in the opposite direction and repeat the same maneuver.

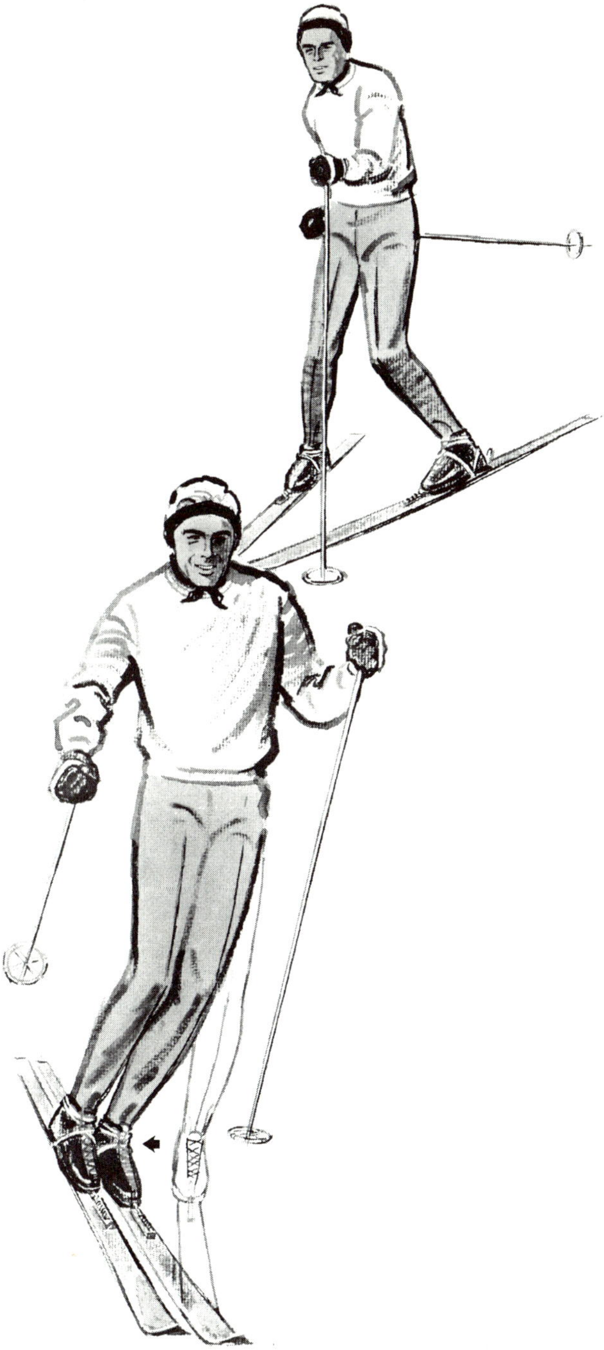

Turning Made Easier

by John Church, Certified Instructor, PNSIA, Mount Spokane Ski School, Spokane, Wash.

Skiers, talking about their lessons, have often commented that the "down-up-down" movement is most valuable to them in overcoming problems such as encountering moguls, shifting weight from one ski to the other, and developing rhythm.

"Down-up-down" simply involves sinking down by pressing the knees more forward just before a turn (when you are stemming or counter-rotating), rising as your skis hit the fall line, and sinking down again to follow through at the end of the turn. As you sink down before your turn (whether it be a snow-plow turn or a pure christie), you are getting yourself set for the up movement; then, when your body rises, the skis are unweighted and it is easy for you to change from the old direction across the fall line and into the new direction. Your final down movement is linked to the shift of weight onto your downhill ski and your follow-through of rotation to complete the turn.

"Down-up-down" is a rhythmical flowing movement, not a jump or a hop. It is particularly important that the "up" phase not be made so far in advance of the fall line that it causes a shift of weight onto the uphill ski. The "down-up-down" movement is helpful in shifting your weight as well as making it easier to turn your skis. It facilitates turns in heavy powder, over the edges of moguls, and on sticky snow. Linking turns, so that the "down" movement at the end of one turn is the preparatory movement for the next turn, gives you a smooth rhythm in skiing.

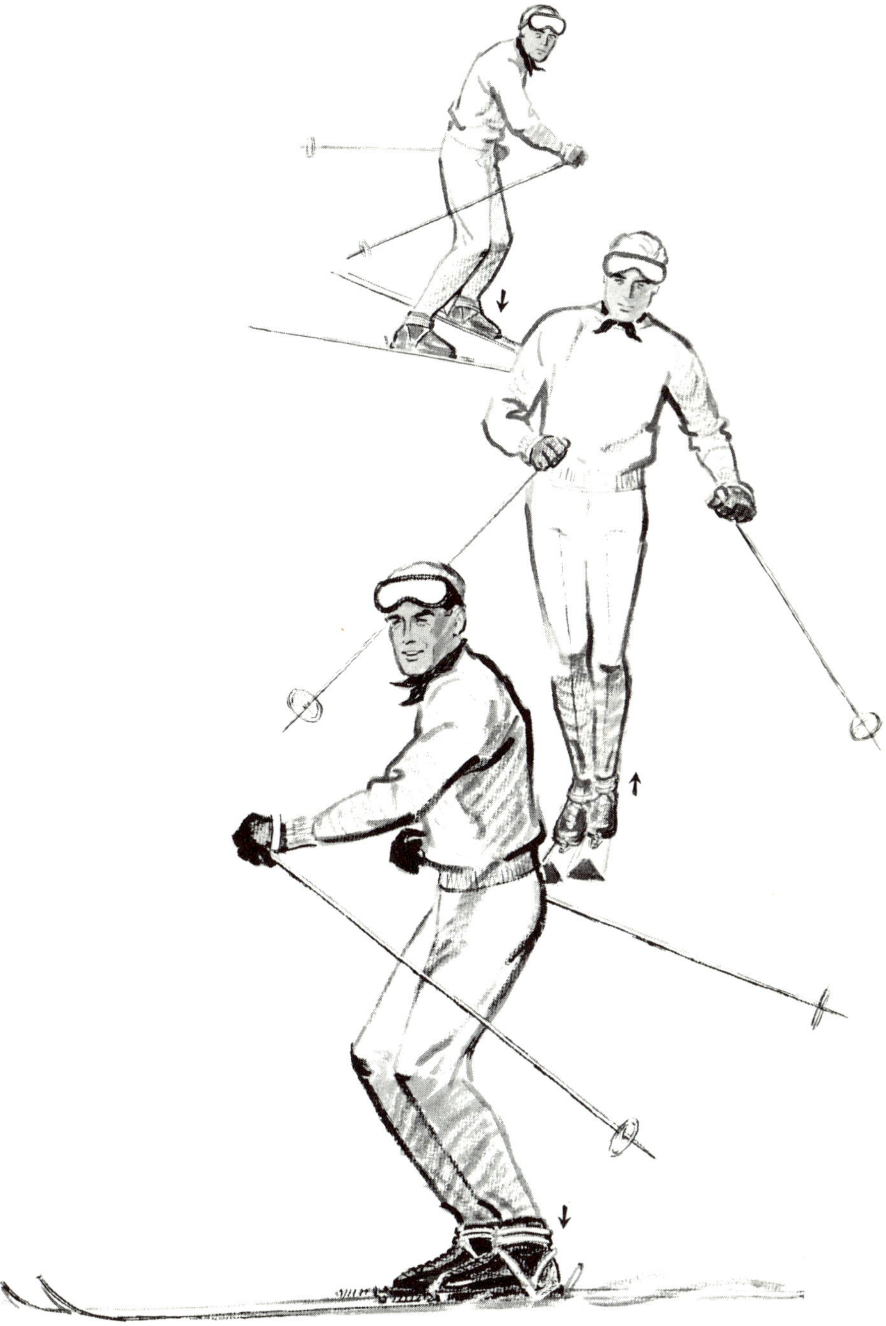

When Unweighting Should Vary

by Merlin Bingham, Assistant Director, M. Earl Miller Ski School, Snow Basin, Utah

There are three main elements in a turn: unweighting, edge change, and turning power. By unweighting your skis, you facilitate edge change by reducing the amount of weight on the skis and suspending that weight above the skis for the period of time necessary to change the edges and start the application of turning power. *The amount and type of unweighting of your skis should vary as the snow conditions, speed, terrain, and radius of the turn vary.*

1. Snow conditions—on well-packed slopes, unweighting is at a minimum. As snow conditions increase in difficulty, from packed powder, through powder, to "crud," the amount of unweighting increases proportionately to the difficulty of snow.

2. Speed—As speed increases, there is less weight acting downward on the snow due to the increase in momentum. Therefore, as speed increases, the unweighting required decreases.

3. Terrain—On flat terrain, more unweighting is required than over moguls where you can take advantage of the skis' natural unweighting caused by passing over the crest of the mogul.

4. Radius of the turn—Long-radius turns require more unweighting over a longer period of time than short-radius turns. In short-radius turns, the use of hip and leg motion unweights the skis, while the upper body remains on a constant level.

The "art" of unweighting skis lies in the proper adjustment to existing snow conditions, terrain, and type of turn.

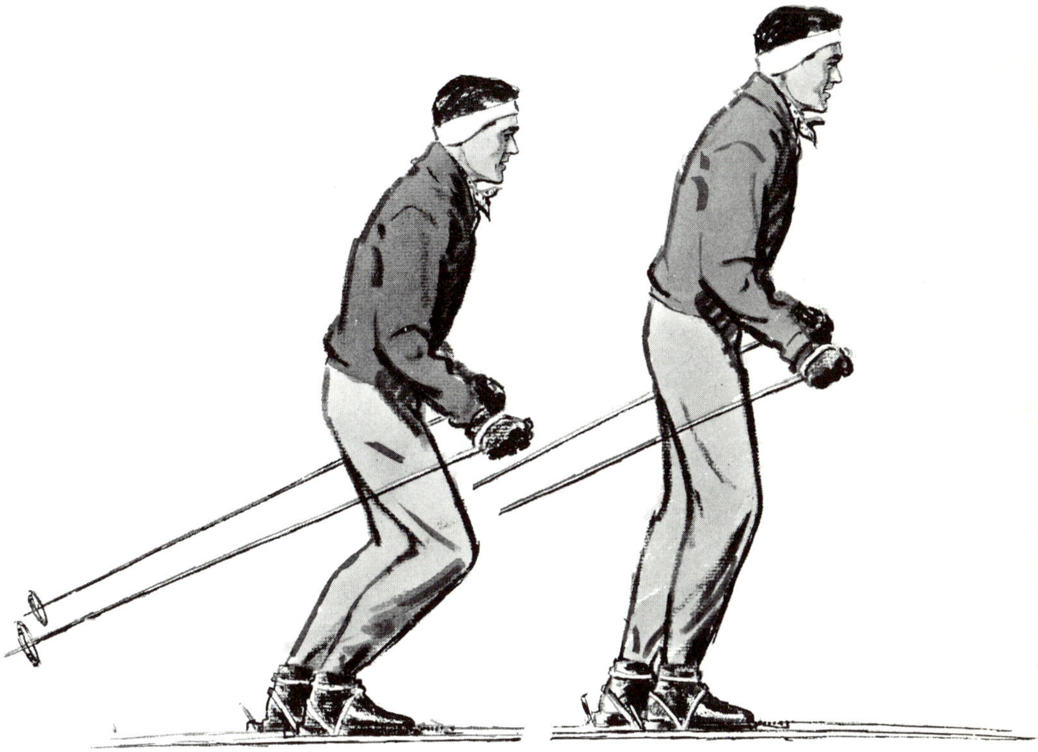

Ski from the Hips Down

by Dick Finlay, Certified Instructor, USEASA, Bromley Ski School, Manchester, Vt.

Most novice and intermediate skiers tend to brace against the pressure of a turn, and, while it is true that a snow-plow turn will come around when done with stiff legs, the intermediate's stem christie will be short, jerky, and will leave a track like an "L" rather than a nice, smooth curve like a "C." *It is the flexing of the legs, the down-up-down motion through the turn, the bending of the hip, knee, and ankle joints in an almost slow-motion rhythm that mark the expert skier.* For, as he sinks down in the legs through the turn, he can control the bite of the ski edges with his knees—more bite for a short, fast turn and less for a long, easy turn. At the end of each turn, the expert is in a traverse position again, if only very briefly, ready for the down-*up*-down movement of his next turn.

If you will think back a bit, you can recall that the Arlberg technique taught us to rotate the upper body when turning. The Swiss school taught the uphill stem and the Austrians to tilt the shoulder down and out over the turning ski. The French taught us to turn with the shoulders and upper body directly over the skis. Who is right? Everybody. For all techniques, the most important movements of the body—from the hips down—are the same.

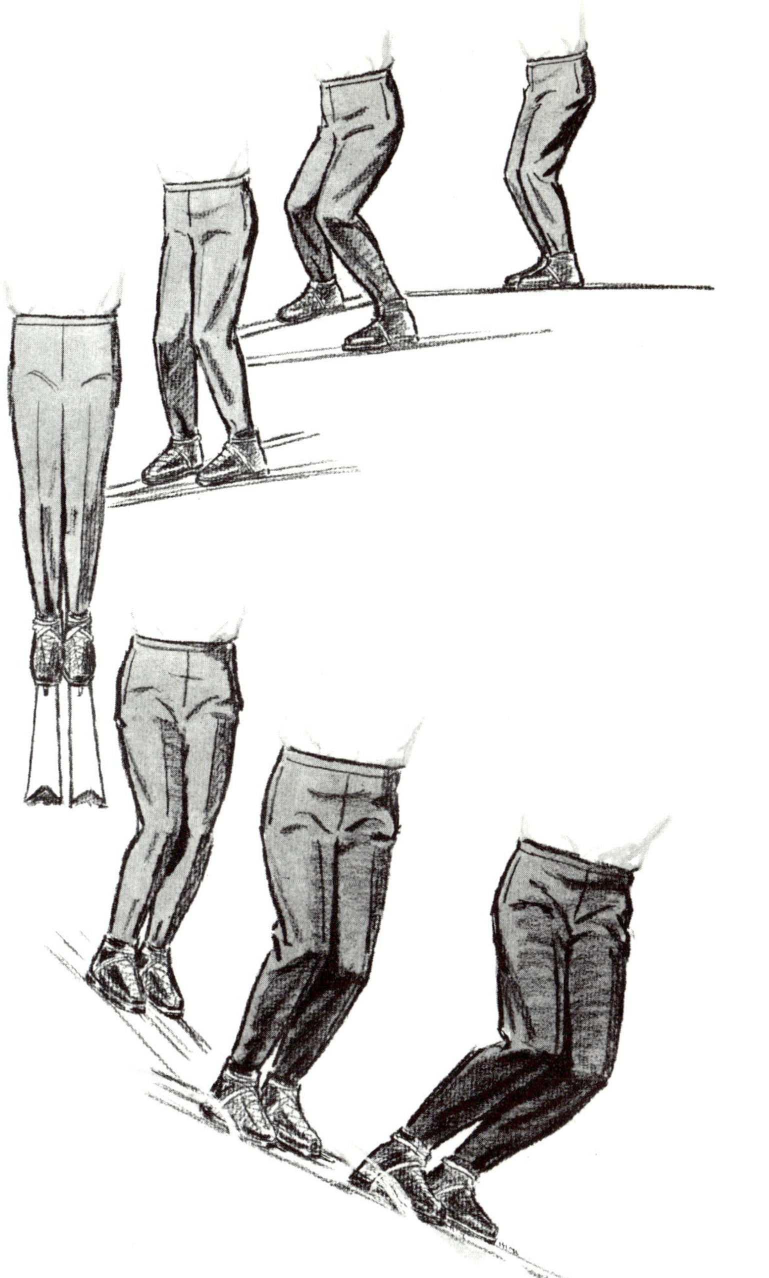

Learning by Exaggeration

by Don Powers, Certified Instructor, USEASA, Whiteface Mountain Ski School, Wilmington, N.Y.

If you have ever experienced the thrill of floating effortlessly down a mountain in a foot of new powder snow, carving long, sweeping turns, then you know the ultimate in skiing pleasure. You are also using one of the basic principles of skiing—controlled exaggeration of your movements such as lifting and unweighting the skis. *For, to ski on any surface which is not completely packed or groomed, you need to exaggerate, to a certain degree, most of the exercises learned in skiing.*

Many people term exaggeration as hard work over and above the normal maneuvers in skiing. It is. You expend a great deal of energy at the beginning but, once you get the feel of each new maneuver, the energy required decreases. Since each new maneuver in skiing is a relatively new sensation, you must first become familiar with it in order to feel comfortable with its execution. Controlled exaggeration is an excellent expedient to this familiarity.

You may have noticed how certain instructors demonstrate each maneuver with seemingly exaggerated motions. This is for your benefit, so that you may clearly see the positions and results. It would be well for you to overexaggerate, too, so that you can feel for yourself each motion necessary to the particular maneuver. Once you are relatively familiar with the maneuver, you can gradually lessen the exaggeration until you find the most effective and comfortable position for yourself. For instance, how much lift do you need in order to change edges and direction for a new turn? The more you lift off the snow, the longer you have to make these changes. You must experiment with and experience your own individual balance and timing, become acquainted with your own personal "feel" of your skis. Exaggeration aids in this acquaintanceship, and its practice will make you more proficient.

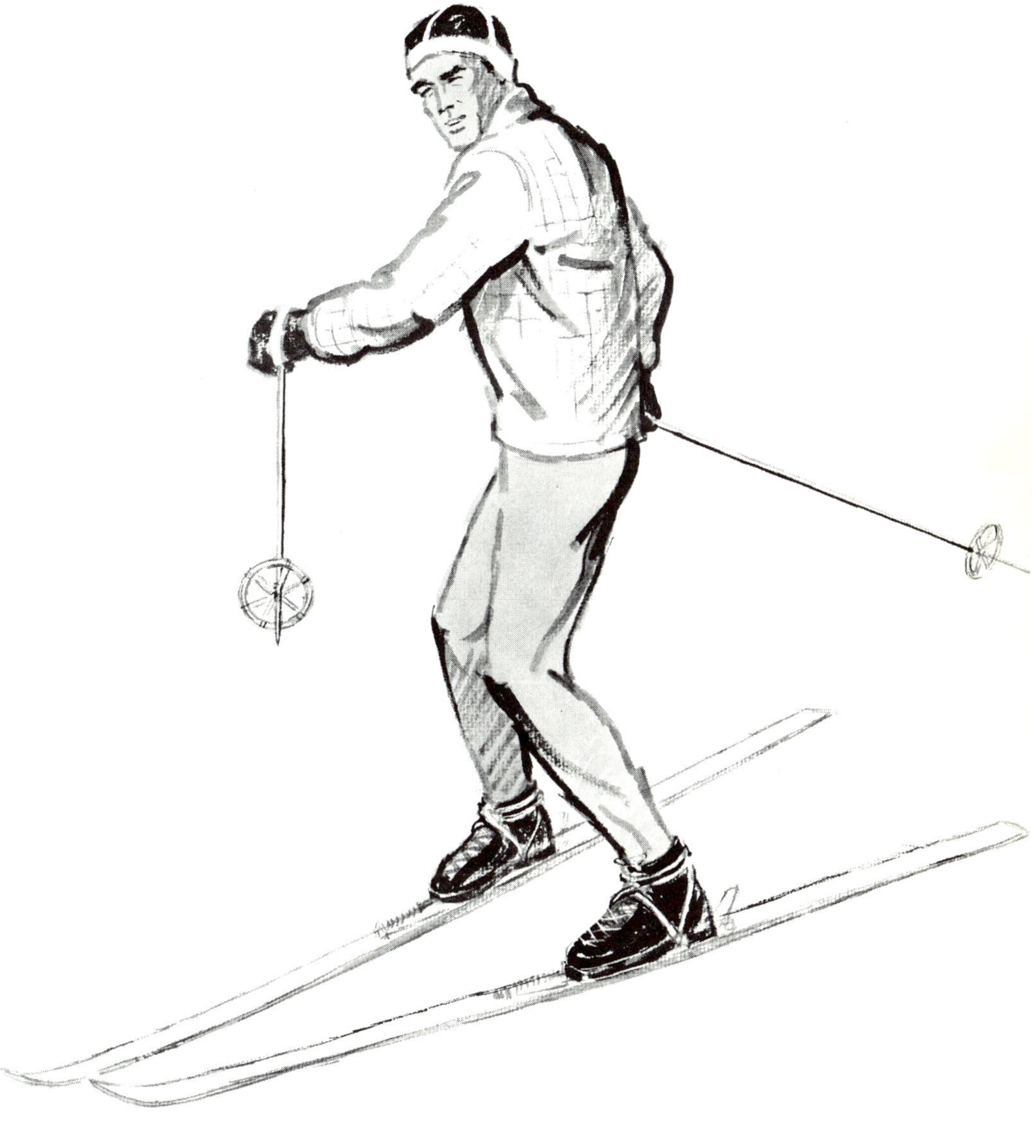

Pole Action on Turns

by Philip S. Miller, Certified Instructor, NRMSA, Grizzly Peak Ski School, Red Lodge, Mont.

Ski poles can be a useful aid when shifting your weight properly in a turn. Many novices have difficulty learning to use their poles as an aid in turning because they either make an incomplete weight shift or do not make the shift quickly enough. This results in the skier drifting down the hill away from his pole and, since he still has his weight on it, he finishes the turn wrongly on the uphill ski.

Here's an easy exercise to help you practice the most effective use of your poles. *Start on a comparatively flat slope, in a very slow snow-plow position, heading directly down the fall line.* Your weight should be equally distributed on both skis with ankles bent well forward and knees pressed toward the ski tips. *To make a right turn, place your right pole in the snow about one fourth the distance from your right ski tip to boot and about a foot out from the edge of the ski. Using the planted pole for support, straighten up from your knees and completely unweight the right ski.* All your weight should now be on the left ski and the planted pole. *Bring your right ski parallel to the left ski and immediately sink down and forward with your ankles and knees.* The down-and-forward movement will complete the turn. At this point, all weight should be taken off the pole and it should be withdrawn from the snow. Then repeat the same exercise to the left, using the left pole for support.

When this exercise has been mastered at a very slow rate of speed, you should attempt it at a faster speed by edging less in the snow-plow position. Then practice it on a steeper hill. As soon as you achieve an easy, relaxed use of your poles starting from the snow-plow position, practice the same exercise using a stem christie to begin the maneuver. Start your first stem christie close to the fall line and each succeeding turn farther away from the fall line. Practice until you can link a series of christies across the fall line with ease.

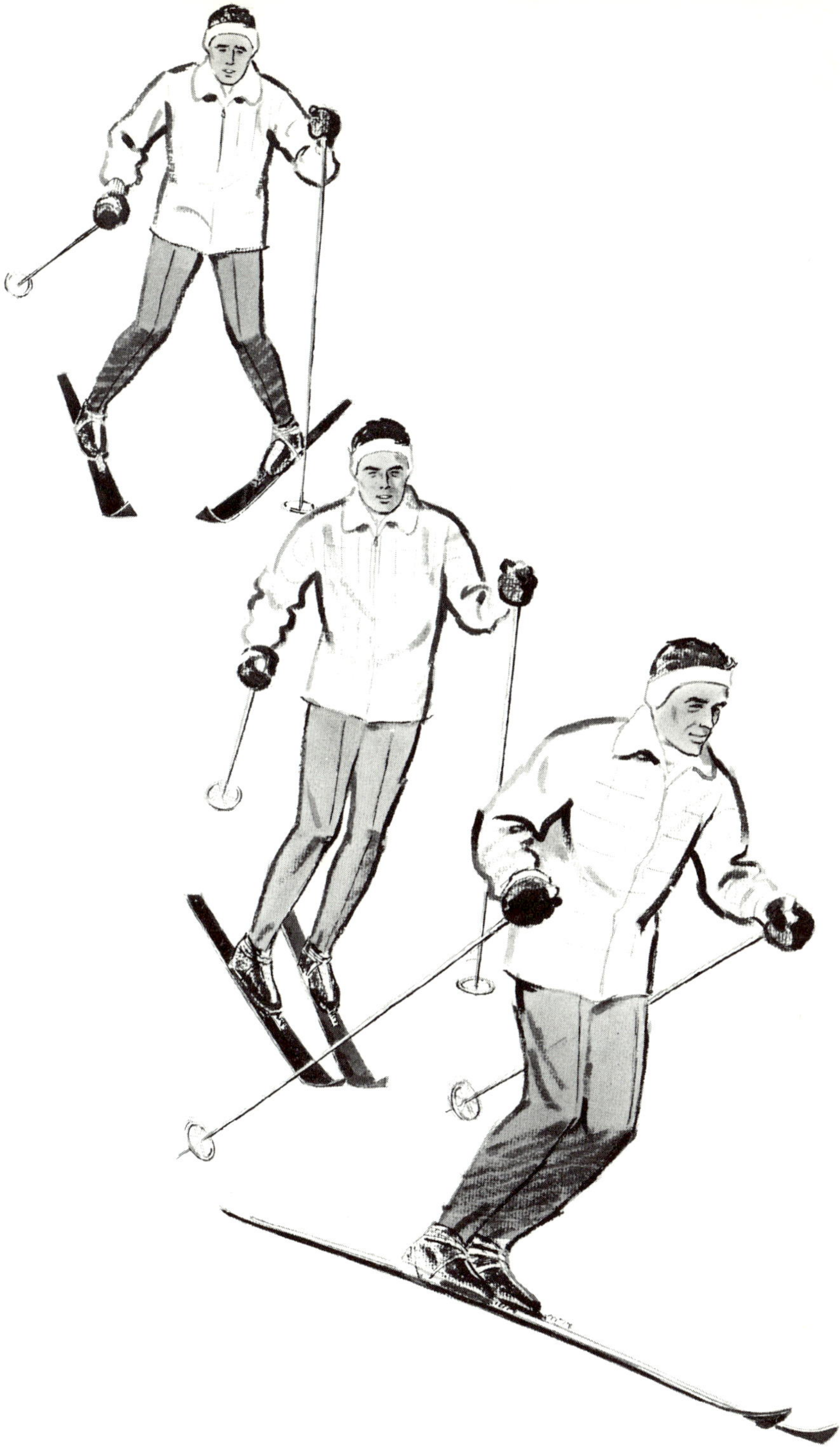

Controlling Length of Turn

by John Wheeler, Certified Instructor, USEASA

Many skiers find themselves turning to a greater degree than they wish. This is caused mainly by not transferring their body weight to the outside (downhill) ski as they cross the fall line.

The radius of any turn is controlled by the amount of pressure put on the front part of the outside (downhill) ski. This front part of the ski acts as a pivot around which the turn is made. In order to shorten the length of your turn, drop forward more with your knees. This forward movement will cause the edges on the front of your downhill ski to bite more deeply into the snow. The quicker this forward pressure is applied to the downhill ski, the shorter the radius of the turn. To discontinue the turn, retreat from the forward position and raise your body slightly. This will reduce the edge bite on the front of the ski.

Since the completion of one turn is the start of another, it is essential that you keep up your rhythm and speed. By keeping up your rhythm from the previous turn, you will cross the fall line on your way to another turn. And, with a little practice, you will soon be able to make turns when, and exactly where, you want them.

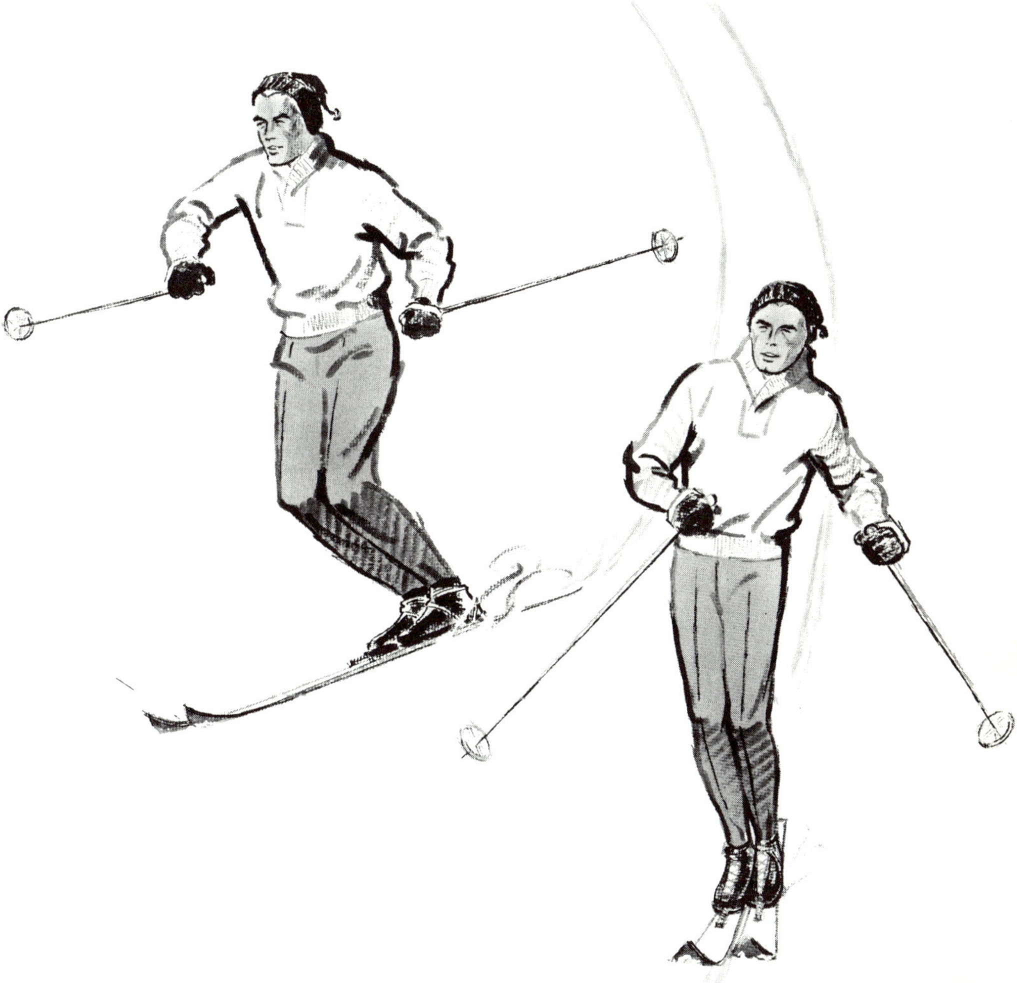

Strengthening Weak Side Turns

by Bob Bourdon, Sepp Ruschp Ski School, Stowe, Vt.

It is an unusual skier who can turn his skis right and left with equal precision and ease. Sometimes this difference is so marked that the skier can scarcely make a turn at all in one direction and consequently develops a serious mental block which just makes it worse.

The simple excuse is to blame your equipment, and sometimes this happens to be the answer. So make sure your skis are not warped and that your feet are properly aligned on the skis. Now, assuming that skis and bindings are all right, then the chances are almost certain that you are simply not weighting your lower ski on the weak turn. To check this out, make a simple traverse in the direction of your weak side and try lifting the upper ski. Then make an uphill turn in the same direction, again lifting the upper ski. If you can't make a traverse and turn while lifting that ski, then you have found the cause of the trouble. One cure is to practice these same exercises, making sure of the following points: *Keep the uphill ski at least six inches ahead of the downhill ski at all times and your knees and feet close enough to touch each other most of the time. Make certain that your lower hip is held a little behind the upper hip and that your head is held over the lower ski and not the upper one.* Maintain this position throughout the traverse and turn. Don't let habit or instinct make you change it. With proper weighting of the downhill ski, the turns on your weaker side are sure to improve.

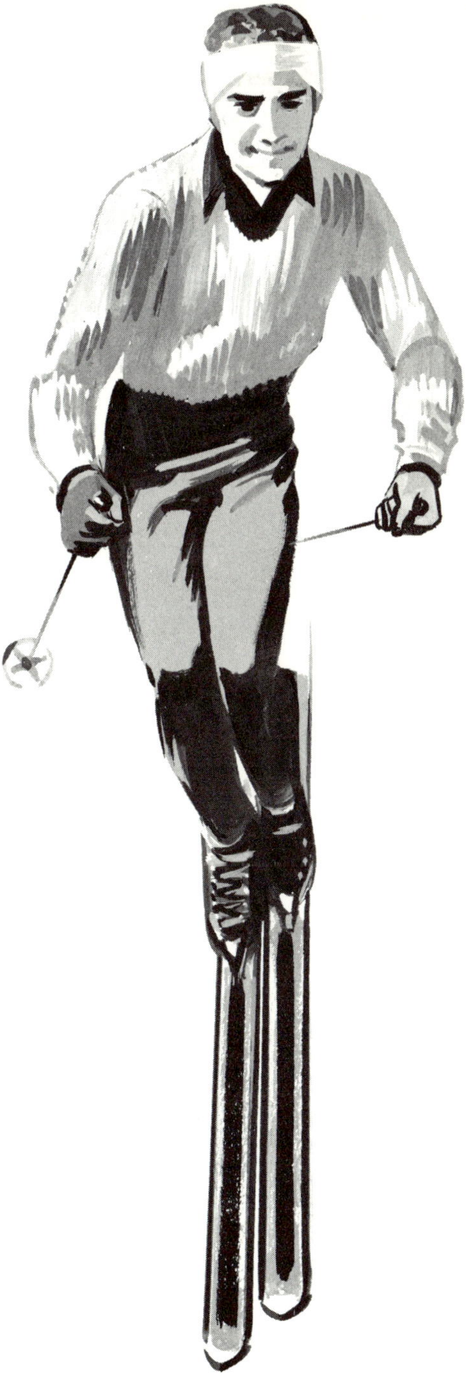

Improving Balance

by Bob Beck, Certified Ski Coach, NRMSA, Montana State College, Bozeman, Mont.

Regardless of the technique used, balance plays one of the most important roles in skiing. First, to find your point of balance, put on your skis and stand erect. Relax in the knees only to the extent that they are not locked. Lean back until there is pressure on the top of your toes against your boot. Rock forward until you feel a definite pull on your heel. Now that you have experienced both extreme positions, relax your knees a little more in a kneeling position and rock back and forth until you settle your weight evenly over your skis in a comfortable position midway between the two extremes. This will be your balance point.

Now practice balance while skiing. First, try traversing the hill on one ski. *Start in a normal traverse position, then lift the heel of your uphill ski to a level with the top of your downhill ski boot. Let the tip of the uphill ski rest gently on the snow.* Practice this exercise until you feel comfortable and relaxed while traversing on one foot in both directions. Edge control plays an important part. Be sure you make a straight track. If your ski slips, adjust your edging to a point where the ski holds again. Experiment with this edge control. Once you have mastered this, look for bumps and continue your practice across a bumpy slope. You should be able to master traversing on any type of terrain on your downhill ski alone. Next, repeat the same exercise but this time let the ski drift (side-slip) across the hill. Set up a drill of traverse, slip, traverse, slip. Now you're ready for the supreme test. Start your turn, shift your weight to the new downhill ski, and complete the turn on one ski!

Any time you feel rusty in your turns, or you are having trouble making turns hold on hard snow or bumps, go back to one-foot skiing for balance.

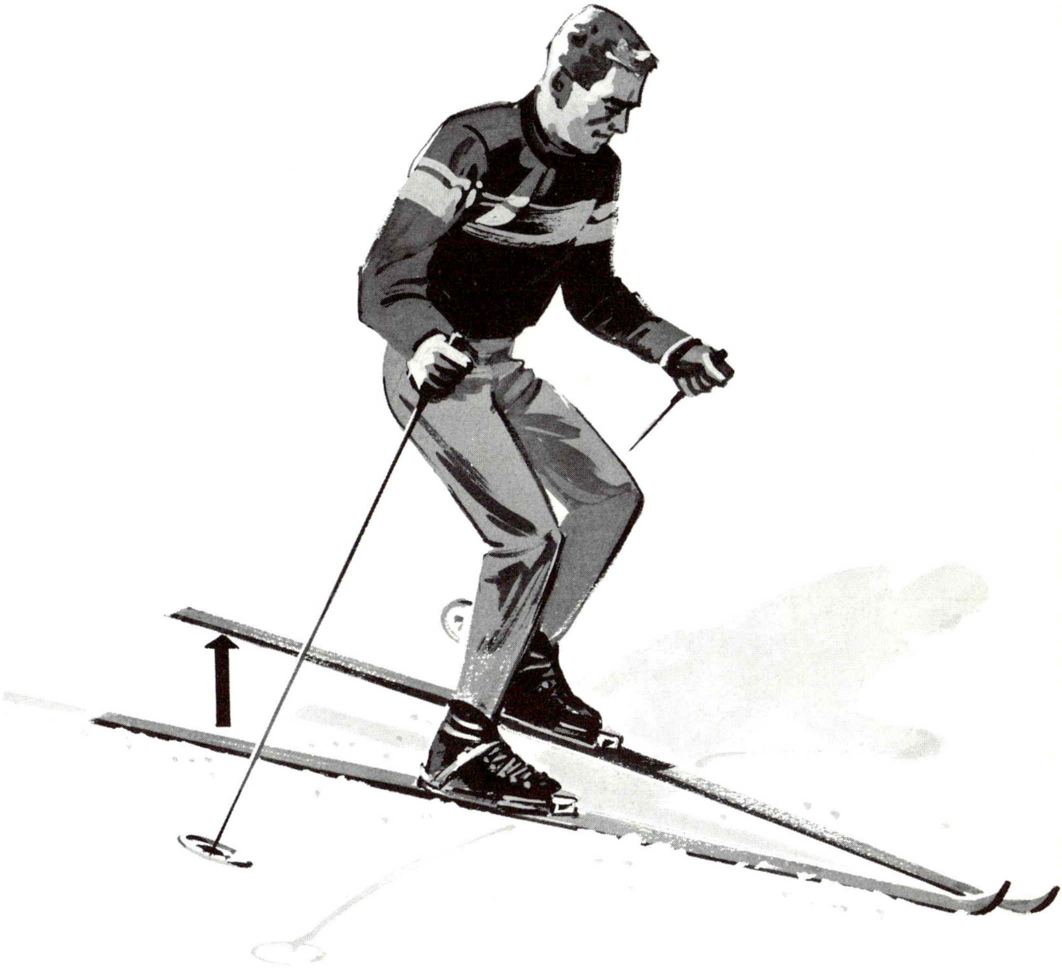

Skating on Skis

by Clifton Taylor, Certified Instructor, USEASA, Hogback Ski School, Brattleboro, Vt.

Whether you are just learning to ski or have been skiing for many years, you will improve your ability by skating on snow.

Skating is one of the basic downhill maneuvers and every skier should include it as part of his technique. It is a quick way for the beginner to get the feel of his skis, and *an excellent exercise for all skiers because it incorporates many of the components of a sound downhill skiing technique—balance, rhythm, knee action, edging, and proper weight distribution.*

Skating is one of the best exercises for balance and rhythm because it teaches you to ride and glide on one ski at a time and to shift weight from ski to ski in a rhythmical knee action, as you spring from one step to the other (bending the knee with each gliding step), and of edge control, as you edge the ski to push off and flatten the ski to slide.

You can use skating steps to accelerate over a long, gradual downhill slope, or between slalom gates when racing. It is also a quick way to change direction on a straight run. Or you can use skating as a warm-up maneuver.

Today's modern ski lifts give you easy access to long downhill runs where there are usually plenty of gradual stretches to practice skating steps. Skate on skis as you would on ice skates or roller skates. Push off with one ski, take an oblique step and glide on the other, then reverse the procedure. Work up a smooth rhythm as you skate from ski to ski. With each step, keep your body centered over the weighted ski. Be sure to keep the tip of the unweighted and "stepping" ski higher than the tail to prevent catching a front edge. Push off from an edged ski and glide on a flat ski. Use a strong push-off or spring-off motion at the completion of each gliding step.

Notice how the figure in the diagram lifts his left ski and takes an oblique step to the left, then shifts his weight to that ski and balances and glides on it, making a complete sliding-skating step. To continue skating, he will take another step in the opposite direction with the right ski.

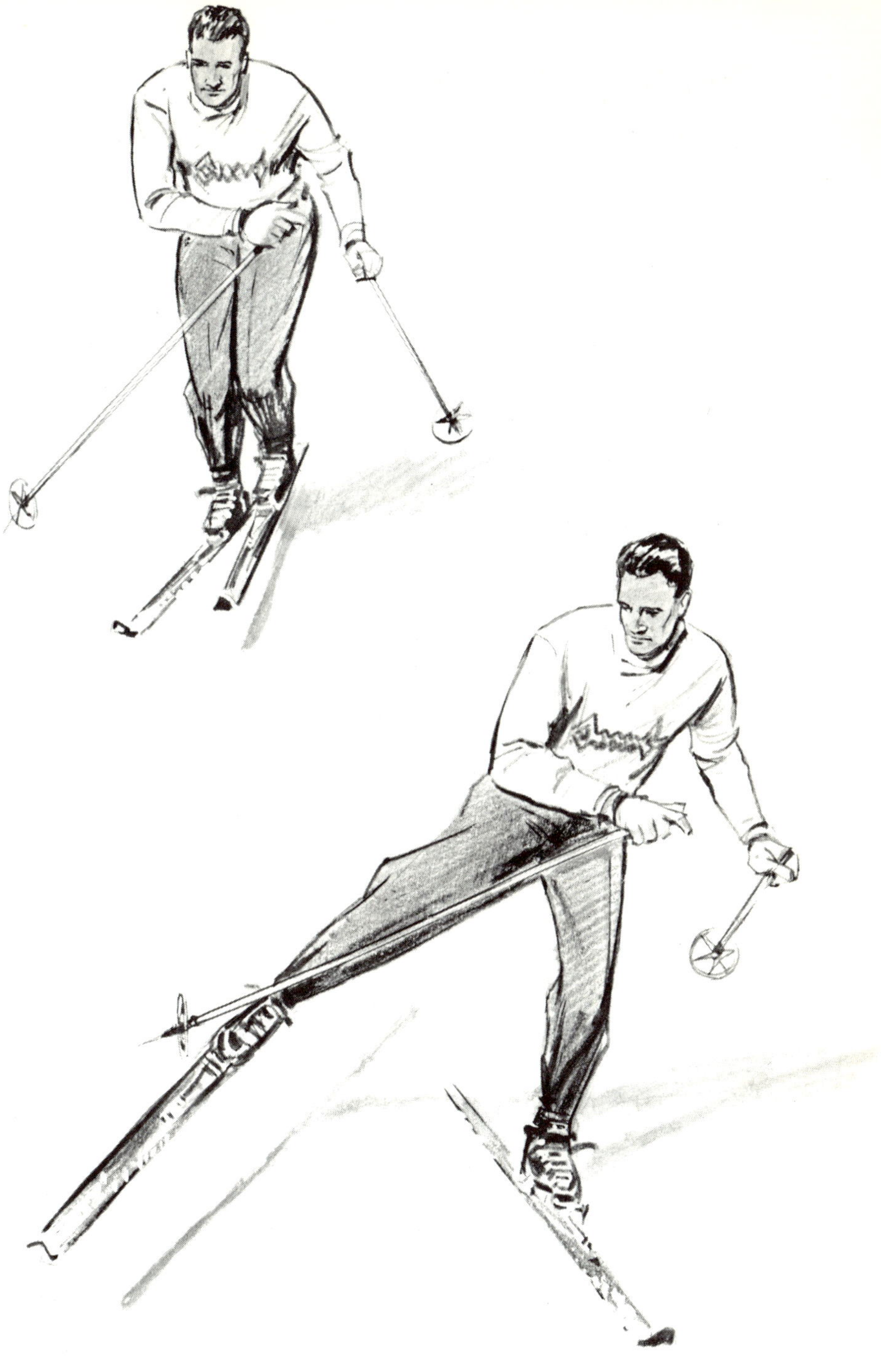

Breathe—and Ski Better

by John Church, Certified Instructor, PNSIA, Mount Spokane Ski School, Spokane, Wash.

If you are completely worn out or breathless at the end of a long run, your problem is probably inadequate breathing. Strange as it may seem, many skiers, experts as well as beginners, sometimes forget to breathe.

Skiing, literally, can be a breath-taking sport. Ski areas are usually at an elevation higher than the altitude to which you are accustomed; therefore, for the same amount of movement in your diaphragm, you get less oxygen. However, you can learn, almost automatically, to adjust to different elevations. Other breathing problems take a conscious effort to solve. For instance, when learning a new maneuver, you will have a tendency to become tense. In so doing, you also brace the muscles with which you breathe. Then again, you might be skiing a trail on which you do not feel confident of your ability. You get "butterflies" in your stomach and hold your breath until you reach an easier slope. You might also become so intent on performing a certain maneuver that you might actually stop breathing for a while.

These instances merely indicate some of the problems you might encounter. The solution, simply to tell yourself to start breathing, is often not enough. Even after giving yourself many lectures on the subject, you will find that you will still forget to breathe when performing new maneuvers, or in tight spots on the trail. *The best treatment you can administer is consciously to practice steady, regular breathing as you ski down the slope.* For this, you will need some specific action to make you breathe. Many skiers look on in amazement at international racers when they run through an entire slalom course panting vigorously and noisily. *These top skiers have the right idea. They consciously force themselves to breathe by panting aloud.* Some racers even make a low whistling noise as they methodically exhale through their teeth. Singing, too, helps to develop steady breathing.

Once you train yourself to breathe fully, you will find yourself automatically relaxing more on your runs. Indeed, proper breathing can put new life into your skiing.

INTERMEDIATE PROBLEMS: CAUSES AND CURES

Traverse

PROBLEMS	CAUSES	CURES
Can't run straight	Weight on uphill ski	Center weight over downhill ski. Try to pick up tail of uphill ski
	Sitting back	Move weight forward by pressing downhill knee forward
Skis wander	Sitting too far forward or back	Move weight forward or back as indicated
Skis cross	Sitting back	(*See* above)
	Wrong ski leading	Move uphill ski half boot-length ahead of downhill ski
Skis separate	Weight on uphill ski	Center weight over downhill ski
	Sitting back	Move weight forward by bending knees and pressing forward
Skis slip downhill	Insufficient edging	Roll knees and ankles into hill
	Weight on uphill ski	Center weight over downhill ski
Downhill edges catch	Overexaggerated comma	Modify position; downhill shoulder never beyond downhill ski
	Stiff lower leg; downhill ski too flat	Flex downhill knee and bend it forward and in
Uphill edges catch	Overedging	Roll knees and ankles out
	Leaning into hill; weight on wrong ski	Shift weight from uphill to downhill ski

PROBLEMS	CAUSES	CURES
Fall into hill	Wrong ski, shoulder or hip forward	Advance uphill ski, shoulder, and hip
	Weight on uphill ski	Center weight over downhill ski
Fall downhill	Overexaggerated comma	(*See* above)
	Faulty edging; outside ski too flat	Roll knees and ankles equally into hill
Instability	Stiff knees, stiff downhill leg; standing up	Flex knees, press them forward
	Sitting back	Move weight forward

Sideslip

PROBLEMS	CAUSES	CURES
Skis separate	Faulty body position	Uphill shoulder and hip slightly ahead, knees bent; don't sit back
	Too much weight on uphill ski	More weight on downhill ski; bend downhill knee
Skis cross or wander	Weight on uphill ski or too far back	More weight on downhill ski; bend downhill knee; press knees forward
	Wrong ski leading	Advance uphill ski half bootlength ahead
	Faulty edging	Roll knees and ankles into hill
Skis slip separately	Faulty body position	Uphill shoulder and hip slightly ahead, knees bent; don't sit back
	Unequal edging	Edge both skis together
	Weight on uphill ski or too far back	More weight on downhill ski; bend downhill knee; press knees forward
Downhill edges catch	Overexaggerated comma	Modify position; uphill hip and shoulder slightly ahead, knees and ankles in
	Faulty co-ordination of arms, body, and legs	Arms, body, and legs move as a unit in normal comma position
Uphill edges catch; can't start sideslip	Faulty co-ordination	Arms, body, and legs move as a unit in normal comma position
	Overedging	Flatten skis by rolling knees and ankles out a bit
	Weight on uphill ski	Bend downhill knee and press forward. Try to pick up uphill ski
Skis slip too far backward	Weight too far back	Bend knees, press them forward. Lean body forward

PROBLEMS	CAUSES	CURES
Skis slip too far forward	Weight too far forward	Shift weight slightly to rear. Relax forward pressure in knees
Loss of speed control	Faulty edging	Roll knees and ankles into hill
Loss of slip control	Skis not parallel	Keep knees and skis together, weight on downhill ski
	Faulty weighting	(*See* "Skis slip too far forward or backward")
Instability	Stiff body, arms, or legs; faulty co-ordination	Arms, body, and legs move as a unit in normal comma position
	Faulty weighting	(*See* above)
	Skis not parallel	Keep knees and skis together, weight on downhill ski

Uphill Christie
(Christie-into-the-Hill or Off Fall Line)

PROBLEMS	CAUSES	CURES
Can't start turn	No unweighting	Keep skis together; sink into downhill knee
	Skis not parallel	Keep skis together, weight on downhill ski
	Failure to release edges	Flatten edges as skis are unweighted
Can't turn	Skis not parallel	Keep skis together, weight on downhill ski
	Weight on inside ski	Bend outside knee and press forward
	Overedging	Release edges at start of turn
Jerky turn	Overexaggerated comma; too much wind-up at start of turn	Modify position. Inside shoulders and hip lead. Don't lean out too far
	Rotation	Maintain comma position
Can't stop	Edging too slowly	Edge set should be completed by end of turn. Roll knees and ankles into hill
	Faulty weighting	Weight forward over downhill ski
	Body stiff and not centered over skis	Sink down into knees. Don't overrotate
Overturning	Rotation	Maintain comma position
	Edging too quickly	Set edges gradually as turn is completed
No heel slip	Faulty weighting; overedging; skis not parallel	Weight forward over downhill ski. Keep skis together. Flatten skis in turn
	Insufficient knee action	Push knees into hill, heels downhill

PROBLEMS	CAUSES	CURES
Skis cross	Wrong ski leading	Advance inside ski half bootlength
	Faulty edging or weighting	Weight forward over downhill ski. Release edges at start of turn
Downhill fall	Edging too quickly; over-exaggerated comma	Set edges gradually. Modify position. Inside shoulders and hip lead. Don't lean out too far
Uphill fall	Faulty weighting; weight on inside ski	Weight forward over downhill ski
Instability	Faulty weighting	Weight forward over downhill ski
	Stiff body, arms, or legs	Flex knees; bounce if necessary. Keep arms and hands down. Stand solidly over skis

Stem Christie

PROBLEMS	CAUSES	CURES
Can't start turn; can't stem	Weight on uphill ski; leaning into hill; sitting back	Bend both knees and press downhill knee forward. Don't shift weight until stem is completed
	Overedging	Flatten skis before stemming
	Too much weight on heel of stemmed ski	Bend uphill knee
Can't turn	No weight shift	Transfer weight to stemmed ski and keep it there. Press outside knee forward
	Rushing turn	Stay in "up" position until fall line is crossed. Don't drop down until then
	Overedging	Release edges until fall line is crossed
Can't complete turn; jerky finish	Overrotation	Inside hip and shoulder lead throughout turn.
	No heel slip	Keep weight on outside ski; don't overedge
	Faulty weighting	Sink down into downhill knee; press knee forward
Poor rhythm; jerky turn	Faulty weighting; standing up in turn; no "down-up-down" motion	"Down" at start of turn, "up" during turn across fall line, "down" at end. Keep weight on outside ski after stemming. Knees always bent and forward
	Rushing turn or overrotating	Inside hip and shoulder lead throughout turn. Don't drop down until fall line is crossed
	Faulty pole plant	Plant inside pole midway between boot and ski tip when ski is stemmed at start of turn. Pivot around it when coming up

PROBLEMS	CAUSES	CURES
Can't unweight	Standing up	Keep knees bent and forward
	Weight on inside ski	Keep outside knee bent and forward
	Faulty rhythm; poor "down-up-down" motion	(*See* "Poor rhythm" problem, above)
Skis run straight	No weight shift	Transfer weight to outside ski after it is stemmed
	Overedging in turn	Flatten skis during turn
Can't keep skis parallel in turn	No weight shift	Transfer weight to outside ski after it is stemmed
	Faulty unweighting	(*See* "Can't unweight" problem, above)
	Faulty weighting	Keep weight on outside ski
Inside ski drags	No weight shift; overedging; skis not parallel in turn	Transfer weight to outside ski after stemming. Flatten skis and keep them together
Edges catch	Faulty unweighting; overedging	(*See* "Can't unweight" problem, above)
	No lead change	Advance inside ski half bootlength while coming up during turn
Skis wander or cross	No lead change	(*See* above)
	Sitting back	Keep weight forward, knees bent, proper comma
	Unequal edging	Edge both skis equally
	Overedging	Flatten skis during turn
	Excessive stem of downhill ski at start of turn	Stem the uphill ski

87

SKI LIFE EXTRA

The Fine Art of Falling

by Doug Pfeiffer, Director, Snow Summit Ski School, Big Bear Lake, Calif.

Almost anybody with a hearty, adventurous spirit would be likely to fall head over heels for skiing the first time he tried it, but that same person would show far less enthusiasm for the prospect of just falling head over heels. Yet only when a skier resigns himself to the idea that falling is as much a part of skiing as downhill running—and learns the proper way to fall—will he truly become a good, safe, and confident skier, who is equipped to tackle any slope under any conditions.

To ski well, you must stay alert, with your eyes open, and be able to size up quickly the conditions of the snow and slope ahead of you. You cannot do this if you are the least bit preoccupied with fear, or even concern, about falling. What's more, when you are afraid or concerned, it's likely that your muscles will be tense, your limbs less mobile. When that's the case, you can't possibly expect to be able to ski with the quick responses necessary for today's tricky slopes, dotted with moguls and people.

To become a good skier, then, you must lose your fear of falling. And to do this, you must learn to fall without getting hurt. Here are some of the ways we use to teach the rules of safe falling at our ski school.

The basic beginner's fall is first. While traveling slowly across a gentle slope covered with soft-packed snow, prepare for the fall by holding the ski poles about parallel to the snow, with the points away from your body. This position of the poles is important and basic to all controlled falls. It ensures that you will neither stab yourself nor catch a pole in the snow which could cause a wrenched shoulder. As you move your poles to the safe position, begin to sit back, as if you were going to sit on a low chair. As you sit back, twist your hips and shoulders so that your upper body will face downhill. Your hands should remain about the same distance from the snow at all times. There is a good reason for this. You should avoid all uncontrolled movements of the arms since a jerky arm movement will throw you off balance. Your hips should be just a few inches away from the snow and well to the uphill side of the skis. Now, prepare to land.

As you sit all the way down, lean back. At the moment of impact lie flat on the snow, keeping your chin close to your chest to prevent your head from receiving a possible hard knock. Slam your forearms against the snow just as your back is about to hit. (If you've watched judo experts, you've surely seen this forearm slam done to perfection.) Such a slam takes up any undue stress which your back might receive.

This basic beginner's fall is painless and easy. Therefore, it is ideal for learning some of the characteristics common to all falls. For example, after a few preliminary warm-up falls, never let your muscles go limp. You must not overrelax, nor should you cause your muscles to stiffen. To fall safely, your muscles must be in good tone; they must be supple and relaxed. Gymnasts use the phrase "stay pulled together with your muscles ready for immediate action." This takes practice.

Another common rule for a safe tumble is this: Keep your eyes open when you fall. You will always have better balance and react faster if you can see. When you "know where you are" (to borrow another phrase of the gymnasts), you can usually make the right movements to come back right-side-up. Perhaps you've read of the psychological experiment where a cat is dropped upside down from a few feet above ground and always manages to land feet first. Yet, when the cat is blindfolded and again dropped, it is as helpless as a bird in a blizzard. So it is important always to keep your eyes open when you fall.

There is a good deal of truth in the statement that if you don't fall, you won't get hurt. But it is also just as true that if you don't fall, you are not learning a hard fact of skiing. It's one thing not to fall because you are a great skier, but it's quite another thing if you never fall because you avoid all challenges. You will never become a really good skier, or good at anything for that matter, if you constantly avoid challenges. To become a good skier, accept challenges and, as you gain confidence and skill in overcoming them, you will become an expert. You may lose your footing along the way, but you will pick up many tricks to regain your balance before a fall actually occurs. Let's look at a few of these.

Suppose you catch an uphill edge, as I have done at times. It looks like I'm going to fall into the hill. However, there are at least two things that I can do to prevent a tumble. If I have control of my arms, I can quickly stab my uphill pole into the snow to prop myself back to a balanced position. Or, I can make a quick, forceful push-off from the leg on which I am standing. Then, while my skis are free of the snow, I can swing my legs back under my hips to land in a balanced stance.

Perhaps I've caught a downhill edge and am about to land on my right ear. If you were in this position, you, too, could use a ski pole, outrigger fashion, to prop yourself back up. Or, you could quickly push off from your standing leg, swing your skis and feet under you, and land in a good, balanced position. The next time you are on the slopes, try these exercises. You will be well rewarded for your efforts in terms of new confidence.

The trickiest of all falls to cope with are those in which you either cross your skis in front, dig a tip, or somehow get your skis caught on a twig or rock. These clobbers pitch you forward and happen so fast that you've seldom much chance to try to regain balance. When you feel you are about to be thrown forward in an ungraceful dive, the safest thing to do is to go with the momentum of the fall. Don't fight it. When you get thrown violently forward into the egg-beater type of tumble, just strive to keep your legs together and your skis parallel. Try to attain a compact, pulled-together feeling.

With a little practice, you'll soon become an expert at recovering from a forward fall. And once you completely lose your fear of falling, you'll find skiing any slope easier and much more fun.

III. *Advanced Technique*

What distinguishes the advanced skier is his ability to keep his skis together throughout the turn, eliminating the stem. However, many who reach the stem-christie stage seem to find it difficult to progress into true parallel skiing. In this chapter the first set of pointers builds an easy platform to long-radius parallel turns. The second series leads to the more intricate wedeln (short fall-line turns)—the goal of every modern skier.

Parallel Turn

Starting in the fall line or from a very shallow traverse, lower your knees and hips and plant your inside ski pole in the snow between boot and ski tip.

Your body rises from the hips and knees,lightening the skis, and most of your weight is transferred to the outside ski. With the aid of your pole and a steering action of the feet and knees, the skis begin to move laterally across the slope in the opposite direction.

With a down pressure of your knees, the tails of your skis will continue to skid sideways and, at the same time, the edges will begin to bite into the snow to help you carve your turn.

The down pressure of your knees and a slight follow-through of rotation will complete the turn.

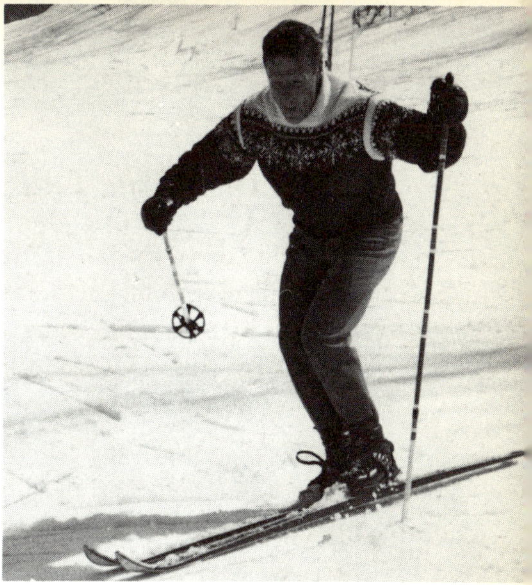

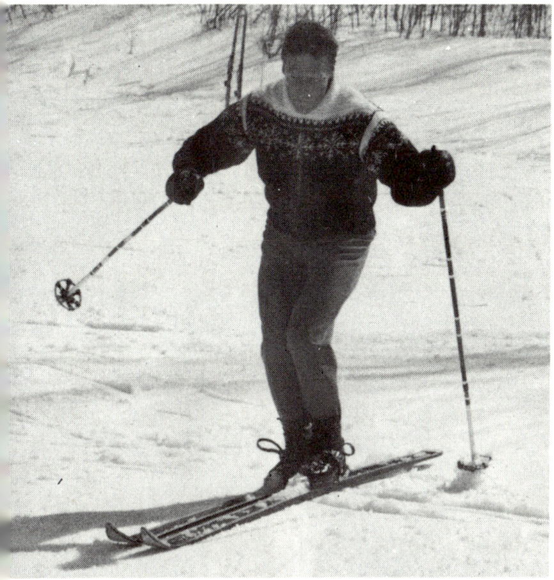

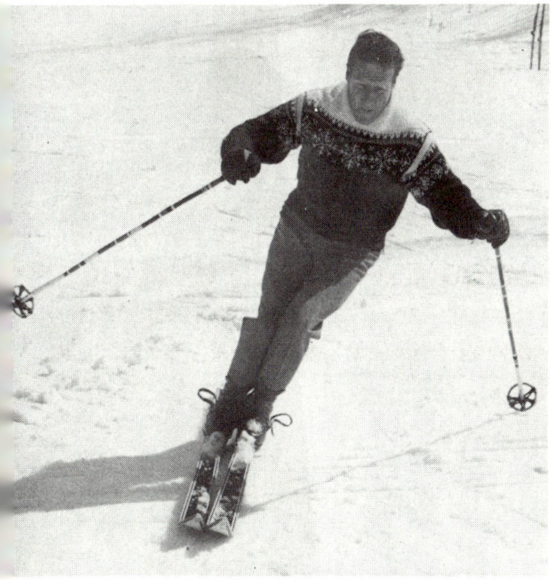

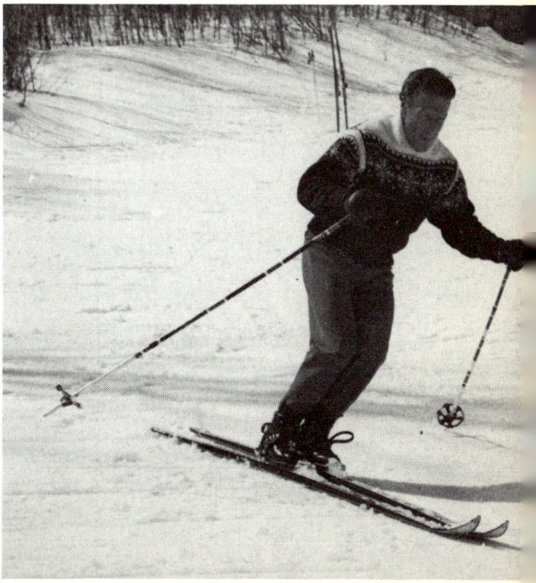

Hop Down the Fall Line

This hop down the fall line while skiing is very close to the wedeln movement. Lower your knees and hips while planting your pole close to the ski tip. Rise from the knees, retracting the skis and moving them laterally across the hill. This exercise, repeated while skiing down the fall line, will result in a fall-line hop.

Start skiing down the fall line or in a slight traverse to the right. Lower your knees and hips and plant your left pole in the snow halfway between your boot and the tip of the left ski.

Retract your skis and, with the support of your pole, move them laterally to the left.

As your skis come in contact with the snow again, absorb the shock by slightly lowering your knees. Now the right pole is brought forward in preparation for the next hop.

Plant your right pole in the snow as you again lower your knees and hips.

With the support of your pole, retract your skis and move them laterally to the right. Repeat this exercise as you ski down the fall line.

Transition from Hop to Wedeln

Begin with the previous exercise, or hop down the fall line. Once you have established a smooth rhythm, lower your body more from the hips. Now, as you rise from the knees and hips, and with the aid of your ski pole, move your skis laterally across the slope by using a steering action of the feet, or heel thrust. It is this combination of heel thrust and greater up-and-down movement, together with rhythm and added speed, that completes the transition to wedeln.

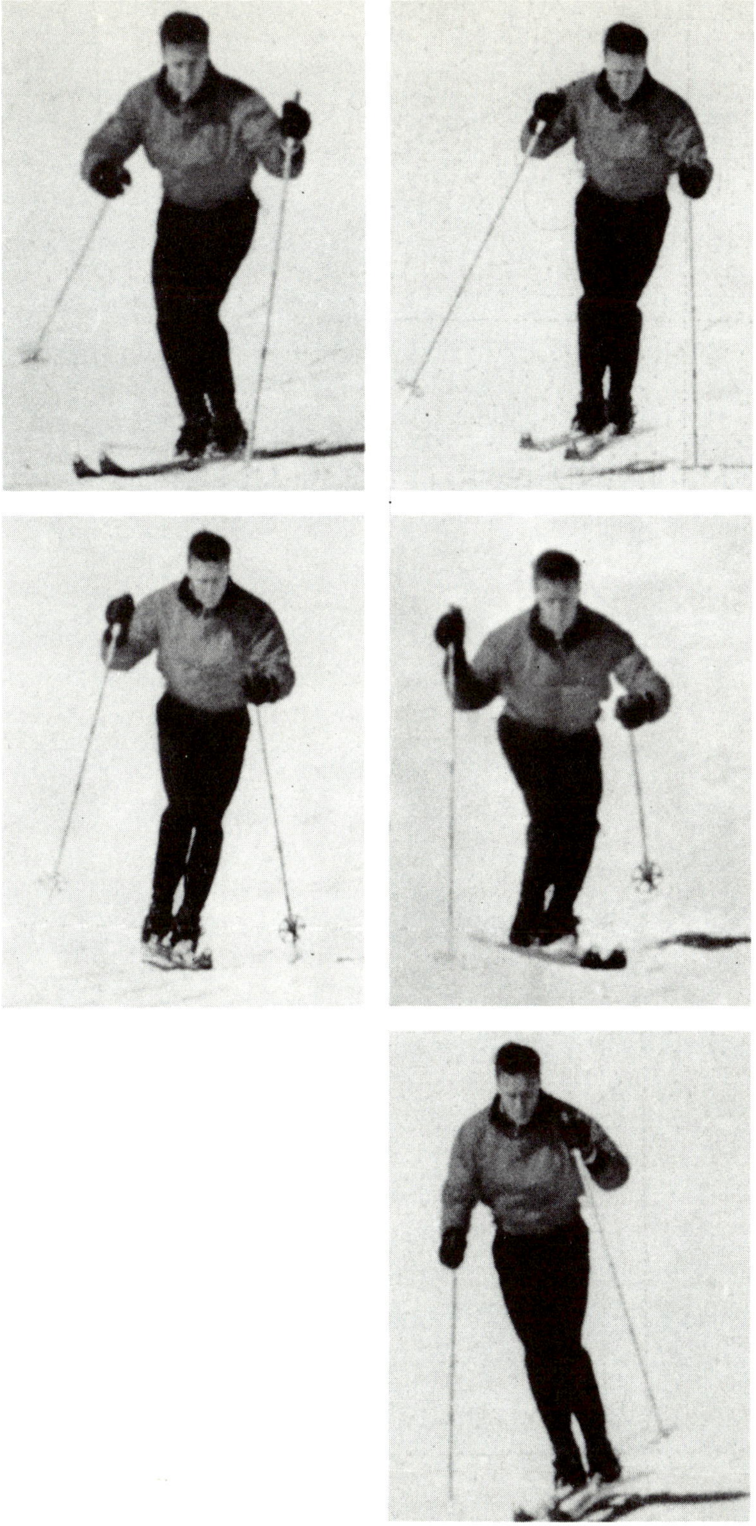

Wedeln

Starting from a very shallow traverse, lower your knees and hips and plant your ski pole in the snow.

As your body rises from the knees and hips, the skis are lightened and, with the aid of your pole and a steering action of the feet, knees, and hips (heel thrust), the skis begin to move laterally across the hill.

As the skis reach the fall line they are almost flat, and your body is squarely centered over the skis.

With a down pressure of the knees, the tails of the skis will continue to skid sideways, and at the same time the edges will begin to bite into the snow to help carve your turn. The majority of your weight should be on the downhill ski.

The outside arm and pole are brought up and the pole is again planted in the snow between boot and ski tip. Your body again rises, lightening the skis, and, with the aid of the pole and a heel thrust, the skis begin moving laterally across the slope in the opposite direction.

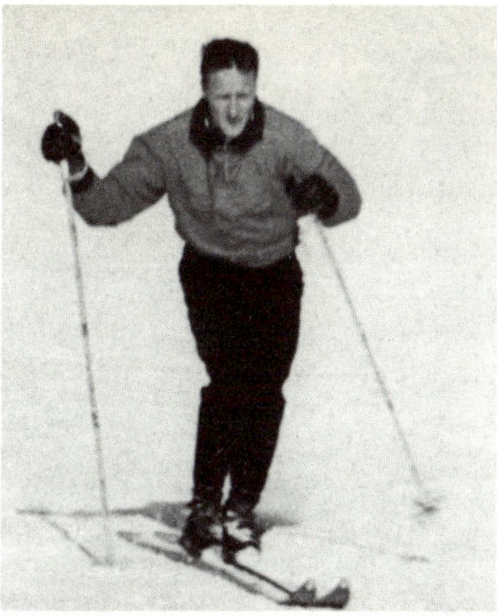
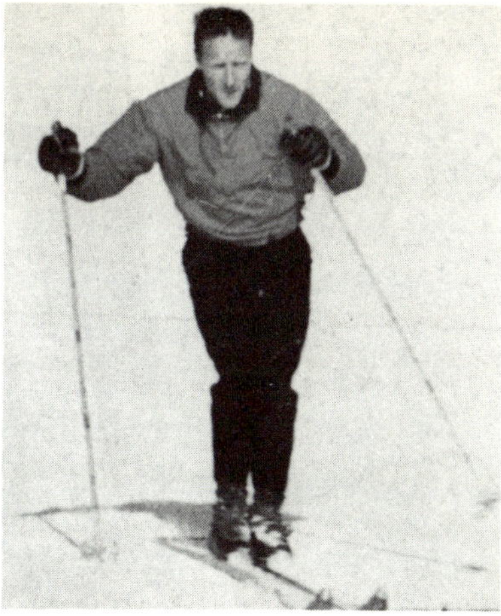
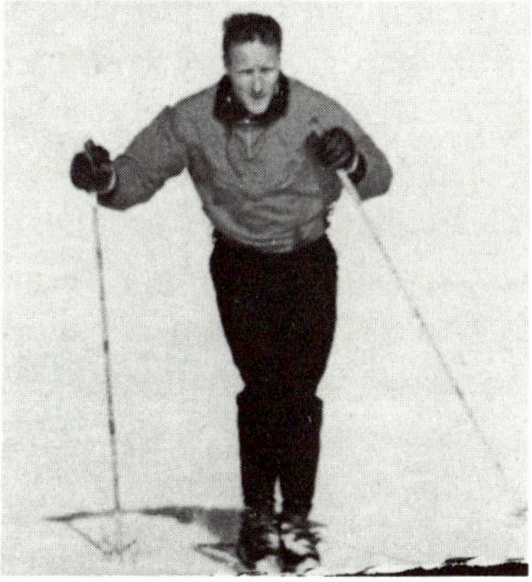
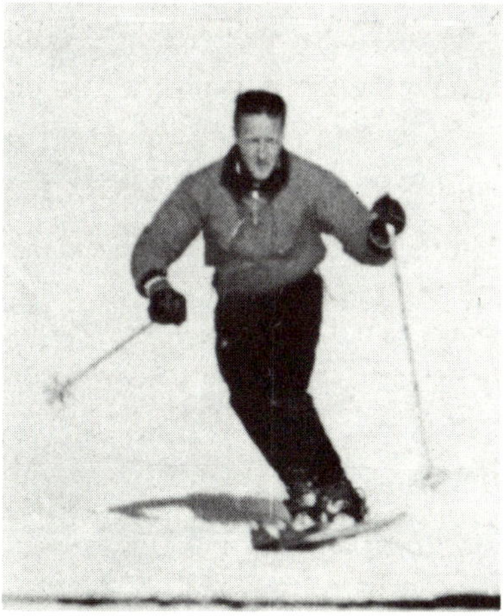
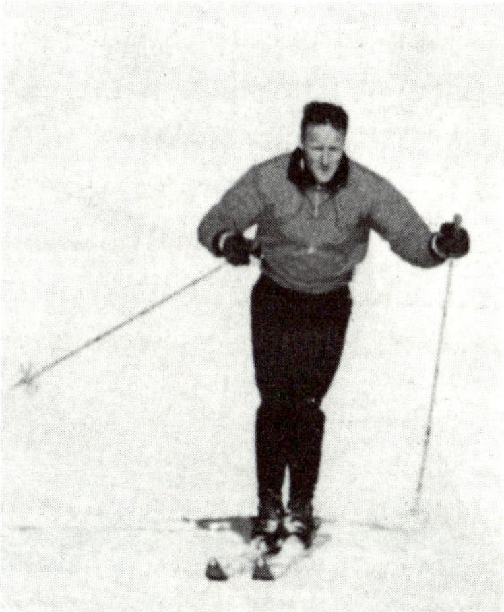

SKI POINTERS ON ADVANCED TECHNIQUE

Break the Stem Habit

by Don Schwartz, Director, Lookout Mountain Ski School, Virginia, Minn.

The biggest hurdle for the average skier who has mastered the basic rudiments of wedeln to overcome is the break from the short stem to parallel skiing. Stemming prevents you from experiencing the full exhilaration of skiing this smooth new style.

There are two factors in wedeln that make the difference between stemming and skiing with your skis perfectly parallel. The first factor deals with forward lean. The popular misconception in wedeln, it seems, indicates that because of the "heel thrust" idea, the weight is carried back on the heels. Actually, just the opposite is true. *It is the forward lean of your body and the forward press of your knees that enable the unweighted heels of your skis to whip from side to side.*

Secondly, it is the up-and-down motion of your knees, combined with the forward press of knees and body, that rhythmically enables you to thrust the skis from side to side. This forward lean and up-and-down motion, when synchronized with pole action (the pole is planted in the snow at the down movement of the knees), completely eliminates the stem and lets the skis work together as one locked unit. Very little edging is needed. The exchange of ski tips, right tip ahead on a right turn and left tip ahead on a left turn, is the only movement of the skis that you should be consciously aware of.

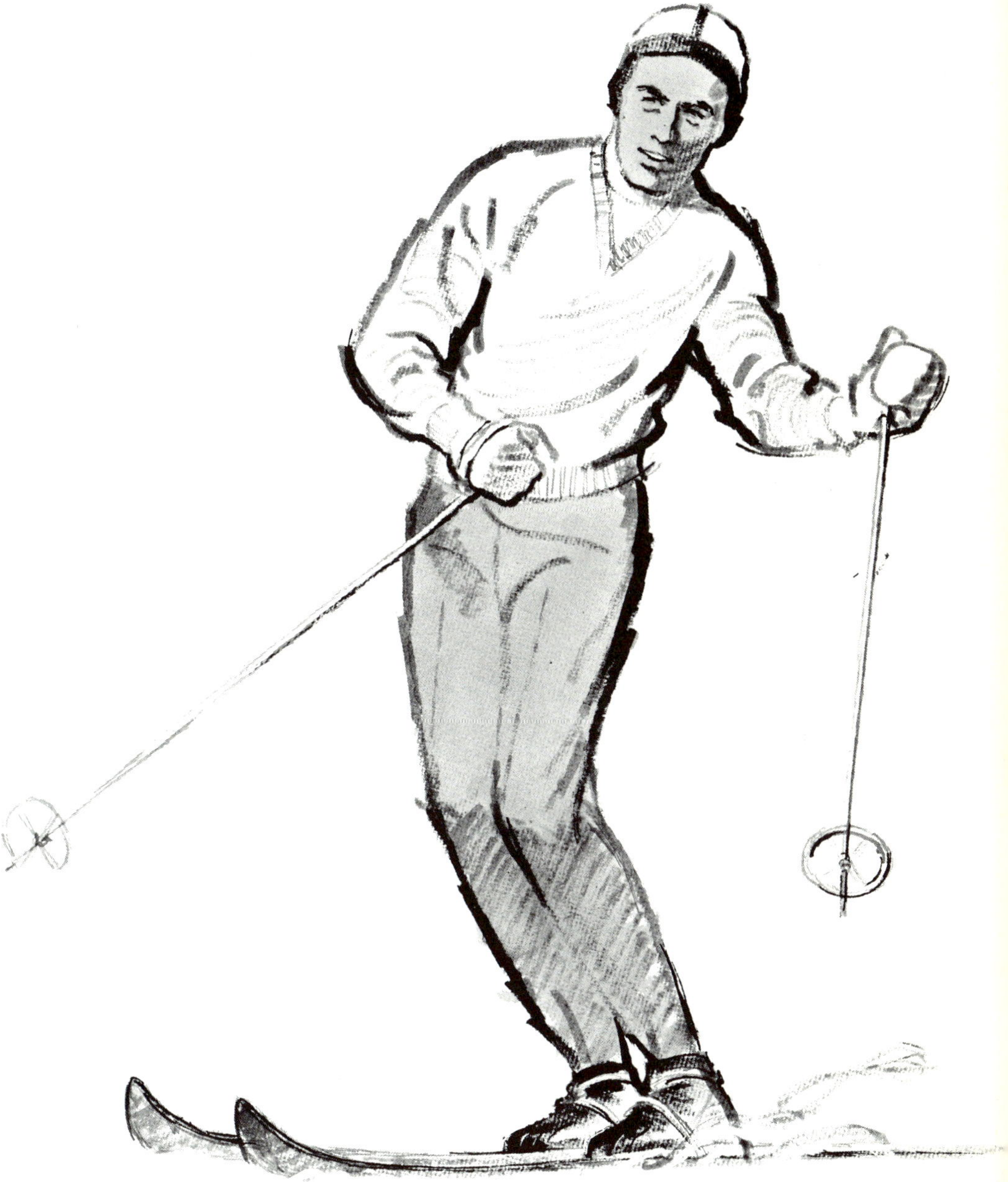

Use More Knee Action

by Robert W. Craig, Certified Instructor, SRMSIA

In short swing, or any swing for that matter, the fluidity of knee and ankle action is probably the single most important factor. I suggest that knee and ankle flexion be taken as one unit rather than as separate body functions. *The essence of proper knee action is that when in a turning sequence you should never, or hardly ever, have to use all your reserve by rising from this flexed position.* In skiing fast through rough terrain, you may occasionally get jarred out of this constantly flexed position, but this is an exception to the rule. Whatever new methods of turning have been developed over the past several years, the knees and ankles have survived most of that mutation. In fact, I like to think that they have become more fluid. To illustrate briefly: skiing through bumps, you effect the rapid change of edges required and maintain control of speed by remaining in what might be called a locked flexed-knee position. To straighten out your knees between changes of direction is to lose control in short fall-line turns between moguls. *It is precisely this fluid knee action, coupled with a very short rotational swing, that makes the so-called "swivel turns"—the latest embellishment of modern slalom technique. The more fluid the knees and ankles, the more sensitive the turn.*

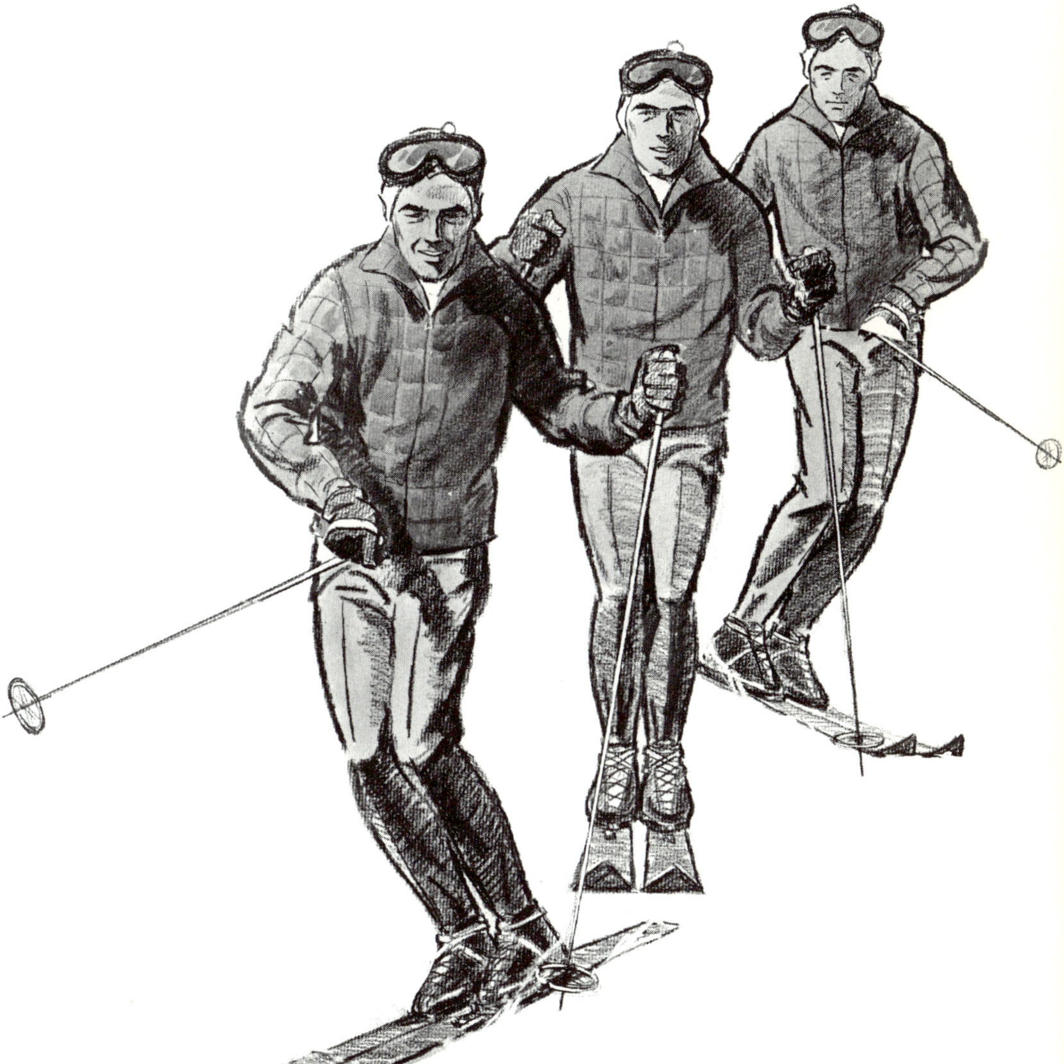

Practicing Knee Action

by Pierre Chauvin, Director, Brule Mountain Ski School, Iron River, Mich.

Wedeln is simply advanced and up-to-date parallel skiing. *But in this new parallel system there is less movement in the upper part of the body, and more pressure exerted by your feet and knees.* Therefore, in order to build up your skiing in this modern technique, it is necessary to drop down a few notches and begin with the snow-plow turn.

Start down the fall line in a snow-plow position with weight evenly distributed on both skis. As your speed increases, start your turn by shifting your weight to the outside ski. Make sure that the pressure you put on the outside ski is caused by increased knee action and not by tilting your whole body to that side. *Get the feeling that it is your feet and knees that cause the turn.*

Now try traversing. Start in the traverse position and pick up a little speed. Roll your knees and ankles outward slightly. This will release your edges automatically, causing your skis to slide. At the same time, turn both feet in toward the hill. Now stop the slide and the turn by going back to your normal traverse position. Do this four or five times on a long traverse, in both directions.

Now, add the use of your ski poles. Traversing across the hill, lower your knees and plant the uphill pole in the snow between ski tip and boot. Use the pole as a pivot for your heel slip. As you become more proficient in this maneuver, increase the angle of your traverse until you start your slips closer to the fall line. Start each one with an up motion of your knees and feet and follow through with a slight sinking motion. Be sure you don't rise too fast at the start and that you synchronize your "lift" with both feet turning at the same time. As your turns become faster, you will begin to establish a rhythm. This rhythm is the main ingredient necessary to wedeln.

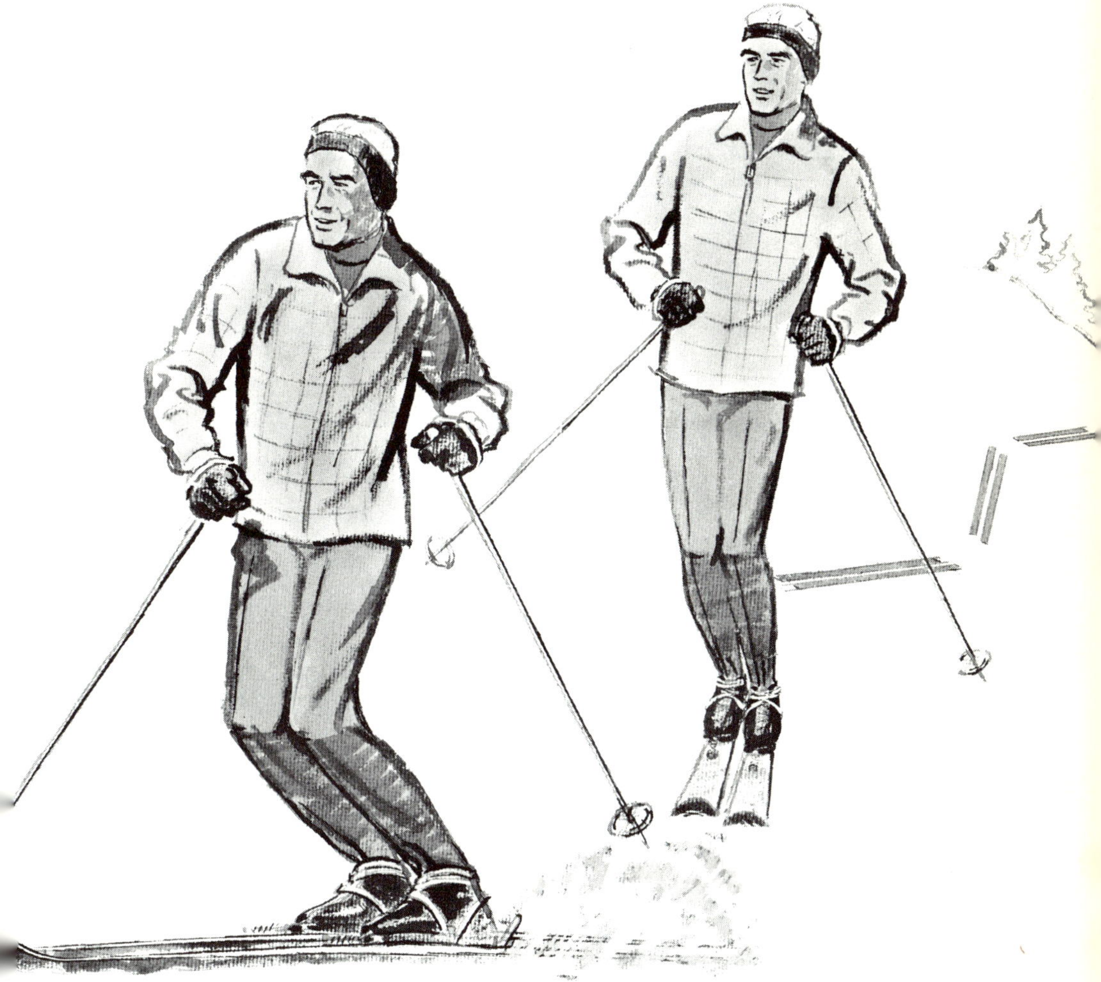

Unweighting the Skis

by *John Yonkow, Certified Instructor, FWSIA, Heavenly Valley Ski School, Lake Tahoe, Calif.*

In wedeln, unlike other techniques, the upper body does not turn the skis. The turning job is done with the legs, while the upper body only performs a function of balance and compensation in the turn. Therefore, *one of the most important elements in mastering wedeln is the proper unweighting of the skis, with a down-and-up movement of the knees.*

Here is a good exercise to practice unweighting your skis. Build a series of artificial humps in the snow, using a gentle slope. Each hump should measure about two feet in height and the humps should be spaced no more than five to ten feet apart. Now try straight running over the humps. Push your knees forward and down just before you reach the top of each hump and straighten your legs again as you start down the other side of the hump. Time these movements so that you establish a smooth down-and-up rhythm as you ski. After you get the feel of this easy unweighting exercise, practice the same down-and-up movement on a smooth slope. You can aid the lift of your body by alternating your poles in the snow. As you quickly sink down in the knees, plant your left pole in the snow, halfway between the tip of your left ski and boot. Remove the pole as you rise again with a smooth "up" motion of your knees. Now sink down again and place the right pole in the snow, near the right ski. Co-ordinate your down-and-up movements with the rhythm of the poles.

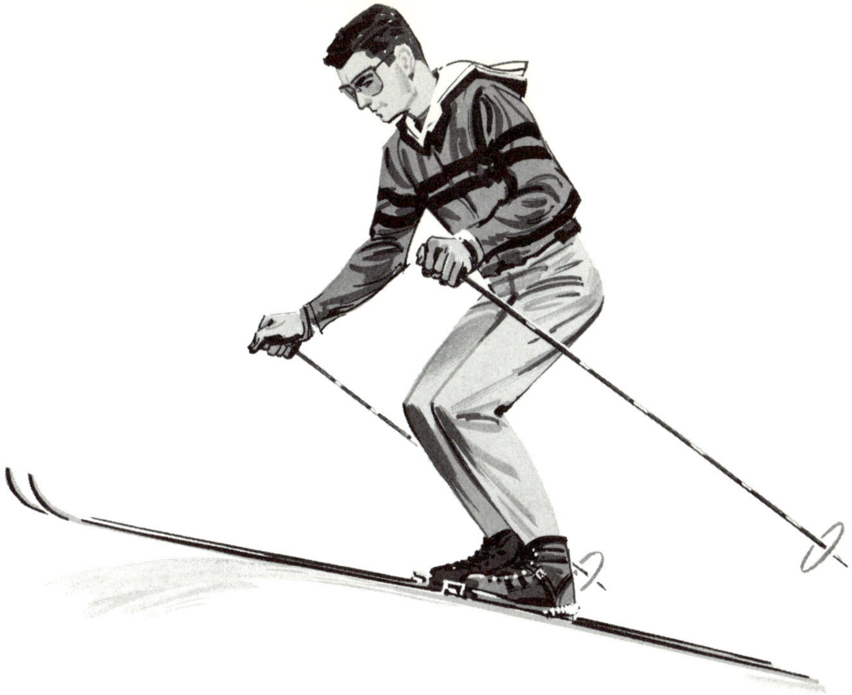

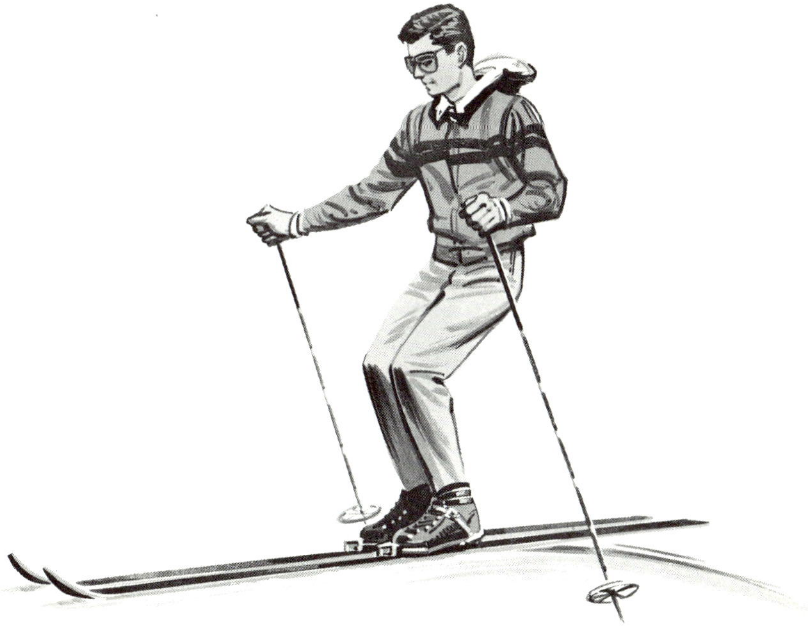

Controlling Speed by Edge Set

by K. Smith, Jr., Director, Brighton Ski School, Brighton, Utah

Most skiers make the mistake of trying to control or check speed *while* turning. This is wrong—no matter what type of turn is involved. Instead, check or control speed *before* you start to turn downhill. For the novice, this can be done by steering your snow-plow turn or stem turn in a longer arc, so that your skis are pointing more toward the hill at the completion of one turn, before beginning the next turn.

The same rule holds true with parallel turns except that here you are more concerned with "edge set." The degree of sharpness and abruptness depends on the arc of the turn and the amount of speed that has to be killed. Always plan to gain speed while turning. Then you won't sit back on your skis, fighting speed and trying to hang on with premature edge setting. Remember, in order to start a turn, the edges must be released to allow the ski tips to brush toward the fall line. But if you edge to hold back speed in the turn, then you frustrate the very thing that makes the turn easy and graceful.

Again, if you set your edges too soon after the skis turn through the fall line into the new direction, your drift will stop and your trip across the hill will be just as fast as it can possibly be. Instead, *keep the skis slipping or drifting until just before you want to turn in the new direction, and then set your edges again.*

Learn to Bank Your Turns

by Clifton Taylor, Certified Instructor, USEASA, Hogback Ski School, Brattleboro, Vt.

Downhill skiing is one of the most effortless sports. You do not have to create your own momentum; snow and gravity do this for you. Thus it always amazes me to see a skier come schussing downhill and suddenly stem a ski out in preparation for a turn. *All you really need to do is to take advantage of momentum and simply lean in the direction you want to go—like a motorcycle rider banking around a corner.*

Whether you ski short swing or Arlberg, the principle of the lean is the same. Using a short-swing turn, you lean your hips laterally toward the center of the turn. Using an Arlberg swing, you lean your entire body. Proper lean in a turn does two things. It gives your skis a smooth edge change from one turn to another and it offsets centrifugal force (the force that causes a turning object such as a pencil on a spinning recording disk to be thrown outward, away from the center of the disk).

Since a turn in one direction puts your body at an inward lean, a series of linked parallel turns would give you the sensation of swaying—your hips in wedeln, your body in Arlberg—from side to side. Naturally, you will use less lean on hard-packed or icy slopes and exaggerate your lean when skiing in deep powder, because of the increased resistance of the skis. Once you get this dance-like rhythm, your turning technique will have improved considerably, and will be more graceful with less effort.

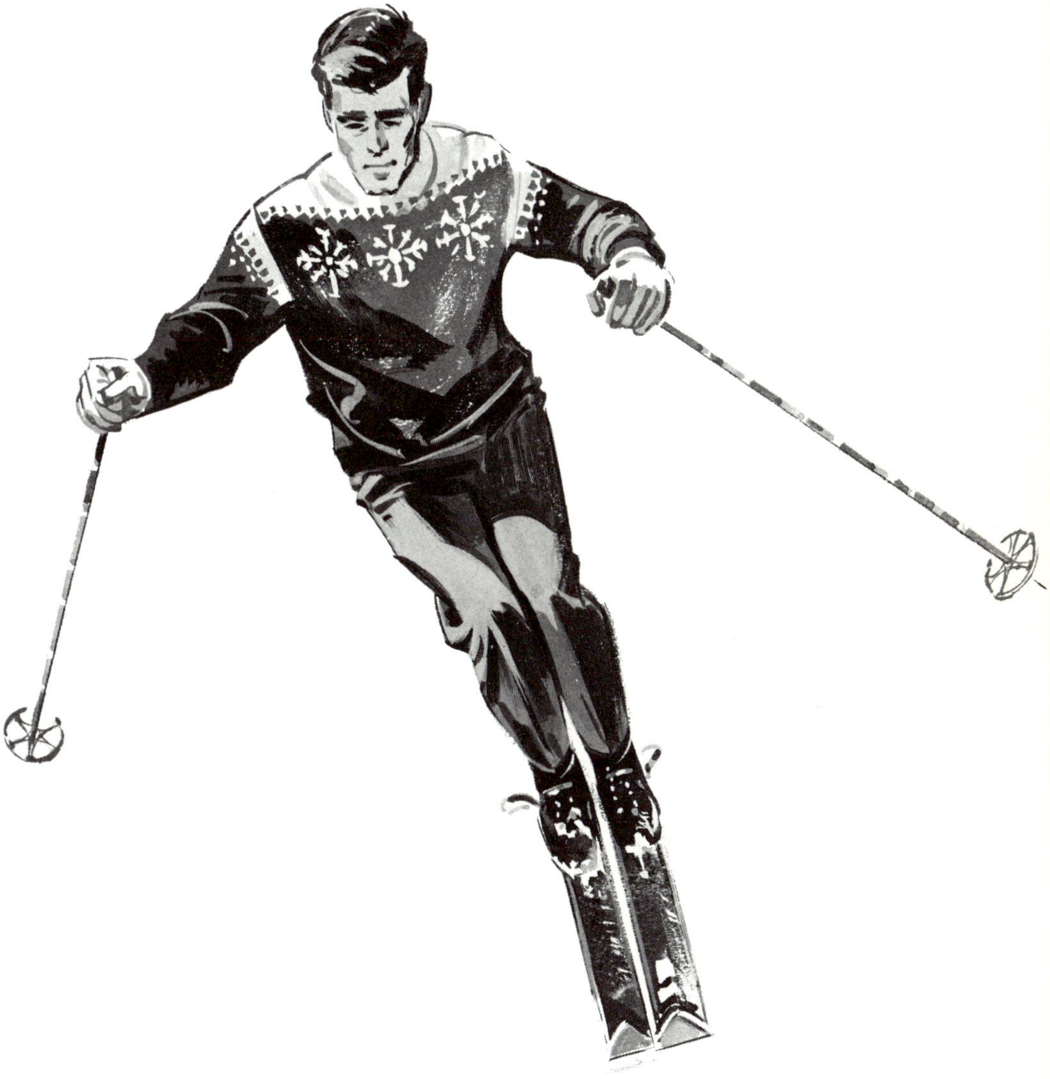

Exercise for Wedeln

by Alex Petrie, Certified Instructor, USEASA, Bromley Ski School, Manchester, Vt.

Wedeln has often been defined as a "series of fast turns executed on the fall line of a slope." That's a rather simple definition for a difficult ski maneuver. More than any other ski maneuver, wedeln demands rhythm and balance. Here is an exercise that you can practice to help achieve that balance and rhythm. Before describing the maneuver, however, I must caution you that this is not intended to be a complete series of turns. Rather, it is an exercise to gain balance and rhythm, plus good practice in shifting your weight by leg action.

Begin on an intermediate slope, directly in the fall line. Keeping your body erect, assume a modified snow-plow position by pressing your knees forward and inward, and pressing your heels outward.

As you start down the slope, put your weight on the right ski by pushing the right knee forward and inward and getting your body out over that ski. Keep your right heel pushed outward. The weight you have put on the right ski will cause you to turn toward the left. Now, before completing that left-turn motion, shift your weight to the left ski by pushing the left knee forward and inward. The weight shifted to the left ski will turn you back toward the right. As your downhill speed increases, the left-to-right swing rhythm will increase, causing the skis gradually to become parallel and close together and leaving a trail of snake-like turns (see illustration).

When you feel that you have achieved the rhythm and balance of this exercise, it is time to add the use of your ski poles. With your weight on the right ski and your body out over that ski, set your right pole in the snow between boot tip and ski tip and close to the right ski. Let the pole help you unweight the ski, shifting your weight out and over to the left ski. This will change your direction toward the right. Now set the left pole in the snow and shift your weight back to the right ski, causing a turn toward the left. Again, this is not to be considered a full turning motion, but an exercise in the fall line.

Once you have achieved the necessary rhythm and balance by proper use of this exercise, it will be of untold value when you begin to adapt to wedeln.

Stem Approach to Wedeln

by Walter Blaesi, Certified Instructor, USEASA, Winter Park Ski School, Winter Park, Colo.

For teaching wedeln, I have a special exercise which I find a quick and easy way to learn this most difficult but exciting maneuver.

Start with the stem christie but change the turn preparation from uphill to *downhill* stem. This downhill stem is more a break of your speed and that is the most important point in wedeln, since you ski in the fall line. This downhill stem will also teach you automatically how to set your edges once you bring your skis together.

From a traverse position, bring your downhill ski into a slight stem position. Then, with a quick unweighting motion, bring your skis parallel again and resume the traverse position. Practice this exercise a few times in both directions. Now find a very gentle slope and start out in normal straight-running position. Stem your right ski, unweight the ski tails and bring them together by jumping them sideways to the left. Do the same exercise to the opposite side, then link turns, right and left.

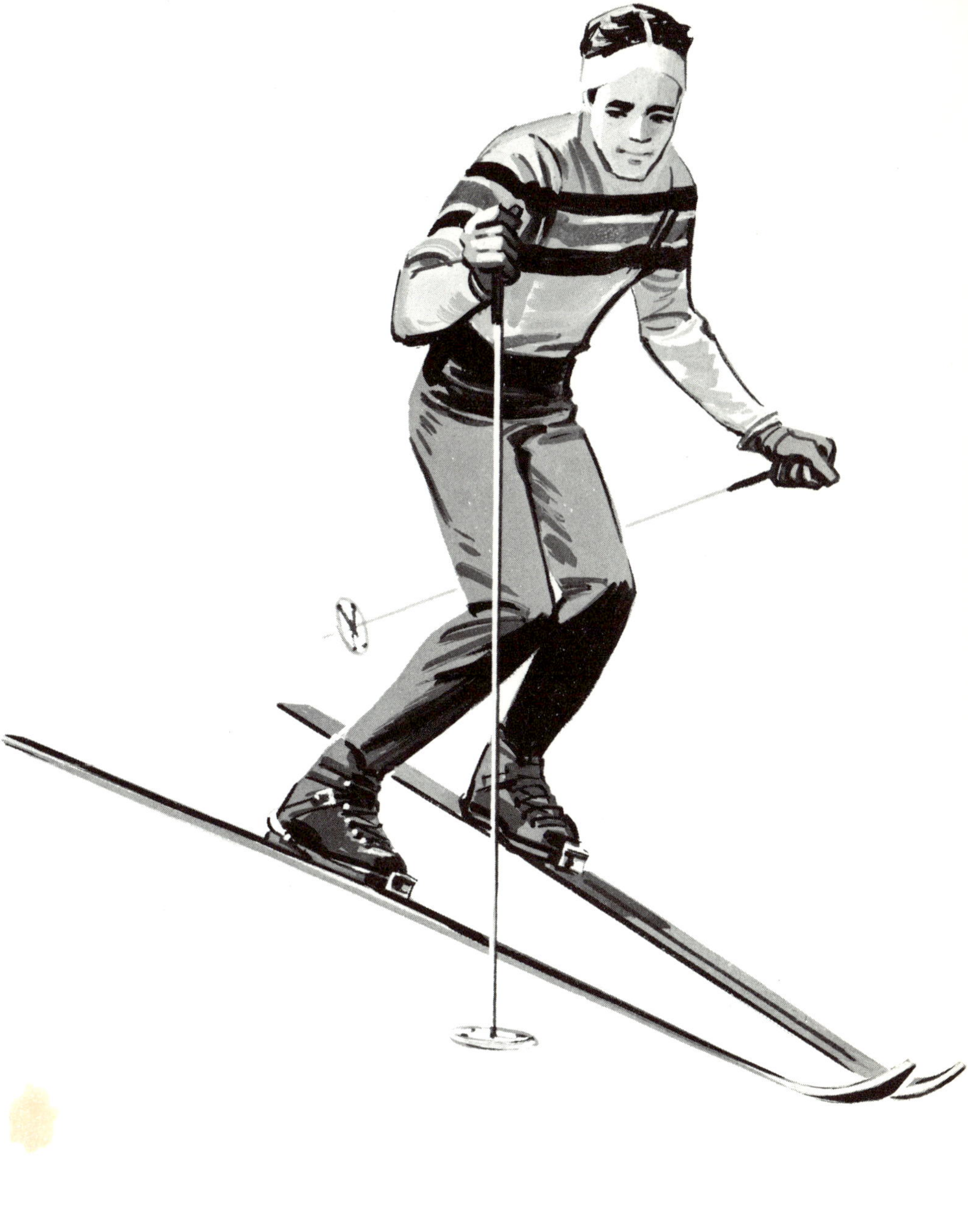

Parallel Approach to Wedeln

by Lutz Aynedter, Director, Edelweiss Ski School, Twin Bridges, Calif.

There are two different approaches to wedeln—the ultimate maneuver in skiing today. Some schools teach it from a stem or snow-plow position, and others start out parallel immediately. Both methods, however, eventually lead to the same final product.

Assuming that you have achieved a good deal of experience and sureness in all the maneuvers leading to advanced skiing, here is a short run-down on our own particular method. Sink down and rise up with the lower body (hips and knees) to weight and unweight the skis. *At the top of the body lift, while the skis are unweighted, flatten them and thrust your ankles opposite to the desired direction of the turn.* Thrust right to turn left, thrust left to turn right. Synchronize the setting of your turning (inside) pole with the ankle thrust (using your left pole for left turn, right pole for right turn). The pole acts as a turn indicator, stabilizer, and pivot point. Practice this maneuver across the hill, in both directions, and keep approaching the fall line until the fall line is crossed with every turn. Choose fairly flat, well-packed, easy terrain for practicing. Make it a rule to use less edge on this easy, flat terrain and more edge on more difficult terrain, keeping the skis parallel at all times. As you grow more proficient at practice, gradually progress to steeper terrain.

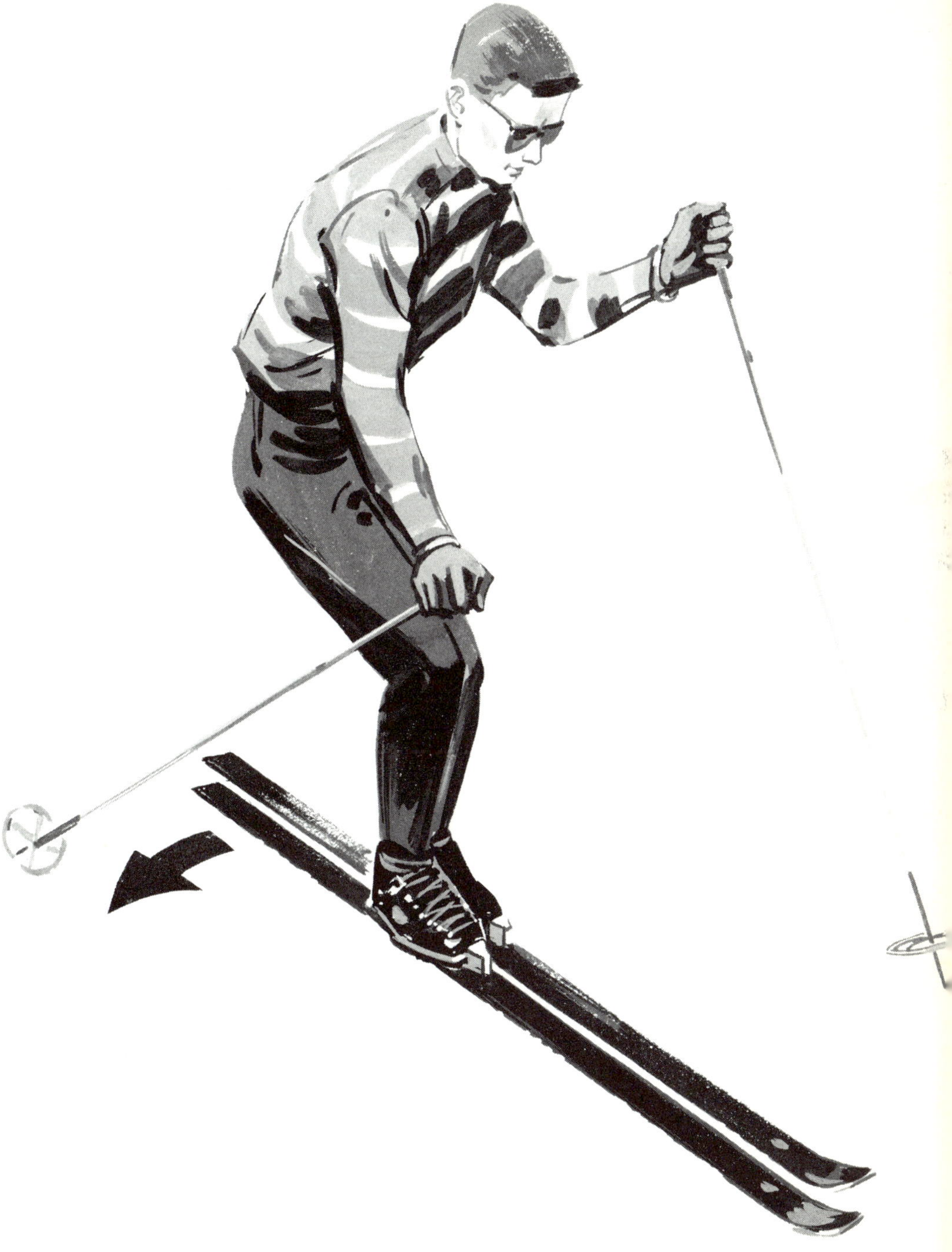

Tips on Schussing

by John Church, Certified Instructor, PNSIA, Spokane Ski School, Spokane, Wash.

One of the most basic maneuvers of skiing is the schuss, or going straight down the slope. *However, even the experienced skier can benefit by a few suggestions on schussing properly—your body in a natural, relaxed position, your ankles bent, your knees pressed forward, arms held as though they were holding a small barrel. In powder snow, the skis should be kept close together; on a hard surface, they will be a few inches apart.*

Individual variations in style are developed, of course. For control, you will keep your weight forward. If you race, you will sometimes sit back to gain speed. But whether you are schussing to save a walk across a flat or to win a downhill race, it is important that your body be kept very relaxed. Flexible knee action is needed to negotiate bumps, for a mogul will toss a rigid skier into the air. Then too, the person who holds himself stiff will tire more quickly than a relaxed skier. A schuss in the middle of a long run can actually help you to catch your breath and relieve tension on muscles, if you take the schuss relaxed. Don't try to hold your skis so they do not waver at all. Let the skis run freely and if you feel them wiggling slightly from side to side, this is all right—because it shows that you are relaxed. If you try to hold the skis perfectly steady, you can easily catch an edge and fall. Often this wavering will occur as you follow tracks; the best thing to do is to let the skis waver. However, if they waver so much that you go out of control, lean forward and they will become steady again. Lastly, be sure you are familiar with the slope before schussing and that you ski in control so that you can stop or turn at any point.

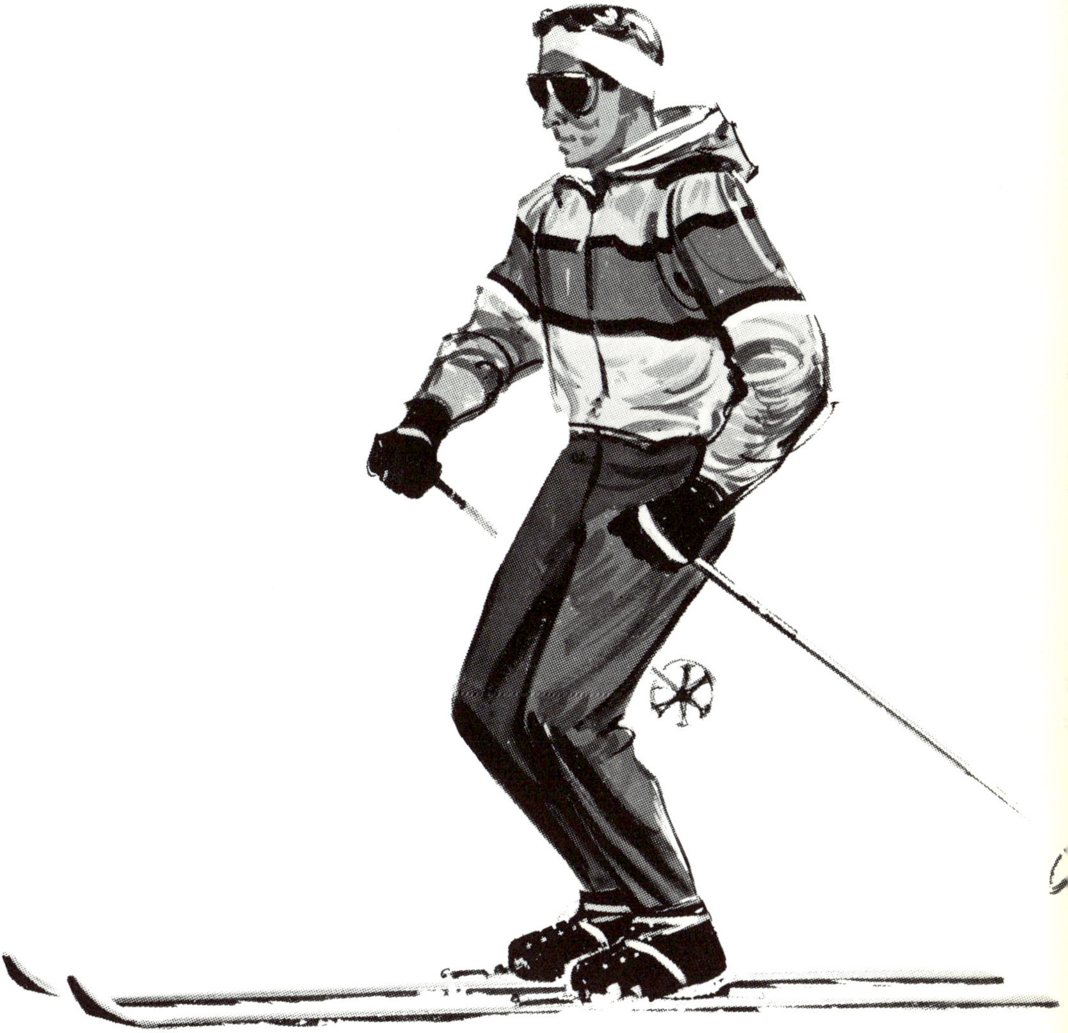

Exercise for "Off Days"

by K. Smith, Jr., Director, Brighton Ski School, Brighton, Utah

All athletes, or participants in sports of any kind, will have an "off day." In skiing, for instance, it's a day when your technique isn't up to par.

Here's an exercise that should improve your skiing on those "off days." Start down the fall line of a gentle slope in a moderate snow-plow position, edging just enough to keep the outside edges of your skis from digging into the snow. Follow the fall line for some distance, until you have attained proper balance and position. Then transfer your weight sharply to the outside ski of your proposed turn and concentrate on holding that ski relatively flat. Now, before the turn is completed, transfer your weight sharply to the other ski, driving your knee toward the tip of the ski, and begin a turn in the opposite direction. Again, do not bring the skis parallel. Practice these turns quickly in rhythm.

Next, follow this same sequence but, as you change weight and start to drive the outside ski around, lift the inside ski of the turn, leaving just its tip on the snow. Use your poles to help your timing. Plant your right pole in the snow (for a turn to the right) between the toe of your boot and the tip of your ski. As you touch the pole to the snow, transfer your weight to the outside ski and simultaneously lift the heel of the inside ski. Don't lean on the pole and don't swing it; merely use it as a guide for the turn. Now, as you proceed with your turns, and the turns become closer and faster, narrow your snow plow with each turn, until your skis are parallel. You'll find yourself back in the groove, skiing as you should be.

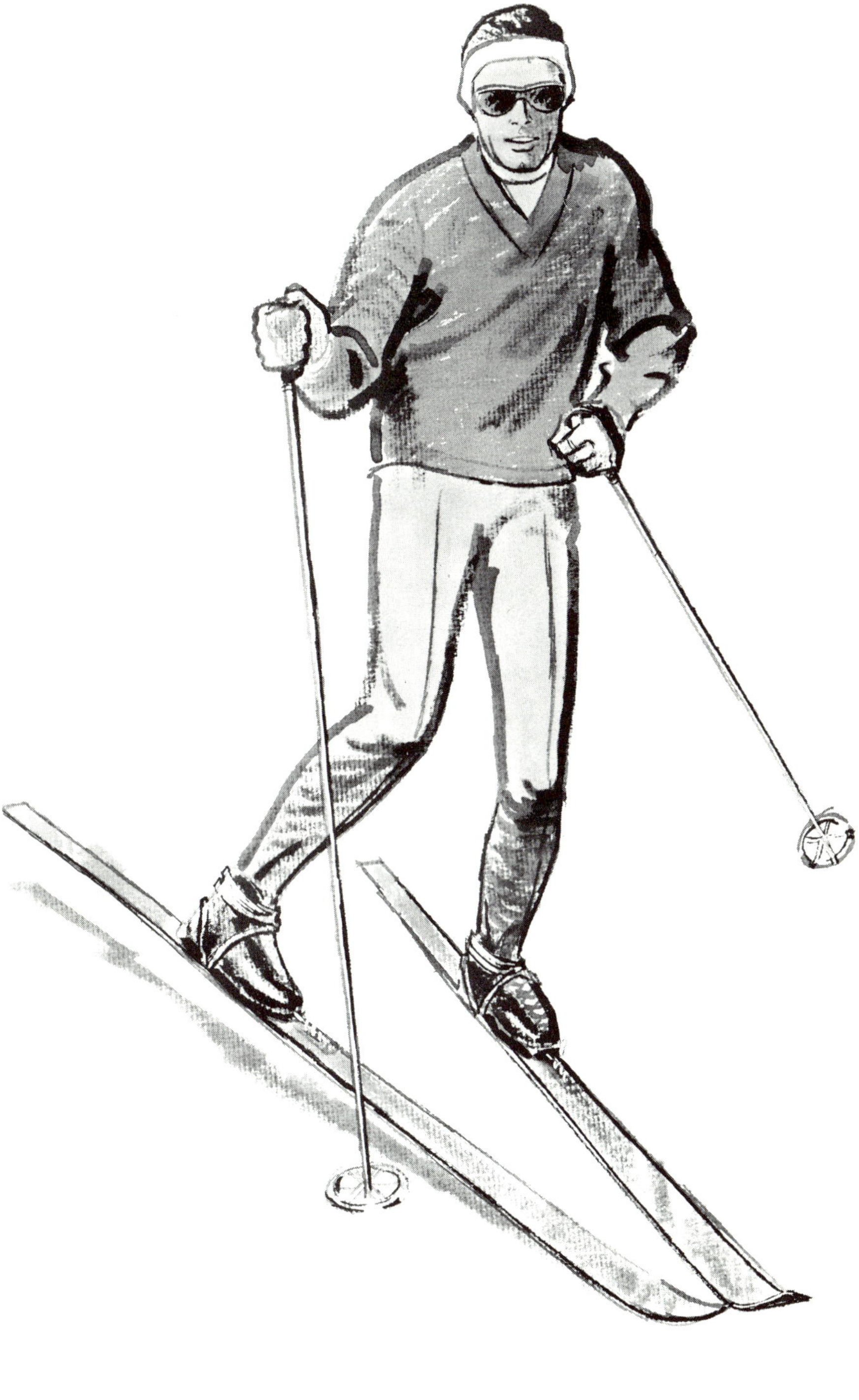

ADVANCED TECHNIQUE PROBLEMS: CAUSES AND CURES

Parallel Christie

PROBLEMS	CAUSES	CURES
Can't turn	Faulty unweighting; faulty rhythm	Emphasize "down-up-down" sequence. Try lifting heels off snow on "up" motion
	Faulty weight shift and lead change	Weight the downhill ski. Lead changes as weight changes
	Faulty edging	Set edges on "down" motion, release on "up"
	Skis not together	Keep knees and skis together. Maintain proper weighting, unweighting, and edging
Turn too early. (Too much check)	Edging too quickly	Set edges after assuming down position
	Overrotation	Inside hip and shoulder lead throughout turn
Turn too late. (Too much float)	Edging too slowly	Set edges in "down" position before rising to "up" position
Inside edges catch	Faulty weight shift	Shift weight in "up" position to new downhill ski
	No heel thrust	Let heels slip throughout "up" motion
	Faulty pole action	Plant inside pole earlier
Outside edges catch	Faulty weight shift	Don't shift weight too early. Slow it down a split second
Can't keep skis together	Faulty weight shift, unweighting, or edging	(See cures for "Can't turn")

PROBLEMS	CAUSES	CURES
Poor rhythm, jerky arm movement	Pole action too early	Slow down pole action
	Insufficient "down-up-down" motion in knees	Sink down and forward into knees before coming up
Uphill shoulder drags or rotates	Pole action too late	Plant pole earlier
Can't link turns	Skis not together, faulty weighting, unweighting, lead change, pole action, or rhythm	(*See* cures for "Can't turn")
Instability, poor balance	Faulty weighting, unweighting, lead change, or edging	(*See* above)

Wedeln

PROBLEMS	CAUSES	CURES
Can't link turns	Faulty rhythm	Check co-ordination of "down, edge, up, slip" sequence and of lead change
	Insufficient pole action	Check timing of pole plant
	Too much pole action	Check for too much arm motion which delays pole plant and upsets rhythm
	Traversing between turns	Shorten turn. Use quicker edge set at end of turn
Too much acceleration in turn	Insufficient pole and edge action	Check timing of pole plant; don't let upper body lag. Use stronger edge action
Faulty rhythm	Faulty pole action	Check for too much pole action
	Faulty edging	Check timing and sufficiency of edge action
	Faulty unweighting	Check "down-up-down" motion for timing and sufficiency
	Poor co-ordination	Check co-ordination of "down, edge, up, slip" sequence and of lead change
Can't check	Faulty rhythm	(*See* above)
	Faulty pole or edge action	Check for too much pole action. Check timing and sufficiency of edge action
	Faulty lead change	Check timing and point of lead change—in the "up" motion as weight is shifted
	Sitting back	Press knees forward
Faulty weight shift	Faulty rhythm	Check co-ordination of "down, edge, up, slip" sequence and of lead change
	Faulty body position	Check for overexaggeration and overuse of comma

PROBLEMS	CAUSES	CURES
	Faulty weight change	Check timing of weight shift—in the "up" motion as lead is changed. Unweighting follows "down" motion as the "up" motion starts
	Sitting back	Press knees forward
Can't keep skis together; stemming	Faulty weight shift	Check timing of weight shift—in the "up" motion as lead is changed. Unweighting follows "down" motion as the "up" motion starts
	Faulty edging	Check timing and sufficiency of edge action
	Faulty body position	Check for overexaggeration and overuse of comma
	Faulty rhythm	Check co-ordination of "down, edge, up, slip" sequence and of lead change
Inside edge catches	Edge change too late	Change edges earlier
Outside edge catches	Edge change too early	Change edges later. Keep edges flat in turn
	Faulty weight shift	Check timing of weight shift—in the "up" motion as lead is changed. Unweighting follows "down" motion as the "up" motion starts
Skis cross	Faulty lead change or edging	Check timing and point of lead change—in the "up" motion as weight is shifted. Check timing and sufficiency of edge action
	Sitting back	Move weight forward
Instability, poor balance	Faulty body position, weight shift, rhythm, late edge change	(*See* above)

SKI LIFE EXTRA

Emphasis on Poles

by Willy Schaeffler, Ski Coach, University of Denver; Director, Arapahoe Basin Ski School; Director of Ski Events, Eighth Olympic Winter Games

Ever since man first began to ski, his basic equipment has always included skis and poles. As his knowledge of their use increased through the years, other items were developed that have since become essential too. The emergence of various ski techniques necessitated advances in boots and bindings and, as these became modified, the importance of ski poles was often minimized. At one point, some people even advocated skiing without poles. Today, however, as we learn more and more about technique, the emphasis is again on poles. As in the early days of skiing, they are again considered essential. Modern skiing methods demand that the pole be used as an integral part of a skier's technique —not merely as an aid to balance, as they were first conceived, or as a "crutch" for the beginner to lean on as he learns to ski, but as a dependable aid to help him ski with greater ease and more proficiency.

In those early days, a ski pole was a necessary evil. The first skiers used a single pole hewn from a convenient branch or sapling. Long and heavy, its blunted tip was manipulated partially as a brake, partially as a steering rudder, partially as a balance rod. Then someone discovered that *two* poles, shorter and lighter, with snow rings attached near the tips, not only aided in pushing forward on level ground, but also helped in climbing and provided more flexibility and balance while in motion.

As techniques made more use of the poles, they gradually evolved to their present size and appearance. First they became shorter, then longer; rings diminished in size; new materials, stronger and lighter, were developed. Today's ski pole represents the product of many decades of experimentation and enlightened knowledge.

In modern technique, pole work is an integral part of the learning process. The beginner first learns to use his poles in walking on skis. Here he learns the proper way to plant his pole into the snow and how to remove it. Only when he learns the proper co-operation of pole and ski action in walking is he ready to move on. Then he learns how to use his poles as an aid to the climbing movements and standing turns. During the snow plow and stem turns and the traverse, the pole is used primarily for balance. But in snow-plow christies and stem christies, the application of the pole as an aid to turning becomes evident. Used as a point on which to pivot, it helps the skier to shift weight, to develop timing, and to master the all-important sideslipping movements necessary for advanced skiing.

In this stage, too, the skier learns to use his poles in a playful, relaxed manner rather than in stiff, tense jabs. He plants the pole with his upper arm relaxed, elbow close to the hip and the forearm pointing ahead rather than to the side. During the plant, the palm is slightly outward. As the skier comes up on his pole and shifts his weight, he brings the palm inward in front of the body. Otherwise, the hand would lag behind the body and pull him off balance.

The intermediate skier soon learns to rely less on his poles and more on weight shift and edge control for smooth execution of turns. But now the poles assume another role. Hop-turn exercises, at first using both poles, then each pole alternately, substitute unweighting for the stem as the skier approaches parallel turns. The less stem he uses, the more christie he gets. Substituting the hop for the stem helps to eliminate the "stem hangover" that plagues many skiers, since it gets the tails of both skis off the snow and across the fall line without dependence on the stem.

In the advanced stages of skiing, the pole becomes a somewhat secondary but nevertheless important factor, since it helps the skier to establish the necessary rhythm and timing required for short-swing turns and wedeln. Used properly, they add the co-ordination demanded for smooth, effortless skiing. They also become indispensable in the execution of the various aerial maneuvers that are a part of any advanced skier's repertoire.

IV. *The Finer Points of Skiing*

What sets the expert skier apart? He is one who can formfully handle any terrain under any conditions. While few skiers reach this ultimate plateau, the refinements discussed in this chapter will not only increase your ability but will add a further measure of enjoyment of the sport.

Variety Is the Spice of Skiing

by Ernie McCulloch, Director, Mont Tremblant Ski School, Mont Tremblant, Quebec, Canada

In the past several years, there has been so much talk throughout the skiing world about wedeln that people have almost forgotten that there are other ways, just as pleasurable and sometimes even more practical, to ski. Skiers do not seem to realize that every top racer or expert uses three or four different techniques in making one single run down the mountain. The *expert* varies these different methods according to the different types of snow conditions and terrain.

The first method, Arlberg, is still very much in evidence in the technique used by most of the world's top skiers today. Through slow-motion photography, it has been shown that many of these top skiers are using a slight stem at times, when it is advantageous. They are also using a certain amount of rotation, which is, of course, the basis of the Arlberg technique.

As most people are aware, the Arlberg technique was originated by the late Hannes Schneider, and it has probably been the most influential technique used throughout the ski schools of the world. When people think of Arlberg, they automatically think of skiing with a stem, and it is true that in this method of teaching the skier learns by using a stem in the early stages. Later on, however, this stem is modified to a point where the skier turns with skis parallel or stemmed very slightly.

As skiing became more popular in Europe and North America, Emil Allais and others of the French school developed a more parallel turn done at slower speeds, which they called the Ruade. In this French system, body rotation is still very similar to the rotation method used in the Arlberg, the main difference being that in the ruade there is more blockage in the hips.

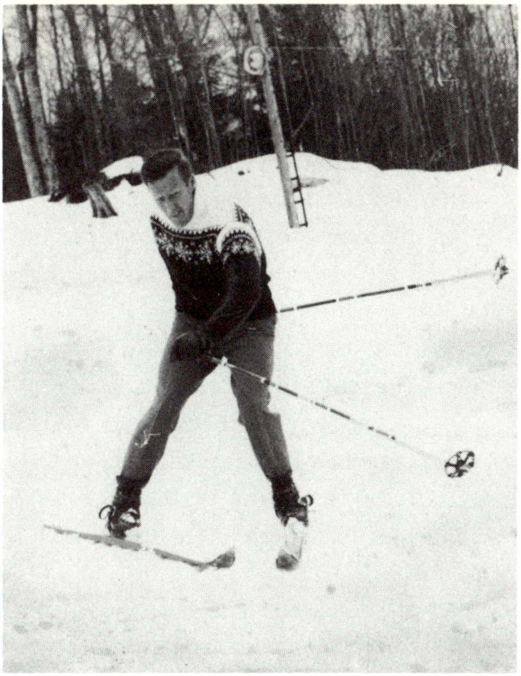

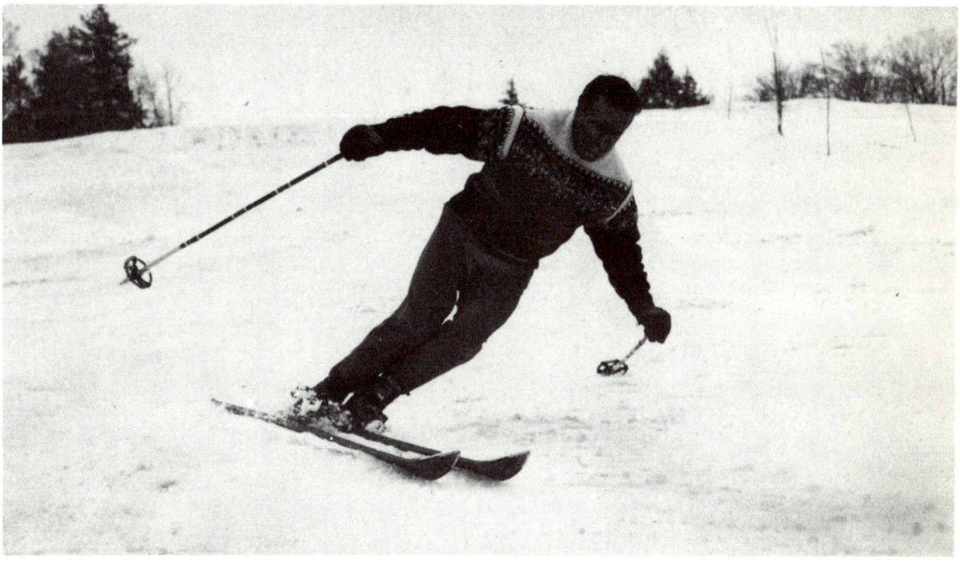

The real difference between these two methods of skiing is that the Arlberg is always started with a countermotion and a stemming of the uphill or downhill ski. (The uphill stem gives a more positive quick change of weight to the outside ski, thus eliminating some of the powerful rotation otherwise necessary at the beginning of a turn. Many schools feel that this is advantageous, since it cuts down on over-swinging, a common fault of many skiers. When the downhill stem is used, the turn is begun by a springboard effect of the downhill ski, followed by a powerful swing or rotation of the body, which causes the skis to turn.) In the ruade, however, a change of direction is begun not by stemming one ski, as in the Arlberg technique, but by lifting or retracting the tails of both skis together and placing them down again close to the fall line. The countermotion is not as exaggerated as in Arlberg, and the body is lowered more in preparation for the lifting of the skis. Upon landing, the upper body follows through to complete the rotation, but, again, with more blockage of the hips.

When it first was introduced the ruade started a trend, since people became more conscious of parallel skiing because of it. But widespread use of the ruade seemed to fade as the years went on and ski technique progressed. Still a very useful turn to know, the ruade does have its advantages, particularly when skiing on steep slopes at moderate speed. It is a great aid in carving a sharp enough arc of a turn to keep speed at a minimum. It will also help you turn with your skis together as a unit.

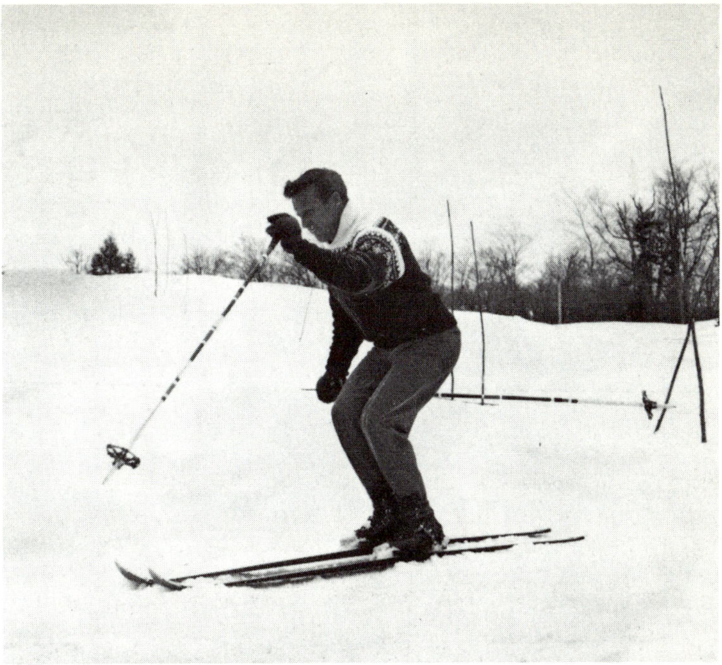

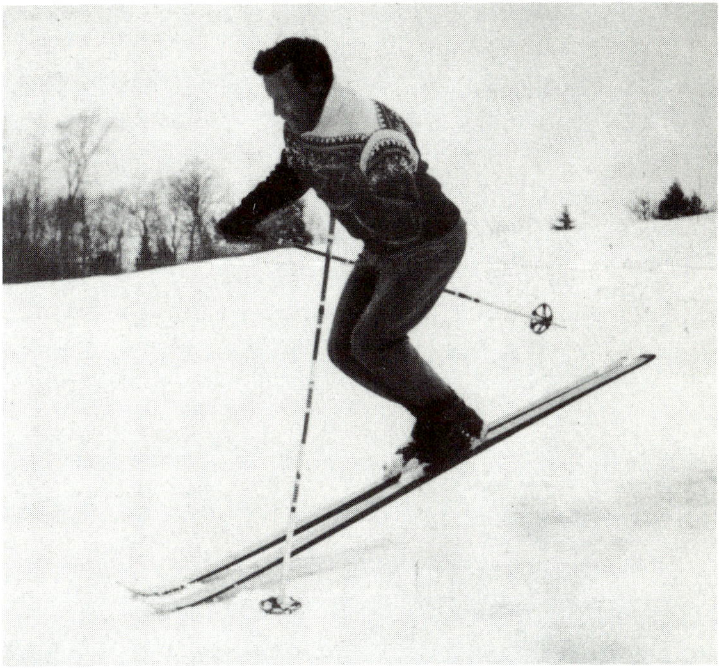

A third method of skiing, the mambo, is more of a fad than a technique. It seems to have been started by the top racers, and it is not a part of any formal teaching sequence. Rather, it is often demonstrated to advanced classes in ski schools for added enjoyment and variety. Even today, you will see several good skiers using it just for fun. In the mambo the skis are kept flat, or almost flat, on the snow, and they are turned by an overexaggerated upper body swing. There is a delayed turning action of the skis because the overexaggerated rotation does not immediately transmit its power to the feet. As soon as the action is transmitted from body to feet, the skis respond and turn in the direction of the overswing. Then, as the skis are turning, the body quickly overrotates in the opposite direction, giving this turn a snake-like effect. Almost any good skier can ski mambo, and it is fun to do on a smooth hill.

Mambo should never be confused with wedeln. Many people who see a skier mamboing down a slope think that he is skiing wedeln because of the popular misconception that wedeln entails this exaggerated, snaky look. Wedeln is completely different. In wedeln, the body never overswings and the turn is started by a powerful down-and-up motion of the knees, which unweights the skis. The inside ski pole is placed halfway between the boot and the tip of the ski, helping the skis to pivot into the turn. A steering action of the feet and knees starts the skis turning. It is true that this steering action will force the upper body to lean to the outside of the turn, causing a slight comma position. Some people have seen photographs of this wedeln position and have confused it with the exaggerated mambo swing. In wedeln, however, this comma position lasts for only a split second, until the upper part of the body catches up to the lower body and is again square to the skis.

62 655

SKI POINTERS FOR REFINING YOUR TECHNIQUE

Using Two Techniques in One Turn

by Fred Lonsdorf, Ski Coach, Michigan College of Mining and Technology, Houghton, Mich.

Too many skiers have a knowledge of the Arlberg method, but they know nothing about other techniques. Therefore, when they run a slalom course and don't have time to counterswing, they ski out of control and run into trouble.

There are many points in favor of the Arlberg technique. In fact, I always use it with my beginning pupils. I believe it to be the best system for new skiers. *However, in slalom running or in skiing difficult terrain, it is my contention that, by combining Arlberg and reverse shoulder in one turn, the skier has better control.*

In order to turn on skis, no matter what method you use, you must get your heels out to the side. Then you must control the amount of slide in the turn. With the Arlberg method, you begin the turn with a windup or counterswing. You step, slide, or hop the heels out to the side and complete the turn with the outside shoulder coming forward. With the reverse shoulder method, however, you begin the turn without a windup. You step, slide, or hop the skis to the side and complete the turn by bringing the inside shoulder ahead. The reverse shoulder turn requires no preparatory movement, hence it takes half the amount of time to get the turn started, as compared with Arlberg.

Many top skiers do not use the Arlberg counterswing, but substitute reverse shoulder to get the heels out, and then follow through with the Arlberg outside-shoulder-ahead. This combination Arlberg-reverse shoulder method works well when you have to get a turn started quickly, but you have room to let your skis swing wide at the finish. If your next turn is wide at the beginning and tight at the finish, you would complete your Arlberg turn (outside shoulder ahead) then snap to the reverse shoulder in the next turn and pull up sharply at the finish. If you are able to ski both methods and can combine Arlberg and reverse shoulder in one turn, you will find yourself more easily able to control your skis on difficult terrain or on the slalom course.

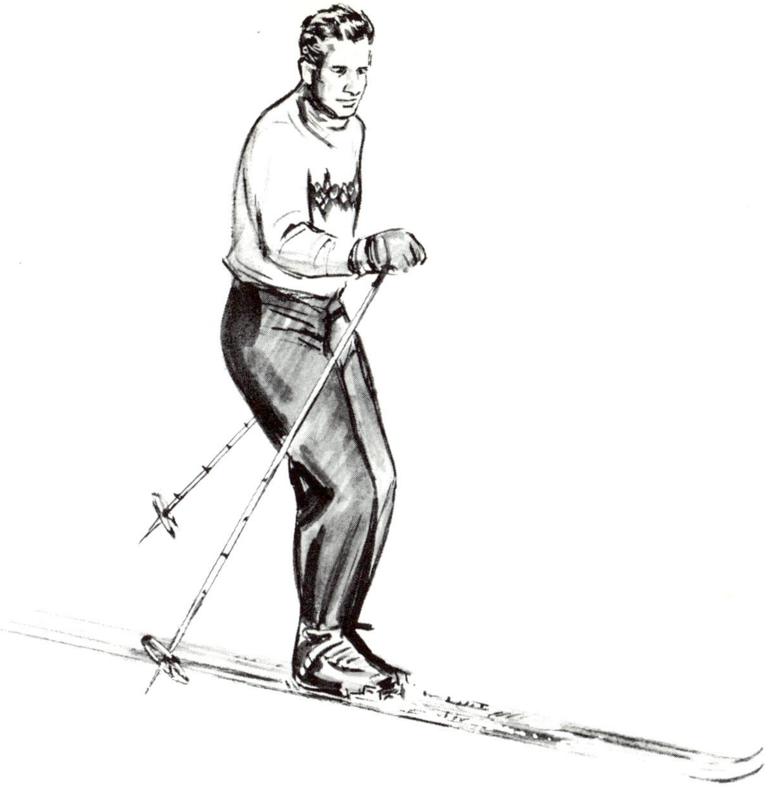

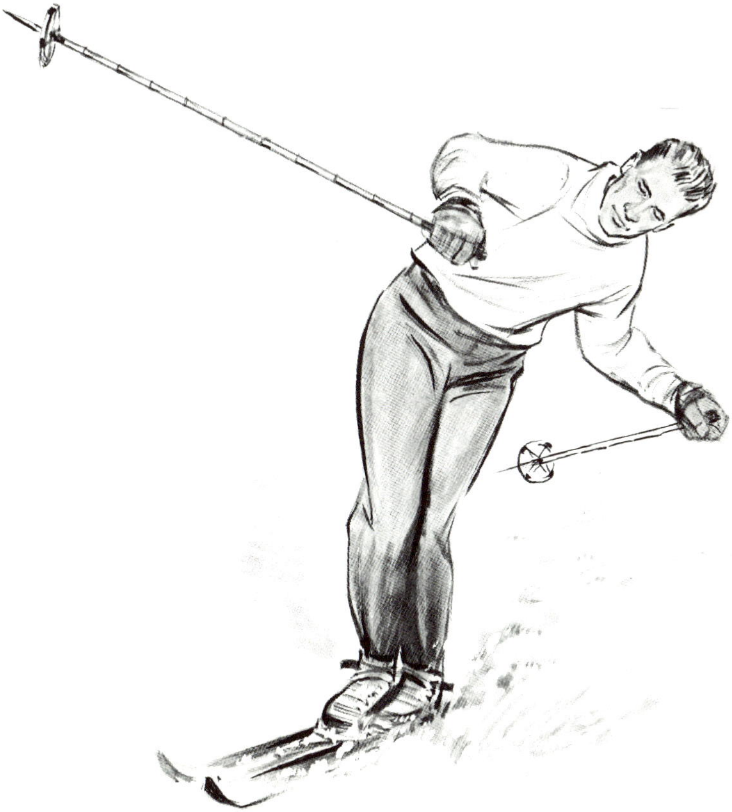

Jumping and Pre-jumping

by Lutz Aynedter, Director, Edelweiss Ski School, Twin Bridges, Calif.

The advanced skier today is often presented with problems of terrain. For, with the ever-increasing number of skiers, all using the same runs, the natural snow surface is worn to a point where it is cut up into thousands of holes, ruts, bumps, ditches, and moguls. Expert skiers traveling downhill at high speeds often avoid these terrain obstacles by jumping or pre-jumping over them.

Jumping is a maneuver used to clear an obstacle such as an abrupt hole or rut. You lift off the snow at the top of one bump and land on the downhill side of the second bump, avoiding contact with the rut in between. The lifting action is accomplished by a slight sinking motion of the knees before the take-off and by quickly straightening your legs again as you reach the crest of the bump. Flexible, bent knees and a slight downward pressure of your heels will help to keep the ski tips from digging into the snow upon landing.

Pre-jumping is the exact opposite of jumping. It is used to hug the ground closely while crossing an abrupt lip at high speed, since jumping too far out may cause a landing in a hazardous area below. The pre-jump is begun by tucking up your knees, feet, and skis shortly before reaching the top of the bump, clearing the top altogether, and landing on the downhill side of the same bump. Both jumping and pre-jumping maneuvers should be practiced first separately, and then alternately. Start in a slow run across the slope and then practice these maneuvers closer to the fall line.

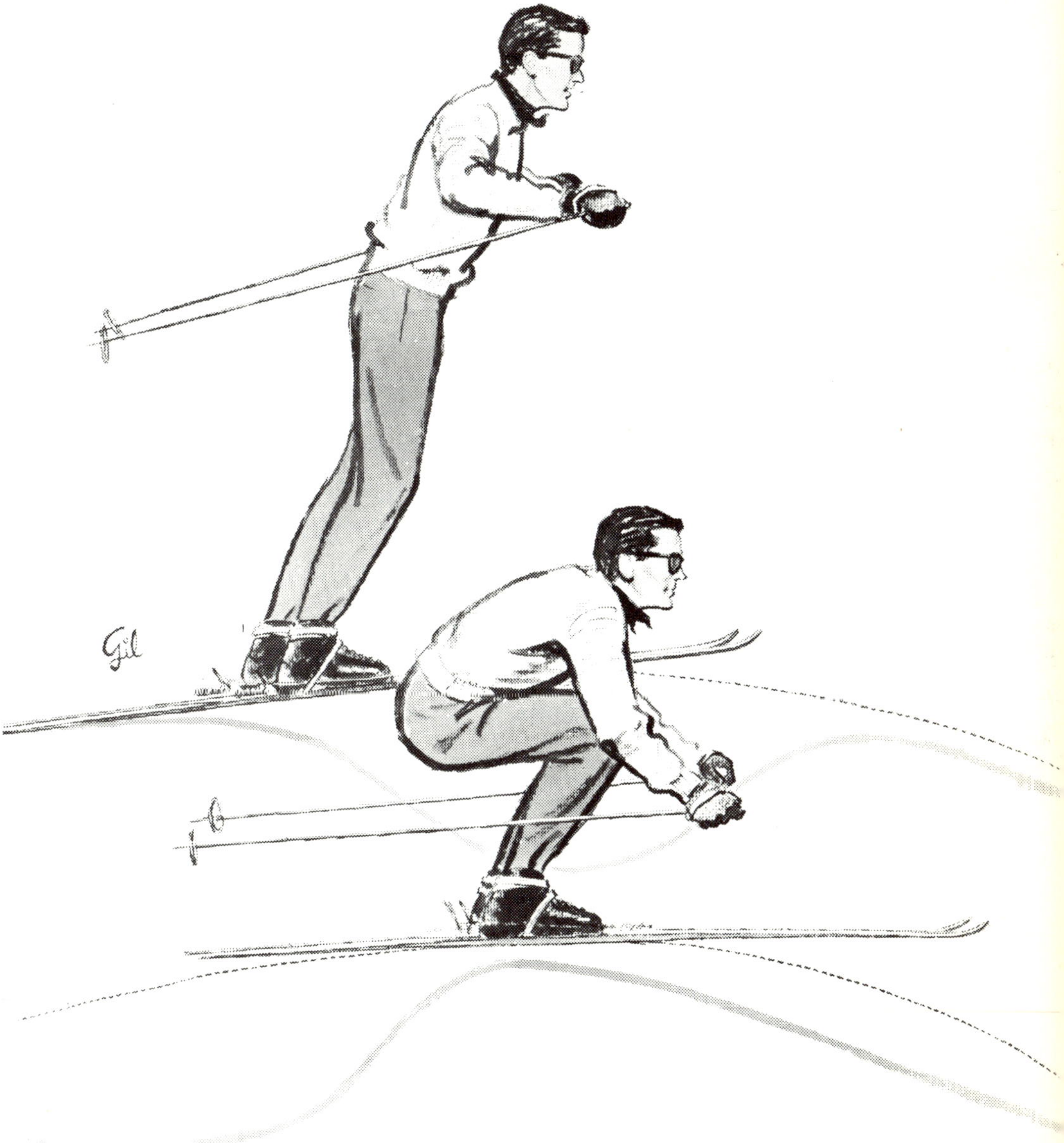
Gil

"Bunny Hop" off Bumps

by Jim Snobble, Certified Instructor, SRMSA, Aspen Ski School, Aspen, Colo.

Part of the great pleasure of skiing lies in the ability to "bunny hop" or do a *Geländesprung* off bumps and moguls. And yet it is surprising how many otherwise competent skiers cannot perform this exhilarating and relatively simple maneuver. They are heavy and lifeless on their skis.

Some of the difficulty, no doubt, is due to an unconscious (or conscious) reluctance to leave the ground. I am convinced, however, that much of this heaviness is due solely to an incorrect approach to the problem. These skiers will almost invariably come into a bump in a low crouch and try to jump upward from this position as they hit the take-off point. The trick is just the reverse. Bounce down into the take-off point with your legs firm and unyielding. Then, push down and then up on the take-off, rather than try to jump directly upward. *The down-and-up movement will almost literally bounce or kick you into the air and will almost automatically force your legs into the desirable tucking position.*

Try this exercise without skis in your home. Jump and try to touch the ceiling. You will note that you won't get nearly the same spring by starting from a crouch as you would by standing from a relatively erect position, then sinking or springing down hard toward the floor. Try to drive your legs right through the floor as you spring upward. This provides you with momentum, a kick, and extra power for the upward spring.

Now try riding over a small bump a few times with your legs firm, rather than letting your legs go soft and thereby absorbing the bump. This maneuver will result in a small hop, without any further effort on your part. One word of caution, however. Start with small bumps and jumps and build up height as your feeling for the snow, the bumps, and the air sharpens. Don't lunge or dive forward as you take off, or you will land tips first. Just try to maintain your basic body position directly over your bindings with your legs in a tucked position.

After a bit of practice, bunny hops will become second nature to you and the result will be increased skiing pleasure as well as increased agility and ability to control your skis under varied conditions.

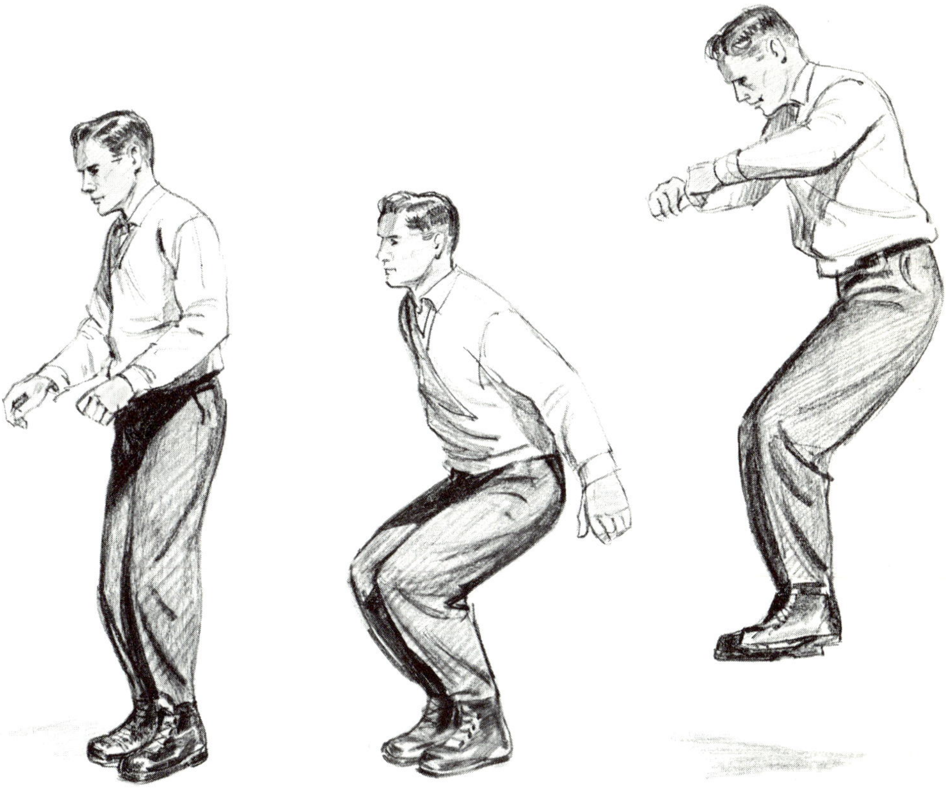

Gazelle Turn

by Max Good, Assistant Director, Grizzly Peak Ski School, Red Lodge, Mont.

The gazelle turn is one of a variety of jump turns that the advanced skier will find fun to perfect. The turn might be considered a combination of an airplane turn and a *Geländesprung,* an airplane turn in which the knees are retracted. The gazelle turn is performed on a mogul, with the use of either one or two poles. With considerable speed, the use of one pole is sufficient. However, at a slower speed, or to gain more height, both poles are used. While practicing or learning, it is advisable to select a single bump on the hill so that you will not get tangled with other moguls on your landing.

Approach the bump from a traverse and set your edges just before the take-off to get an even, spring-like action with both legs. The best way to set the edges is by a simultaneous sinking motion and heel thrust. This will put you in a good "down" position and, at the same time, give you a good platform for the "up" motion or the take-off. *The downhill pole is placed at the top of the bump during the down motion and is immediately followed by an upspringing motion in which the knees are tucked up. At the same time, bank over the pole on the downhill side.*

The banking movement will start the turn in the air. Before landing, straighten your legs, enabling the knees to absorb the shock and ensure a smooth landing. Finish as in a parallel christie by sinking into the knees and ankles, thrusting the heels.

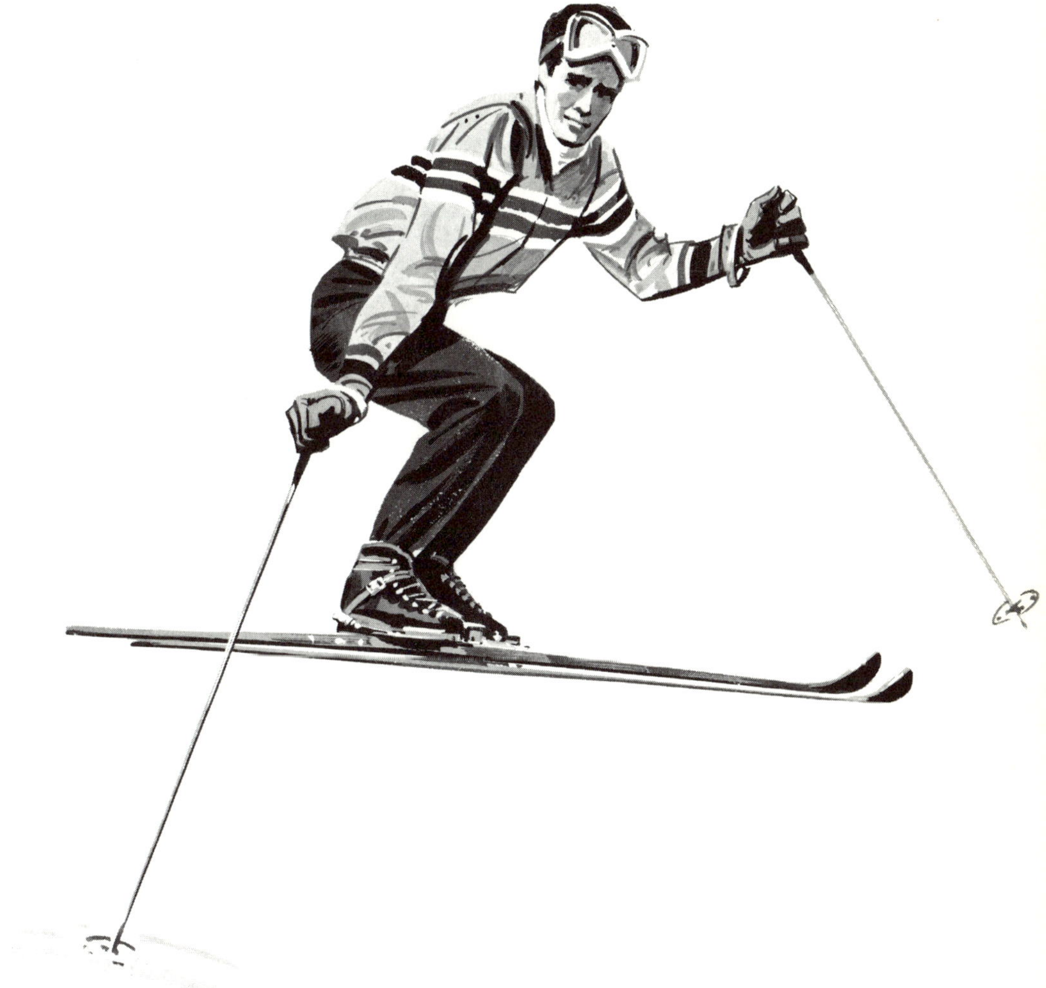

Royal Christie

by Jack Morehead, Certified Instructor, Arapahoe Basin Ski School, Dillon, Colo.

If you are able to "skate" on skis and to maintain your balance well while on one ski, you also can do a royal—one-legged—christie.

First, be sure to pick the right terrain—a concave surface (a shallow gully is perfect) with a gentle slope. Skate off in either direction at a fairly slow and comfortable speed, pushing off with the outside ski and then shifting *all* your weight to the inside ski. Don't ski too fast. Now try rotating your body as you would in a regular Arlberg turn. The first few times you try the turn, lift only the tip of the outside ski and let the tail ride on the snow for balance. Later, as you get the feel of the turn, you will find it more comfortable to bend your body sharply forward at the waist. The outside ski then can be lifted high above the snow. However, the general position of the ski will remain the same—*the tip must be higher than the tail.*

Naturally, linking royal christies is much harder to accomplish. When you have completed one turn, you will find it helpful to plant one, or both, poles in the snow as you go into the next turn. Using the poles for balance, skate off at about a 45-degree angle, trying to shift your weight *forward* onto the new turning ski. Again, the same policy holds: The tip of the outside ski should be held well above the tail.

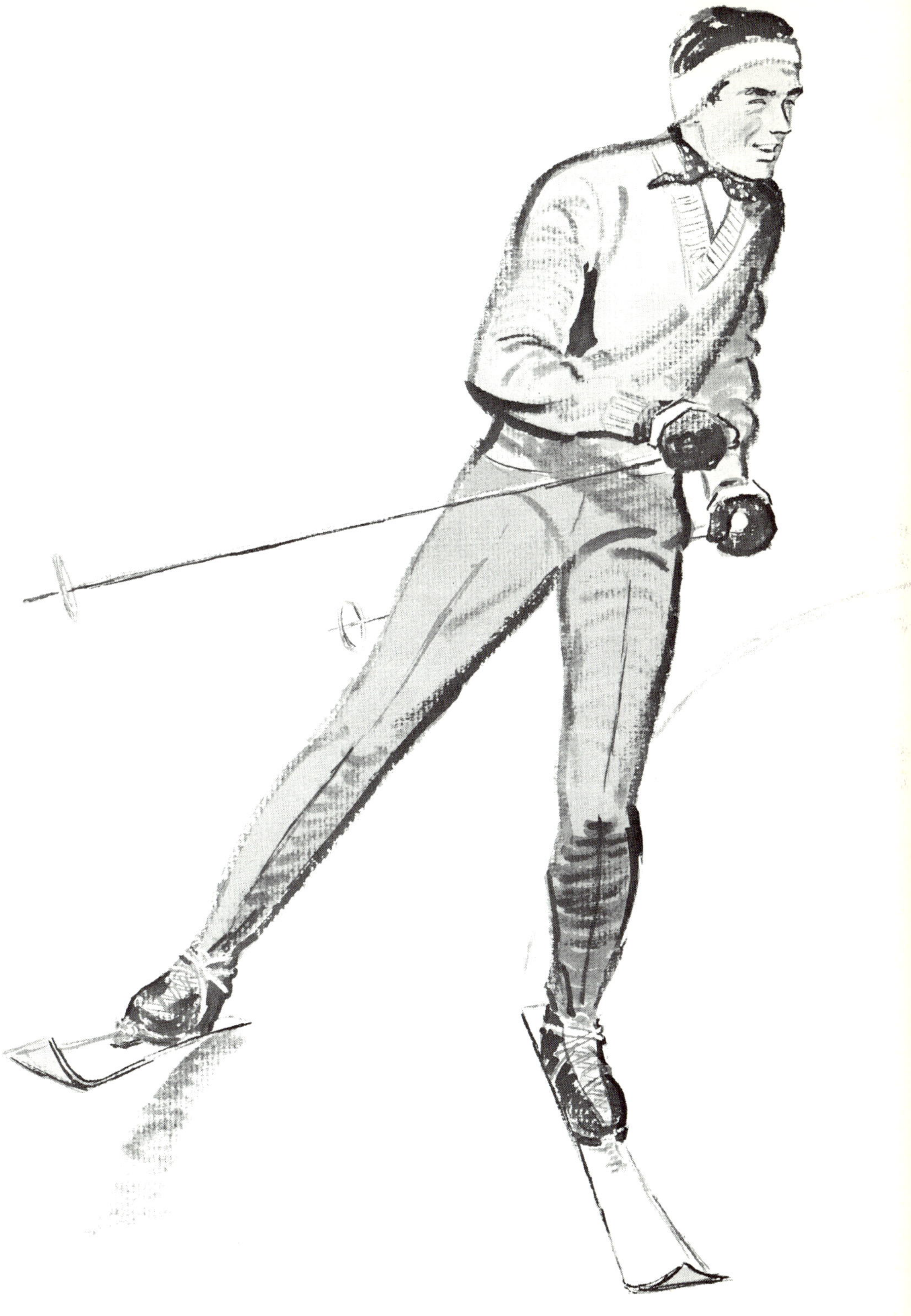

SKI LIFE EXTRA

The Secret of Championship Form
by Charles Bozon, French Olympic Medalist

Skiing is one sport in which man, through his contact with nature, expands his mental and physical qualities. But, in order to utilize the sport to its fullest, he needs the best possible technique, his mental and physical qualities alone not being sufficient.

As is the case in many sports, competition is the best test for improving ski technique. Therefore each winter, with its international races, has brought improvements which will certainly help skiers in the future.

What has caused these improvements? The present competitive skier has to go faster and faster both in a straight line and while turning. The problem, then, is in braking control—in other words, control of edging.

In the principle stages of a slalom turn, the motions of a racer, considering only the precision work of his edges and obtaining their best efficiency, are as follows:

First is the initiation of the turn—the critical moment of edge transfer. The skier executes a leg extension, prepared for a windup. This "up" motion, at its termination, lightens the skis with a minimum of effort and a maximum of efficiency, allowing the transfer of edges. During this leg extension, the upper body leans forward and toward the direction of the anticipated turn. This motion, anticipating the turn, is conveyed to the skis through the legs and ankles, like a pendulum, and causes the transfer of edges. It also gives an impulse to the skis—the front of the skis follow the rotary direction of the tips, describing a slightly wider curve. The transfer of edges then becomes very precise and quick; the skis effect a minimum amount of sideslipping.

The second stage is the leading of the turn. It is a simple motion, if the turn has been properly initiated. The skier controls his turn with a rather increased bend of his legs in relation to the amount of edging. The upper body squares off with the skis. The function of knee bend and edging is to control sideslipping—the less flexion, the less edging, the less sideslipping.

The third stage is the end of the turn. The skier, with legs flexed and upper body square to the skis, increases the amount of inside edging, consequently controlling the end of his turn. Notice that the control of edging is obtained by a combined lateral motion of the ankles, knees, and hips.

The appearance of a racer in a turn goes from an intermediate position, before the turn, to a very forward position as he triggers his turn, progressively losing his forward lean during the leading of the turn. He finally ends up in an intermediate position again. The modern skier skis in a more erect and more forward position than in the past; he is also more in line with the direction of his skis. This is an improvement that competition must bring to ski technique—for the single purpose of a better control of edging. However, with the extreme variety of motions a competitor must execute during a race to keep his balance or to avoid hitting a slalom pole, it is very difficult to see the basic motion. Each racer, having a style of his own, increases the difficulty that an observer has in trying to recognize the motions that will improve his own skiing.

Ski technique, which some day may allow any skier to perform on a trail with as much ease and grace as an ice skater on a rink, is still in evolution and continues to surprise even those who know it well.

V. *Teaching Children to Ski*

Each season, more and more families are flocking to the slopes. Children can be taught to ski and enjoy it as much as any adult. Here are some helpful suggestions for parents to follow.

SKI POINTERS FOR TEACHING CHILDREN

Advice to Skiing Parents

by Paula Valar, Director, Mittersill Ski School, Franconia, N.H.

Over the past five years, the need to keep children of all ages happily occupied at ski centers has become very acute. Major areas have replied to this demand by installing nurseries for the "wee ones" and children's classes for youngsters aged four and over. *These children's classes should not be identified with regular ski school, but thought of, rather, as "play school on skis," where the instructor uses his ingenuity and colorful props to capture the imagination of the children.* The youngsters respond quickly, following their leader around, and thus learning to handle their skis in a playful and enjoyable way.

Children exposed to bad weather and snow conditions become quickly discouraged. Ski lessons, therefore, though intent on keeping to a two-hour schedule, are sometimes cut after one hour for a short trip to the restaurant. Hot chocolate or ice cream puts new enthusiasm into children and the outdoor activities can then be continued for the second hour, unless the children show signs of weariness.

It is very hard to advise parents on just when their children are ready to take up skiing. So much depends on the attitude, aptitude, and body control of the youngsters. Generally speaking, children aged six to eight are ready to be introduced to skiing. But do not *make* them ski. Their skis should be fairly short with good, spring-cable bindings, steel edges, toe plates or toe-release bindings. Rubbers or galoshes are impossible to learn on. Many sport shops have initiated a special service whereby parents purchasing a good pair of ski boots for their youngsters can later trade these boots in for a larger size, thus keeping the child well shod at little extra cost.

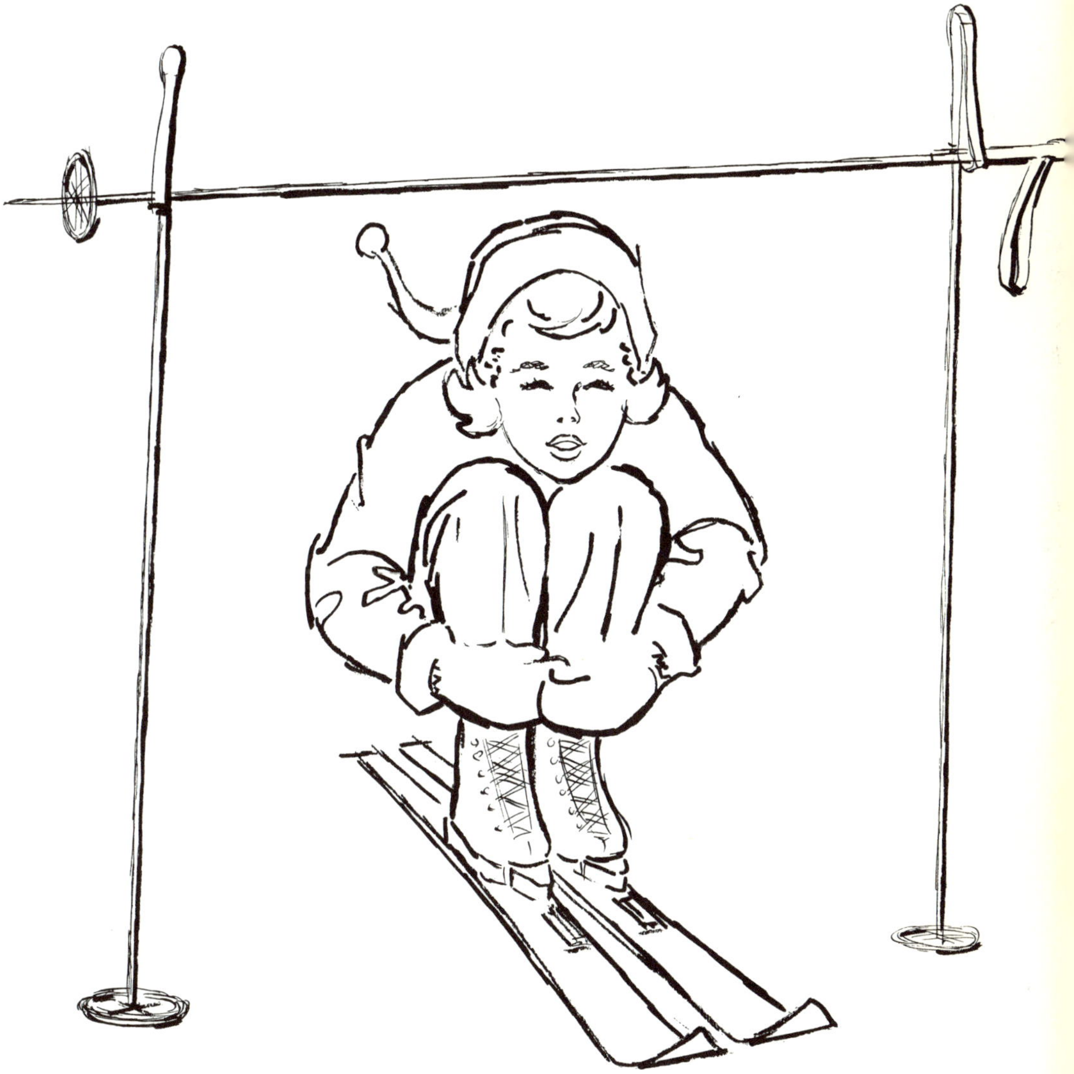

Teaching Children

by Martha Miller, Certified Instructor, FWSIA, Yosemite Ski School, Yosemite Park, Calif.

Do you wonder what to do with your children while you ski? You can solve the problem by taking them with you, placing the older ones in the hands of a ski instructor and keeping preschool children with you. This plan works well and introduces children to skiing at a desirable early age.

Prepare your preschool child for skiing with as adequate clothing and equipment as you would prepare any adult. Gloves or mittens should be waterproofed and should fit well. Wool tends to soak easily and kiddies do like to play in the snow with their hands. Boots should fit firmly, and both dark glasses and suntan lotion are essential. A child should have the shortest skis possible; certainly no longer than he is tall. The bindings should hold his feet firmly and be simply constructed so that he can operate the equipment himself. For preschool children, release bindings are not too practical. Youngsters seem too flexible to hurt themselves and they have an easier time if the skis remain on their feet.

Let the child experience putting on skis and taking them off at home, and let him walk around indoors or in the yard on skis. This eases the new experience when he first reaches the snow. Give him poles long enough to permit walking without bending at the waist. Now, when he is ready to try his skis on snow, choose a sunny day. Help him get started walking but don't encourage downhill running until he wishes it himself. And when he is wet and cold, bring him indoors. Don't force instruction on youngsters. They just aren't as co-ordinated as we bigger folk. At these early ages, children learn by seeing and doing, not by being told what to do. Above all, don't force children to enjoy skiing. They will anyway, soon enough.

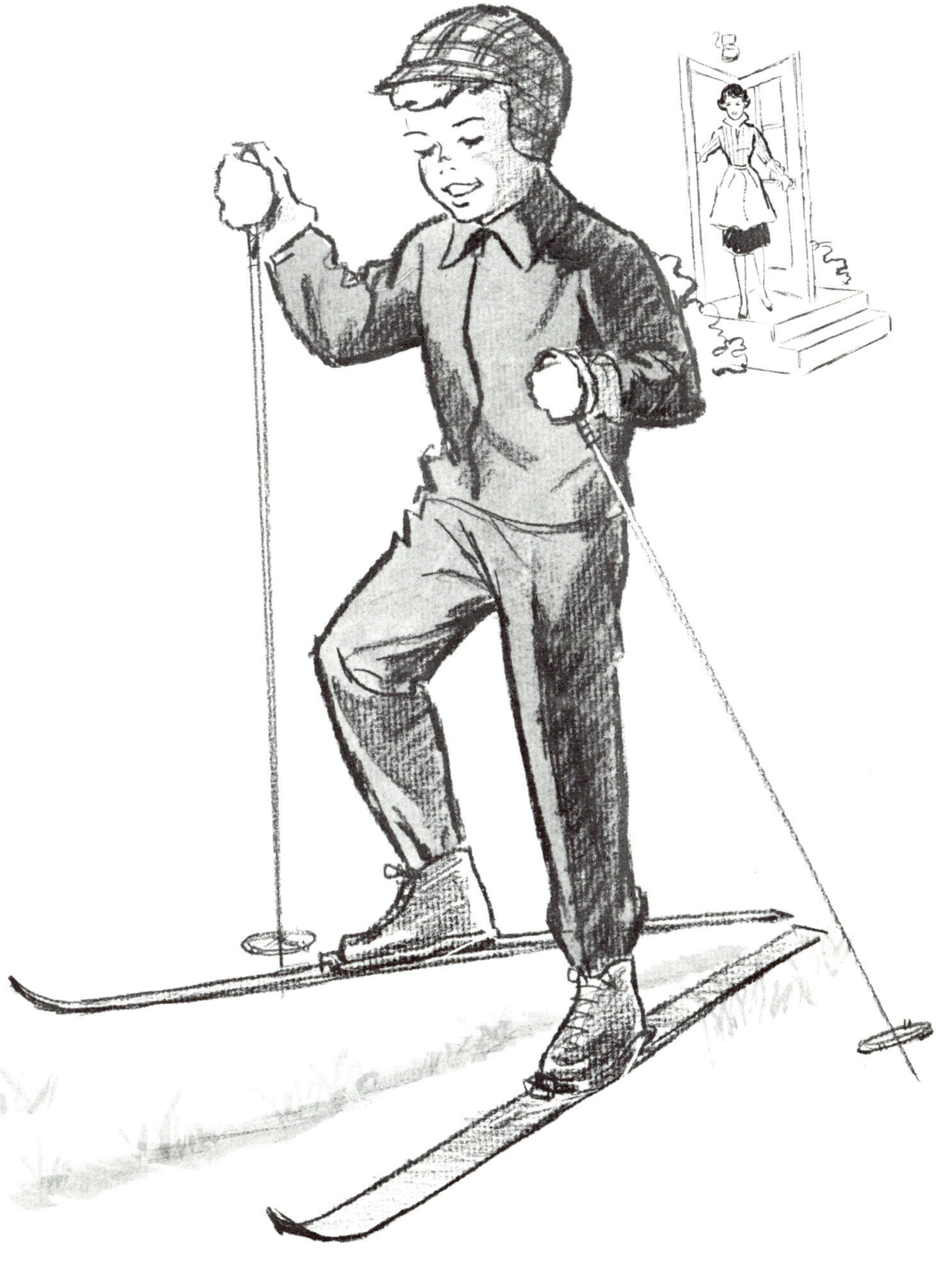

SKI LIFE EXTRA

Pablum in My Rucksack

by Merrill Pollack

One of the immutable facts of life for skiers is that ski slope romances often lead to marriage, that wedlock leads to parenthood, and the presence of one or more small children makes skiing trips so insanely difficult that rational people often give up the sport in defeat. My wife, Barbara, and myself must be irrational folk then, for we've continued to mush out to the slopes winter after winter, although for the past seven years we seem to be dragging more and more children behind us.

Bachelor boys and girls give us affrighted and pitying looks whenever we heave into a ski area and proceed to unload our car of skis and poles and baby carriages, portable cribs, stacks of diapers, cartons of baby food and milk, and kiddy books and toys and miniature skis and sleds. Admittedly, this is odd paraphernalia for skiing, but it's essential if *pater-* and *materfamilias* are to get in any skiing at all. The day will come, we keep assuring ourselves, when all our children will be old enough to require only skiing gear. Until that time comes, however, we've reconciled ourselves to planning each trip like a military campaign, with fine attention to routes of advance, bivouac areas, reserve troops, and routes of retreat.

Obviously, the easiest solution is to leave the kids home and be done with it. We do leave them often, for a variety of social and professional reasons, but we feel strongly about skiing, my wife and I, and we want our children to enjoy it too. So we've taken them along from the start, almost as soon as they started getting born, and they're all learning young how to make the best of long car trips, how to behave in restaurants, how to get along with strangers—and how to ski.

About the only all-inclusive suggestion we can offer to skiing parents who feel as we do is this—learn to be bland when childless skiers stare. You'll often find yourselves doing odd things and occasionally you'll get trapped in bizarre situations.

In the winter of 1953, when our daughter was five months old, we did a lot of letter writing to friends and chambers of commerce, trying to find a place in New England where we could spend a week with our infant. A few ski areas had baby-sitting service on week ends (but no provisions for infants) and no lodges seemed eager to have us, explaining that the season was at its height. We were saved by a friend who has three children of his own and, fortuitously, lives in Jackson, New Hampshire. "Come stay with us," he wrote, and we did. Each day we took our baby skiing with us. We'd set up the folding carriage, tuck the baby in warm, and wheel her over to the bottom of a large open slope. The skiers gawked at the sight of a baby buggy on the slopes and several came over to inspect it, half-expecting, I'm sure, to find the carriage loaded with beer. The sight of a pink, sleeping infant amazed some and amused others and a few laughed so hard they got tangled up in their skis and fell flat on their faces, at great peril to the baby and her carriage. Once the excitement waned, the carriage-on-the-snow routine worked fine—we would take the tow to the top and at the end of each run we'd ski over and make sure the baby was all right. Five-month-old babies can't walk, so we didn't have to worry about our little darling wandering off.

The following winter we skied only once, in one of Philadelphia's parks. This wasn't because we'd run out of friends or because we'd lost heart—my wife was expecting again. "But wait till next year," we promised ourselves.

We did it up big in '55. Some friends of ours, Bob and Lynne, had a seven-month-old son of their own and they wanted to go skiing with us. This sounded fine, but our daughters then were aged two-and-a-half and ten months, and this was a formidable gaggle of toddlers to unload on any ski lodge (our friends living in the ski country were automatically ruled out—few friendships, however strong, can survive a visitation of four adults and three children). Bob lined up for our use a cabin in the hills behind Waterbury, Vermont. It was on the rustic side. There was running water, all cold, and the furnace burned wood ravenously. My wife washed diapers by hand (Lynne used the disposable kind) and waited patiently for water to heat. Bob and I chopped wood incessantly. It kept us in trim for skiing, we kept telling ourselves.

On our first skiing day we took all the children over to the lodge at Stowe, agreeing we'd take turns baby-sitting each other's children. We all got in some skiing and the youngsters found their own amusements. The lodge we stayed in turned out to be the place where the Ski Patrol brought in injured skiers who were awaiting ambulance rides to the nearest bonesetters. There was a succession of wounded skiers through the day and the toddlers (our own and a few others) found these supine athletes fascinating indeed. They picked snow off their boots and ate it, not perturbed by the fact that the snow was occasionally tinged with blood. As parents, however, we found the setup less than ideal and that night Bob and I scoured the back hills near Waterbury until we found a pleasant farm wife who was willing to come up to our cabin and baby-sit during the day, providing we furnished transportation. She never did quote a fee for her services (whether this was out of shyness or canniness I cannot say) and at the end of the week we paid her generously. The children did well, too. We arranged our schedule so we could give them some sledding behind our cabin each morning.

We did it up even bigger in '56. Everyone agreed we'd had enough of roughing it. "No cabins," we said. "It's either a lodge or nothing." Bob and Lynne, having begat their second child by then, decided they had earned a real vacation, so they parked their children with their grandparents. Barbara and I, being made of sterner stuff, brought our daughters, now aged three-and-a-half and twenty-one months, with us. This involved a bit of logistics since, as we now knew, parents with babies are not in demand at ski lodges, where young men and women are not supposed to see what comes after the ritual dance of courtship. Therefore, we arranged to arrive at the lodge, just outside Stowe, on a Sunday evening, after most of the guests were gone, and we promised to slink away ourselves on the following Friday, when the gay, young unmarrieds would begin to arrive again. I don't know what Bob and Lynne did without their children. As for my family, we'd carted along two camp cots and extra blankets and we all slept in the same room to save money. There wasn't much floor space left after the cots were set up but, what the hell, we were together, weren't we?

There was one hitch in all this serenity. About two weeks before this trip we'd begun weaning our younger girl from her nighttime bottle and by vacation time we thought she was off it without any visible trauma. When we checked into the lodge the owners—very sweet grandparent types—asked my wife if she'd want any milk during the night. "Oh, no thank you," Barbara answered proudly. "The little one doesn't need her bottle any more. She's getting very grown up."

Thus it was that at 2:30 that morning the little girl woke up in a crowded, cluttered, and unfamiliar room and forgot how adult she was supposed to be and began bawling for her milk. It's a hair-raising sound even in your own home. In a ski lodge, where such bellowings are rare, it sounds even more blood-curdling. "She's regressed," I moaned, ducking like a coward under the pillow. My wife, who keeps her head in such emergencies, leaped across the two cots and trotted down the hall to

156

the kitchen door. It was locked, bolted, impregnable. The lodge owners never did appear. My wife hurried back and rocked the child for a half hour until she fell asleep again. And the next day we acquired a milk bottle—sweet-talked it away from a young mother we met at the warming hut—and there was no more damn-fool talk about weaning on that trip.

It was a good vacation for all. The children spent each afternoon with a friendly farm wife who had a little boy of her own. Each morning our kids got in some sledding and skiing and the eldest girl, after learning to walk on the flat, demanded permission to take the lift to the top of Mount Mansfield so she could ski down the Nosedive. "Not this year," I murmured.

Our third child, a son, was a proper skier's baby. He was born in November, 1956, which should have given everybody time to toughen up for the tail end of that skiing season. We planned to take off at the end of February. All arrangements were made, baby-sitters had been lined up, milk supply had been guaranteed. But the thaws came early to New England that year and all the slopes washed out on the day we were supposed to start. The only place that got any snow was Bucks County, Pennsylvania, where we live—so we skied that winter on a hillside a few miles from our home. The girls picked up the rudiments of downhill sliding and our son, stuffed in a car crib, yelled bloody blue murder because the only thing he cared about was food, and skiing clearly constituted a threat to his ravenous appetite.

Meanwhile, should there be any readers left who've taken courage from this recital and are now toying with the notion of going skiing *en famille,* I pass along a list of suggestions prepared by my wife, Barbara, who speaks from a great deal of experience, not necessarily bitter.

SURVIVAL TIPS Carry your own folding cots or travel beds, as well as extra blankets, rubber sheets, linens, diapers, etc. This way you avoid being beholden or apologetic to anybody.

If you're staying at a lodge or tourist home, you may be able to arrange for laundry service or the use of a washing machine if you mention these needs in your preliminary correspondence.

Take only dark-colored clothing for the children; they don't look bedraggled quite so quickly.

Be well supplied with Kleenex, paper towels and napkins for emergencies top and bottom.

To keep youngsters diverted in the car or ski lodge, have a supply of their favorite books and toys. Also have a few crayons and paper—and something new, a toy or book.

Save all your old, worn-out, and mismated woolen socks and mitts. Without even mending them (and don't fuss about whether or not they match) you'll find them useful to pull over your child's own gloves, high up on his sleeves, so they cover his wrists. Use your old woolen socks over your child's shoes before you put on his rubbers or boots. This technique will keep his ankles warm and dry.

Always carry saltines or other dry crackers in the dash of your car. They stave off starvation (which is always imminent with children) and they aren't sticky. Also carry a Thermos of water. Milk is optional; it makes some children car sick.

Take along infant aspirin, an antihistamine especially made for children, and a fever thermometer. With this equipment you can often head off a cold.

Most small children get chilled after about twenty minutes outdoors on a raw day. Plan their sledding and skiing accordingly. Remind the children that their parents will be taking turns skiing. Warn them that stacked skis are not there for their amusement—if they fall on little people, little people may get brained.

Try to arrange an excursion each day for the children—drive to town where they can shop for souvenirs and candy.

VI. *Difficult Snow Conditions and Terrain*

Skiing is easy—on packed slopes. But when the going gets rough or icy, or the powder deep, you'll need to adapt your technique to the particular snow condition and terrain. Here's how the experts handle this difficult phase of the sport.

How to Ski Ice and Like It

by *Jimmy Johnston, Director, Minneapolis Ski School, Minneapolis, Minn.*

Hard pack or ice is all too often the condition you might find at your favorite ski slope on frigid winter days. Even where the base is fifty feet deep, if enough skiers travel the slope without further snowfall, the surface can become as hard as the cement in your basement.

If you are going to confine your skiing to days when there are five inches of powder over a hard-packed base and agreeably cold temperatures, you are not going to ski very much some winters, especially if you live in the East or in my region, the Midwest. Otherwise, you will have to learn to make adjustments in mechanics and technique for various types of snow and weather conditions. It's all part of the sport.

Suppose you've just traveled a thousand miles or more for a two-week ski holiday and you find the area is an ice climber's paradise. There are certain adjustments you can make and still have fun skiing—even on ice. To begin with, the right equipment makes a great deal of difference in your enjoyment of skiing on icy slopes. A narrow, stiff ski is recommended. The more rigid the ski, the more equal the pressure from the heel to the tip of the ski. This will afford you better bite into the snow surface. Steel edges are an absolute necessity, of course. They should be in good condition and sharpened if they are extremely dull. However, you don't need a really fine edge since it will wear down after the first few turns anyway. And, in most cases, waxing is unnecessary since ice or hard pack is very fast and would remove the wax in no time at all.

Probably the most important equipment item is a good ski boot with firm, stiff sides to withstand the twisting sideward pressure of edging and, at the same time, to reduce the strain on your ankles. Your bindings should be rigid, too, so that the ski can be turned on its side and edged effectively. Ski pole tips should be sharp enough to penetrate the snow surface, and points should be bent so that the poles can be lifted easily from the snow.

The most important physical factor in skiing ice is proper weight distribution—the predominant weighting of the downhill ski when your

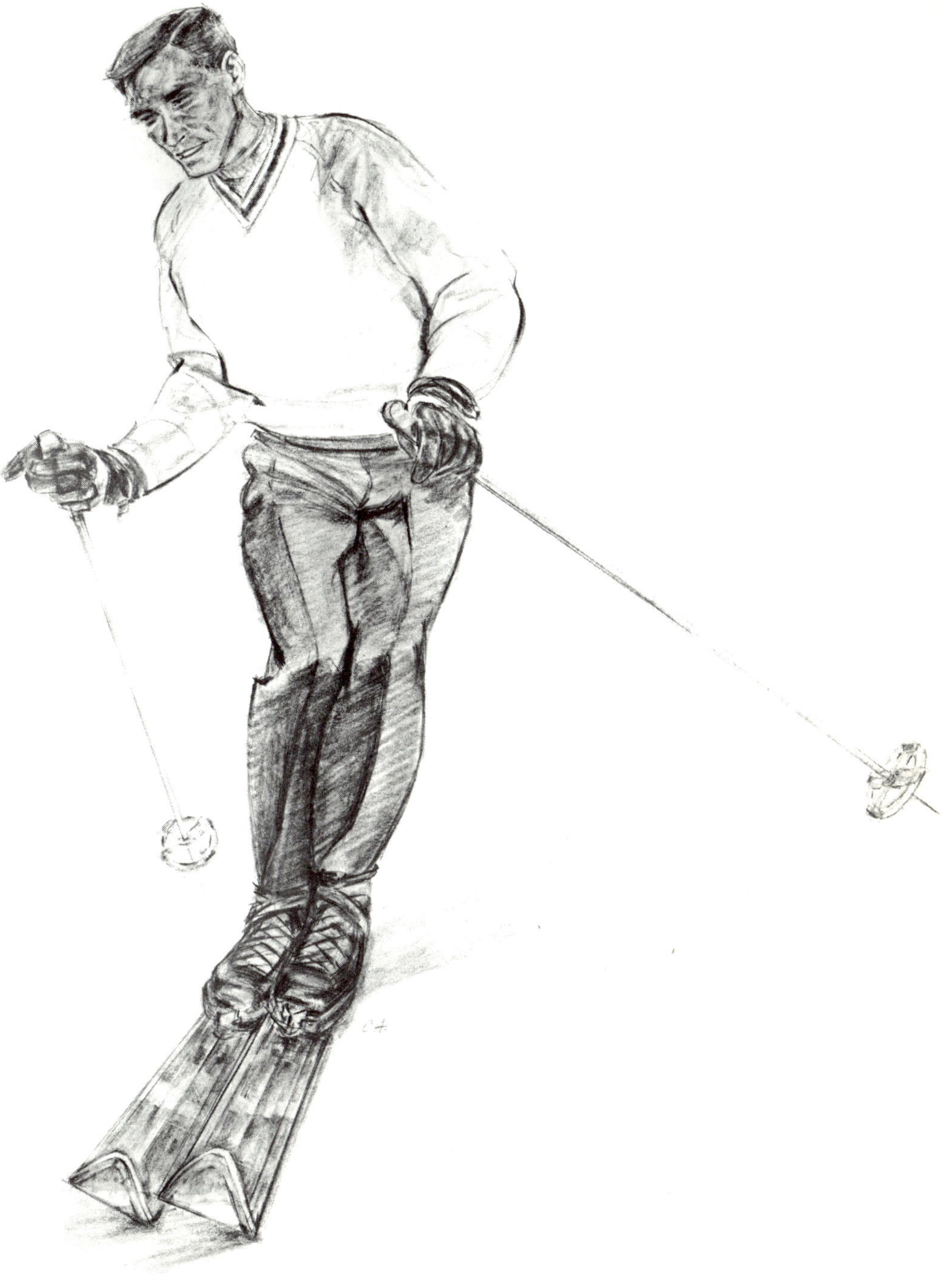

skis are pointing across the slope in a traverse position. You can test for proper weight distribution by lifting your uphill ski and balancing yourself on the downhill ski. This downhill weighting can best be attained by leaning your upper body away from the slope while pressing your knees into the slope. This will give you a faint "reverse-shoulder" appearance and it will help keep your weight on the downhill ski.

While it may seem that evenly weighted skis would give better edge control since the edge of each ski would bite into the snow, this is not so. By placing most of your weight on one ski (the downhill ski), you give that ski sufficient power to cut into the hard snow surface effectively. If the skis were equally weighted, neither ski would have the power to cut into the hard snow or ice. Weighting the downhill ski also helps overcome the tendency most skiers have of leaning into the hill, which results in poor stability. It is also important to feel that your weight has drained to your feet. Don't keep your arms up like a bird and your weight on your toes. Keep your hands down and your knees pressed forward. This position will give you a firm, sure-footed feeling. Your skis should be kept close together when traversing so that you can easily maintain a proper body position over both skis. This is especially necessary when skiing ice, since the skis will have a tendency to sideslip away from you. Weighting the downhill ski properly is the most important factor in skiing ice. Downhill weighting can best be attained by leaning upper body away from the hill while pressing knees into the hill.

Placing most of your weight on the downhill ski will give that ski sufficient power to cut into hard surface. To test for proper weight distribution lift uphill ski and balance completely on downhill ski.

When turning on hard pack or ice, accept the fact that your turns will have a longer radius and a larger curve. Allow for this by giving yourself plenty of room to turn in. Stay on the wide-open slopes where you can traverse between each turn. You can't fight ice by overedging and leaning into the slope. This will only result in your skis sliding out from under you. Keep your body positioned over both skis at all times so that you can exert your weight and power directly *down*.

The turning method I have found most effective could be characterized as a streamlined uphill stem christie. When skiing on ice, it is of definite advantage to keep your skis weighted and biting into the surface all the time you are turning. The up-and-down motion of unweight-

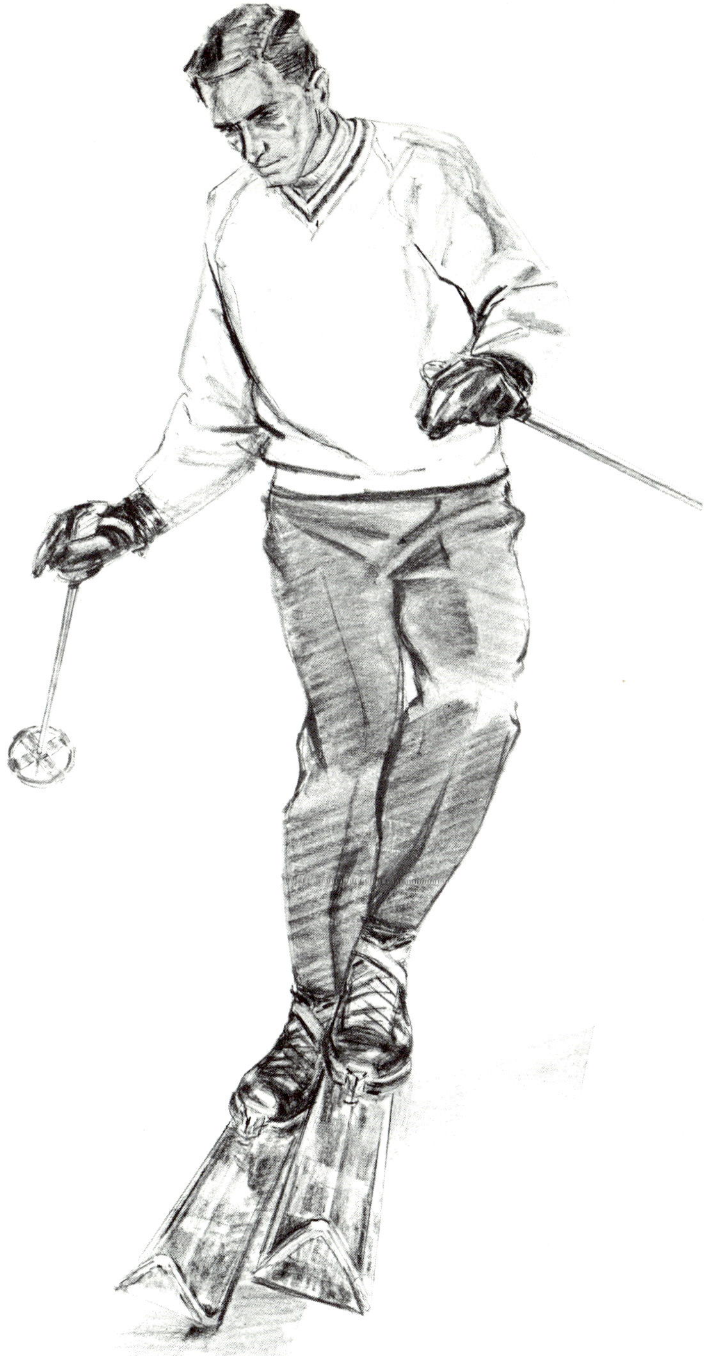

ing your skis to change direction, while being very effective under normal conditions, builds up your speed too quickly and makes you change direction too rapidly when you are skiing on ice. This up-and-down motion usually results in a great deal of sideslipping in the last half of the turn. By using the streamlined uphill stem christie instead, excess speed and sideslipping are avoided. You traverse with your weight predominantly on the downhill ski; then, to begin the turn, you stem and edge the uphill ski, shifting your weight to that edged uphill ski with a *stepping* motion. The unweighted inside ski is flattened and allowed to drift slowly into a parallel position to the stemmed ski during the remainder of the turn.

It is also possible to use this same method of skiing directly down the fall line, if the slope is gentle enough so that you will not accelerate out of control. This method is used by racers. You feel as though you are in an abbreviated snow-plow position, stepping your weight first on one ski and then on the other, making a slight turning slide each time you weight the ski. Your skis may glide together between each step, or turn, but this is unimportant. The important thing is to be able to enjoy skiing on hard pack or ice and, if you adjust your technique to the terrain and snow conditions, you will.

The Key to Skiing Deep Powder

by Sigi Engl, Director, Sun Valley Ski School, Sun Valley, Idaho

Deep powder! These words have probably done more to generate interest in modern skiing than any other term, including racing. Deep powder whets the appetite of the average skier; it is at once the racer's dilemma and the photographer's delight.

It seems only proper that any instructive article covering such a diverse subject should begin with a discussion of the snow itself. What is deep powder? To skiers in certain parts of the country, it is a foot of any kind of new snow. To the more fortunate skiers who live in areas boasting high altitudes and heavy snowfalls, deep powder is several feet of dry, cold snow that has settled and compressed itself sufficiently to make a feathery carpet with a spongy firmness. The spongy quality of the snow affords a fairly solid platform under the skis and allows the skier, exercising proper technique, the greatest amount of deep-snow control.

But these varieties of snow are only the beginning. Also to be encountered is the season's first snowfall which produces a dry, cold, feather-light powder and falls to great depths over a snowless base of rocks, stumps, logs, and sagebrush. It is a beautiful white carpet, but treacherous, due to its many hidden air pockets. Even an expert will flounder waist-deep in this type of snow, providing he is still upright.

The varieties of powder already discussed may be complicated by a thinly crusted topping, created by wind or snow. This truly provides a challenge for the powder-snow skier. But to simplify matters, we will concern ourselves here with those varieties of powder whose solid snow base lies more than a few inches under the surface and that are defined by the word "deep."

Choice of equipment is not as complicated as the texture of the powder. Skis of medium length should be used, long enough to support the skier and short enough not to create excessive resistance. The stiffness of the skis should be in accord with the skier's ability. However, even experts tend toward medium, uniform flexibility. The thickness and weight of the skis are probably more important. Thick skis are a definite disadvantage. Thin skis, such as metal skis, act much like a cheese cutter under snow. They may mean the difference between a fall or a recovery. Heavy skis are like very long skis in powder. Their excessive weight and resistance prevent recovery from even a slight mistake. Some experts prefer medium-weight skis to very light ones because of their stability and feel in changeable snow.

As in any other successful ski-teaching system, the teaching technique for deep powder starts at the snow line and is taught from the feet up. The effect of the snow upon the skis is determined by speed and resistance to slipping and by the depth to which the skis sink in. So, the first hard-and-fast rule should be: *Ski on equally-weighted parallel skis.* In straight running or traversing, the skis run on a step that they cut in the snow. Therefore, the two skis, weighted alike, offer the most efficient support to the skier. It is advantageous to have the knees as close together as possible. The upper ski should run slightly ahead on a traverse.

Rule No. 2 takes the form of a practice exercise. *Traverse, make forward sideslips, traverse, and repeat.* This exercise cannot be overdone. It is the only way to feel the snow and the skis. In our area every new snowfall has slightly different characteristics. Feel the effect of the snow on the skis and then use your legs and upper body accordingly. The deep snow of perfect density must be compressed. The thin, breakable-crust variety must be forcefully broken and pushed aside. The hollow, very light early season snow must be gently caressed by the skis.

The weight of your body on the skis must be such that the tips will plane up. This is true even in crusted powder, for there is deep powder underneath. In order to maintain the very sensitive balance that causes the tips to plane and still does not immobilize you too far back on your heels, the ankles and knees are bent a little more deeply than normal and never are straightened completely. This rule holds true even in the event of a forceful rising motion of the body.

When traversing deep snow, there is no severe edging as there would be on packed snow. Thus the knees and hips do not angle into the hill as sharply as they do on packed snow, nor does the upper body angle downhill as much. It naturally follows that your uphill hip and shoulder lead only slightly. In all senses of the word, the body is kept more squarely over both skis.

Your upper body is fairly erect under powder-snow conditions. Your arms are extended more than normally for balance, but not to the extent of hindering pole use in preparation for each turn. When making forward sideslips or uphill turns from a traverse, the turns are effected the same as on packed snow—with a slight sinking action in the ankles and knees and with the unweighting and turning of the skis on the rising motion. Your upper body helps the lower body counteract the resistance of the skis. It is used, with the planting of the pole, to supply a balanced preparation for the turn. In this stage, your upper body may actually turn in the opposite direction of the intended turn in the so-called "countermotion." But in no event should you be twisted to an extreme in one way or another. It is obvious that this would cause loss of balance.

At this point, I would like to caution skiers who want to "wedel" or "short swing" that this method of skiing will work only in the perfect, desirable variety of deep snow described earlier. This is when the snow can be compressed efficiently under the skis and when the snow surface offers no resistance. With consistent terrain and speed facilitating rhythmical linked turns, this can be the acme of deep-powder skiing. However, except in perfect snow, it is much sounder technique not to let the upper body wind or "reverse" against the lower body in the so-called motion of angulation. Instead, the upper body is more square to the skis. The upper body should follow the lower body in the turn, in the same direction, with a motion of partial or complete rotation, according to snow resistance, speed, and turning radius. Traverse, make a slight uphill turn, then traverse more steeply and make a sharper uphill turn. Make linked traverses and uphill turns. Feel the snow.

At this stage, with more confidence, you will attempt downhill turns. Let us ski together, down one of my favorite powder-snow runs at Sun Valley—Lefty Bowl Ridge into Lefty Bowl and into Broadway.

It is early February and the bowls fanning from the top of Baldy have not had a ski track on them since the storm. Today they are still unmarked, except for the carefully placed tracks of the ski patrol on their testing run. We allow ourselves one more long look at the winter-white valley below, and then let our skis take a rather steep traverse to the right.

We are on a slope facing the north, and because it is still untouched by wind we hope that the powder is of the very best and most desirable variety. We make a couple of uphill turns to test the snow and find that it is of best quality. With the feel of the snow comes confidence, and we immediately wedel down the fall line with a series of deep-powder short-swings. The turns unwind like corkscrews from the feet up, and the upper body is allowed to wind against the lower body. We are definitely aware of the accordion-like action of ankles and knees as the skis are alternately floating on the powder and slowing as they sink and compress the snow. Our tracks seem to descend straight down with short turns of only slight radii. It actually feels effortless when—look out! The snow is changing, for there was no slowing-down or braking action of the skis at the sinking stage of that last turn. With this realization, we immediately recover by a forceful sinking "down" and an extended "up" motion in a long slowing turn that takes us farther from the fall line. We have exhausted our North Slope and are in the Bowl itself.

Now a thin sun crust covers the powder; having adjusted to this, we make a series of longer radius, fully rounded braking turns. The down motion is made more forcefully to break the crust and the up motion is more extended for the longer turns. Our metal skis slice through the crust like sharp knives. Our arms are held out farther from the body for balance, and our knees and ankles are more deeply bent. To open the skis here, at our speed, would certainly cause a fall. We feel that we are breaking the crust with our boots, not our ski tips, although the tips are visible. There is a definite relaxed counterswing of the upper body to prepare for the intended turn. In the turn itself, the upper body follows the lower body with a rotating motion in the direction of the turn. To stand over the skis as squarely as possible is our goal.

We approach the lower, narrower section of Lefty Bowl and we come to the climax of our powder-snow instruction. Our right turns are made on sun-crusted powder while our left turns are made on the tree-shaded north side in perfect powder. Here you feel the snow with your feet as an artist feels brush strokes with his fingers.

Finally, having mastered these last two hundred yards of sun and shade, we glide on to the shady side of Broadway and a three-quarter-of-a-mile easy schuss over cold, untracked powder, and into the sunshine at the bottom of Cold Springs Run and the lift terminal.

Deep powder is for experts, you say? Not any more. With the high caliber of today's average skier, and the excellent equipment available, deep powder is an enjoyable possibility for everyone.

Skiing in Heavy Spring Snow
by Alf Engen, Director, Engen Ski School, Alta, Utah

Spring is that time of the season when skiers are confronted with wet, heavy, and sticky snow. In ski slang, spring conditions are often called "crud" or "junk." These conditions are difficult to ski and can be dangerous. The instructor or expert skier may be able to ski under all snow conditions because of his experience and excellent physical conditioning. But the inexperienced novice or intermediate week-end skier may find the heavy snow a nightmare.

To find a solution to the problem of spring conditions, we must start with the snow itself. Why is this snow difficult and dangerous? Why is this "crud" so hard to turn in?

As soon as the snow falls in the spring, a perpetual transformation begins. Rising atmospheric temperatures, evaporation, humidity, wind, sun, and the heavy water content of the snow itself cause the branches of the snow crystals to adhere. Eventually, this process results in the crystals forming a firmly packed, wet, heavy snow. It is because of this wet, solid pack that a skier meets increased resistance. Skis will not slide. Tips will not plane on the top of the snow, and turning the tips and tails through the snow seems impossible. Obviously, it becomes necessary to alter the ski technique.

Starting with the proper equipment, skis used for heavy snow should be of soft flexibility—especially in the tail. Stiff skis are very difficult to turn in wet, heavy snow. Metal skis are best for spring conditions because of their torsional rigidity (the little amount of twisting in the tip of the ski). The type of running surface and wax is important, too. There must be a good sub-base of the lacquer variety and a medium-to-soft base wax applied with iron or cork. This will bind the top layer of silver or paraffin running wax to the skis. Wax combinations are many for spring skiing, but in general, soft, wet snow requires a soft type of wax. Consult the shop at the area where you are skiing for the best wax to use on a particular spring day. Ski shops will melt wax combinations that can be painted on the skis with a brush. "Paint jobs" last longer than the rubbed-on variety. But in any case, be sure to carry a piece of paraffin or silver wax in your pocket when skiing.

A last requisite is a good release binding. Be certain that it is properly adjusted. You can ski out of your bindings in crud snow if the bindings are too loose, while at the same time, the heavy crud can create extreme leverage that could cause you to break a leg. Be sure to clean your bindings from time to time while skiing, since the snow will have a tendency to "pack" in the binding and disturb the release adjustment.

Spring skiing requires excellent physical conditioning, and co-ordination. This means work. Lazy ski habits will cause trouble in rough snow. Then, too, the mental attitude of the skier is important. Heavy snow naturally causes a skier to be afraid. And since spring snow should be skied in the fall line, a skier can develop a mental block. As long as the skier is afraid of the snow and the hill, there is little hope of skiing spring snow effectively. These fears must be overcome by building up confidence and ability.

Developing spring snow technique is similar to learning how to ski again. You review many fundamental maneuvers and practice them in logical steps. In essence, these are the important rules:

1. Whenever possible, the skis should be equally weighted and parallel. Snow resistance can cause a single unweighted ski to wander, resulting in a dangerous position. And since it is unnatural to maintain equally weighted skis in a traverse, weight must be forced upon the uphill ski by use of muscular pressure.

2. In heavy snow, the skier's center of gravity should be placed in a position that will cause the tips of the skis to plane out to the snow. Edge control is not as critical as on packed slopes. Edges are applied in crud snow to effect a banking of the skis, rather than a gripping action.

3. The most drastic change in crud snow technique is the unweighting of the skis. The down-up-down movement in the knees must be exaggerated, and the unweighting must be limited to the legs, not the upper torso. Bending forward from the waist will only cause the ski tips to dive under the snow.

4. Learn to ski in the fall line because there is less resistance and increased momentum there.

Observe how these fundamentals are applied in practice. First, choose a shallow slope with a runout. Try running this slope straight a few times until you have the feel of skiing on parallel, equally weighted skis. Now try the same position in a traverse. Be sure you apply enough pressure to the uphill ski so that it will not wander. Don't turn—use a kick-turn to link traverses. Steepen the angle of traverse while practicing the unweighting exercises. Drop down, rise up—hold the up position—and drop down again. Keep your chin tucked in and your back straight.

The next maneuver requires good timing and co-ordination—the pole plant with the down-up-down movement. The ski pole is planted in the snow at a point approximately halfway between the boot and ski tip, out to the side of the ski. Plant your pole at the end of the down motion, as you start the up movement. With a slight push on the pole, you can help diminish your weight on the snow and this will greatly assist you in unweighting the skis. Pole plant has other advantages—helping to co-ordinate timing and providing a pivot for the turn. Practice this pole exercise while traversing, being careful not to gain too much speed in the traverse.

Next, try a christie-into-the-hill from a traverse position. This maneuver is done by planting the pole and unweighting the skis with a down-up-down motion. Turn the skis by initiating a hip rotation, causing the heels of the skis to slide downhill and the ski tips into the hill. This last movement will also cause a slight reversing of the shoulders.

Because spring conditions offer extreme resistance, you will often need upper body rotation (shoulder follow-through) to aid in the final turning of the skis. In this manner, the competent skier is able to utilize many sources of turning power to change the direction of the skis. Remember to start the turn of the skis at the top of the up motion in your unweighting movement. When the skis are lightest on the snow, they are most easily turned.

Practice christies-into-the-hill until they can be executed from the fall line. This is similar to a stop christie. Now try turning the skis into the fall line from a traverse position. Sink down to start the turn, rise up to unweight the skis, and sink down again with most of your weight on the new downhill ski. Since the critical problem of any turn is to start the skis turning downhill, this exercise will build up fall-line confidence. Now it becomes a simple maneuver to make a complete downhill turn.

If you have difficulty with the parallel approach, try using a limited uphill stem. This is called stemming-to-the-fall-line and is finished with a christie-into-the-hill. Be careful, though—stemming can be dangerous in crud. Thus, the stem maneuver is done very quickly. From a traverse, with skis equally weighted and parallel, shift your weight to the lower ski and push out the tail of the upper ski. Now quickly place your weight on the stemmed upper ski and bring the downhill ski parallel to the uphill ski. Both skis are equally weighted again, in the fall line, and the turn is finished by a christie-into-the-hill. The transition from parallel skis to stemmed uphill ski and back to parallel skis again should be done rapidly. Practice this exercise, as all the exercises, from both directions. Link maneuvers and turns with as little traversing as possible. The finish of one turn should be the beginning of the next turn. Thus, you are able to utilize the momentum from one turn as the springboard for the next.

A parallel turn on crud snow is a combination of all the forementioned maneuvers, executed down the fall line with more equally weighted and parallel skis. The skis are turned on the up movement, with the pole to aid this lifting action. Turning power will come from the hips, feet, and shoulders. Unweight the skis using the hips to push the tails outward at the end of the turn and follow through with the arm and shoulder. Don't overrotate or swing. When skiing crud, you should learn to delay your shoulder follow-through so that you will always have a reserve turning power to finish the turn.

Crud snow is not easy skiing. Attempt to understand what you are trying to accomplish, and seek the help of a professional instructor. Shy away from well-meaning friends who offer free advice. Incompetent instruction can be disastrous in heavy spring snow. Above all, don't be discouraged. Learning to ski spring snow will require time and practice, just as skiing in deep snow or on icy slopes—but once mastered, it can be immensely satisfying.

Don't Let Moguls Throw You

by Olaf Rodegard, Sun Valley Ski School, Sun Valley, Idaho

Few spring conditions seem more hazardous to skiers than the mounds of soft mid-day mush, or slippery late-afternoon snow which are known as moguls. Many intermediate and some advanced skiers flounder when confronted with an entire slope of high moguls and deep ruts. Actually, they are easy and fun to ski—if you use the proper technique.

Good knee action is the most important factor in skiing moguls. Many skiers keep the downhill knee stiff, trying to use it as a brake to control their skis when sideslipping down the side of a mogul. This is completely wrong. Good down-and-up knee action is the best form of control. It provides a basis for turns, gives edge control in traverses and sideslips, and puts rhythm into your skiing.

For intermediate skiers, approach the mogul from a traverse position, your body square to your skis, with the uphill shoulder kept slightly forward to insure weight on the downhill ski. Knees should be flexed and held slightly into the hill, for edge control. Now sink down in your knees, at the same time bringing either the left pole forward (for a left turn) or the right pole forward (for a turn to the right). Stem your uphill ski and plant your pole in the snow at the top of the mogul. As your skis reach the top of the mogul, start your turn by rising from the knees to unweight the skis and change direction. Now, as you slide down the lower side of the mogul, in the direction of your turn, immediately sink down again in the knees. This up-and-down timing must be practiced—the idea being to unweight your skis at the very top of the mogul (which offers least resistance) and to let your skis down the lower side of the mogul in a controlled sideslip. With the turn completed, you will be in a traverse position again, uphill ski slightly ahead. No body or shoulder swing, other than the use of your pole, described above, is necessary. The pole movement starts a slight counterrotation and, as a result, the rising and sinking in the direction of the turn are all that are necessary.

For the more advanced skier, a turn over moguls is begun with the same down-and-up motion, but it is not made as sharply. It is easier for the more advanced skier to lengthen each turn, so that the skis slide against and over the top of the next mogul, especially if there are long grooves or ruts between bumps. If you are skiing on a slope consisting mainly of moguls, the turns can be done like wedeln, your body keeping a center balance while the heels of your skis slide from side to side. Use your ski pole as a windup and the top or upper part of the mogul as pivot point for your turn, keeping all the turning motion in your knees and ankles.

Practice a turn to the left and a turn to the right separately, then start linking turns. By linking turns over moguls, you will begin to develop a rhythm which makes skiing both easy and pleasurable.

SKI POINTERS ON DIFFICULT CONDITIONS AND TERRAIN

Battle of the Boiler Plate

by Neil Robinson, Director, Bromley Ski School, Manchester, Vt.

In order to ski hard-packed snow, boiler plate, or sheer icy surfaces, you must have the proper equipment. Particular attention should be given to the condition of your boots and skis. Boots must fit properly and should have enough rigidity to give absolute edge control. Skis need sharp steel edges that will bite well into the surface beneath. For this reason, I personally prefer offset hollow-ground edges. Make certain, too, that your bindings are properly mounted, and that they will hold your feet securely to the skis. Stand on your skis over the bindings, with ankles and knees slightly flexed and forward, your body upright and relaxed.

Start slowly at first, until you get the feel of the snow. When turning, drop your shoulder out and keep it somewhat delayed, to insure more weight on the downhill or lower ski. Just a slight amount of lower body rotation and unweighting of the skis are enough to initiate a turn. The advantage of hard-packed surfaces is, of course, the little effort that is required to turn your skis. The problem now becomes how to stop the skis from over-turning. This is done by controlling the amount of sideslip in each turn. *If you stay in the fall line making continuous turns, you will eliminate a good deal of sideslipping and, consequently, the problem of over-turning.* It is true you will be skiing faster. However, when skiing hard-packed surfaces, you are also bypassing the possibility of catching a ski in loose snow, causing you to fall. This thought should give you the added confidence to ski a bit faster. Another control over sideslipping is found in the tail of the ski. If you place too much weight forward on the skis, the tails will skid downhill and you will find yourself in a long, uncontrollable sideslip—particularly dangerous on blue ice. Control the drift of your turn by maintaining that upright, relaxed body position.

Skiing Deep Powder

by Ed Lynch, Certified Instructor, SRMSIA, Aspen Ski School, Aspen, Colo.

Most Western skiers certainly will agree that "floating a turn" in deep powder snow is one of the most satisfying experiences. However, Easterners and Midwesterners often end up wallowing around in the unaccustomed depth of snow, unable to make a turn.

Instead of giving up in disgust, as many do, apply these pointers on deep powder to your own skiing.

To begin with, flexible to medium wooden or metal skis make skiing deep snow easier. This is so because the tips of the skis will "plane" (or ride above the surface) better. It is advisable to tighten up your release bindings just a bit. Longer ski poles also help, as do snow-resistant pockets, goggles, gloves and clothing.

A long traverse across a steep face is an excellent introduction to deep snow. *The snow will tend to slow you down, so make the angle of descent steep enough to pick up sufficient speed to "plane" the skis.* Stand equally on both skis and try a series of up-and-down bounces or rhythmic movements. Make a few stop turns into the hill. Keep your movements smooth and don't hurry your turns. Using this smooth up-and-down lift, let your natural body swing turn the skis.

Most newcomers to powder invariably place far too much weight on the lower ski, with the following result: the pressure of the deep snow immediately pulls the unweighted ski back toward the rear—an acrobatic position rather difficult to maintain. Keep your skis equally weighted and maintain a sufficient speed to let the skis plane up slightly. Now turn down the hill by counterrotating and *lifting up* into the turn, allowing natural body rotation to swing the skis in a smooth arc. A fairly upright body position should be maintained, with ankles and knees providing the needed sink, lift, and sink to finish.

Skiing deep powder is primarily rhythm. Once you have made a few turns, don't stop. When each turn is completed, you are in position to initiate the next.

One other important idea comes into play. This is a proper frame of mind. Most people laugh off any thought of fear until they actually look down a powder snow face. It's quite natural to feel an attack of acute stage fright. The hill has to be steep for deep snow skiing and the skier must stay close to the fall line. It is a common occurrence to watch someone start a beautiful, flawless turn, get halfway through it, and then give up and crash when crossing the fall line. If your mind falters before your body, stop, take a deep breath, and try again.

Skiing in Flat Light

by Manfred Parker, Certified Instructor, ISIA, Alf Engen Ski School, Alta, Utah

One of the less pleasant phenomena of skiing, for the average person and the experienced skier alike, is the atmospheric condition that causes flat light. Visibility can range from poor on foggy or cloudy days in the East to almost zero in the high open bowls of the West or Europe. And although eyes do help a skier's balance in flat light, other parts of the human nervous system also help to maintain balance. These can be stimulated by the action of the skier himself, in order to counteract the imbalance resulting when visibility is restricted.

Every time you bounce on your skis, pressing against the balls of your feet on the up motion, your nervous system receives stimulus aiding you in keeping your balance point. In addition to a bouncing motion, use your downhill pole like a blind person tapping a cane. Working with your lower pole will not only give you additional stability, but will keep you over your downhill ski, counteracting the natural impulse to lean into the hill when you cannot see the slope.

While in the basic traverse position, touch your pole rhythmically in unison with a bouncing down-up-down motion, the pole being planted at the end of the down motion. The more frequently you bounce and touch your pole, the more stimulus will be received by the nervous system, and the easier it will be for you to keep your balance in the traverse. *Ski in a low crouch with your ankles bent forward so that there is pressure against them from the front of your ski boots. Your hips must also be low. The closer you are to your skis, the easier it will be to keep your balance in flat light.*

Take it easy when the light is bad. If necessary, traverse the slope. Turn between traverses by means of a hop christie, keeping the low crouch position while in the air and while landing. As soon as possible after landing, start bouncing and planting the lower pole as you traverse again.

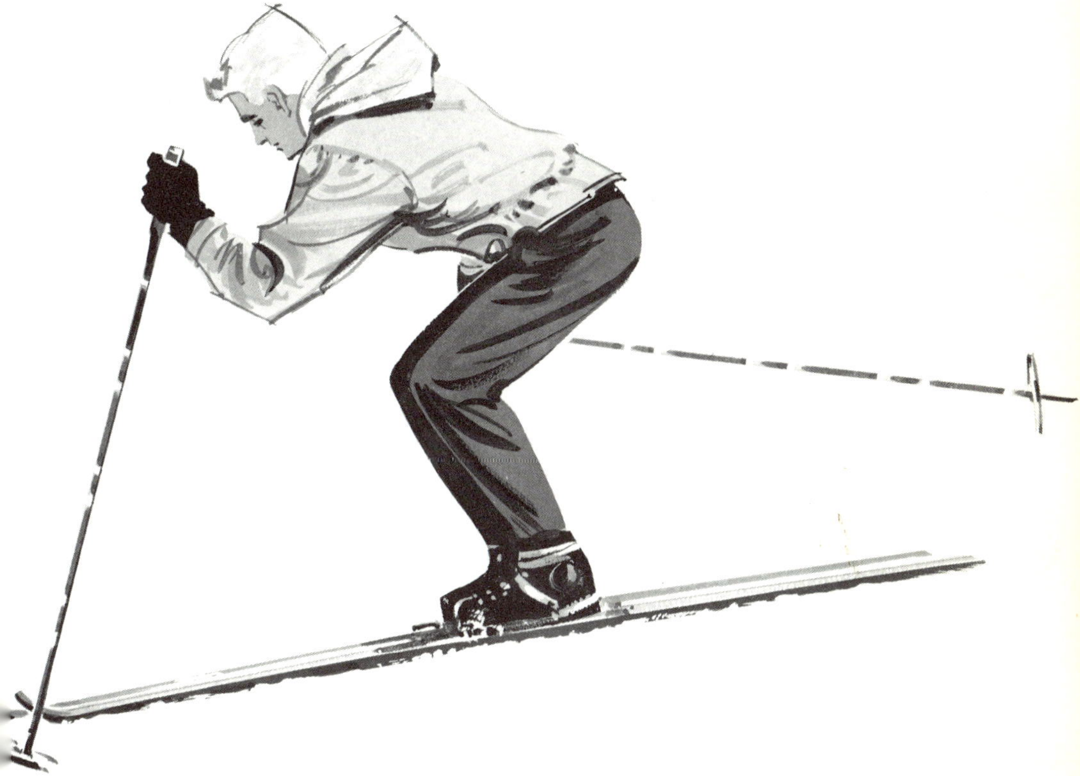

Planning Your Run

by Jerry Wesslen, Director, Mount Telemark Ski School, Cable, Wis.

All skiers, but particularly those in the Midwest and certain sections of the East, are often faced with a problem of terrain—lots of short, steep pitches, followed by longer, gentle grades. This pattern is quite common at all ski areas where large mountain ranges are absent and the long, nearly-constant-grade runs are not available. It has been my experience from watching and teaching skiers that they could derive far more enjoyment from each day's skiing by better planning of their runs. Too frequently I have seen a skier making the same radius turns on the flat, gentle section that he made on a steeper pitch above, resulting in a great loss of speed. This is primarily a problem of controlling the amount of edging and, consequently, the length of the turn. Increased edging is needed on steep portions to keep the radius of the turn short and to control speed, but smoothness should not be sacrificed. Now suppose you come to a long, gentle grade and you make the same length turn you made above. Your excessive edging immediately reduces your speed and a long schuss, skating, poling, or perhaps all three are needed to regain the lost speed which could have been preserved had you made a long, smooth turn with more subtle edging. The correct amount of speed, which depends upon your ability, should be welcomed as a helper, not as an opponent to be feared. A series of linked turns in the fall line can be made on nearly flat terrain if the proper amount of edging is used. *A little preplanning will enable you to get in more real skiing per run, and, in turn, cut down the time it takes to become more proficient.*

Adapt Technique to Conditions

by Tom Hall, Certified Instructor, CSIA, Holiday Hills Ski School, Traverse City, Mich.

I would like to make a plea for the learner to develop flexibility in his skiing. Regardless of what formal technique you wish to pursue, you should learn to accommodate your skiing to suit the contour and conditions of a particular slope.

Learn to "read" the run. For instance, when approaching runs whose hummocks of snow in late season have the formidable habit of resembling tank traps, a carefully chosen course will allow you to filter smoothly down in the troughs between the moguls.

You should also be prepared to adjust to varying snow conditions while under way. When skiing a wind-swept trail, for instance, where the snow may be drifted and untracked along the side, and hard-packed in the center, you can usually take advantage of the whole width of the run if you remember to *sit back slightly when encountering the deeper snow and press forward as you enter the packed area*. On particularly icy surfaces, it is often advisable to forsake style for stability by opening the distance between your parallel skis to approximately a shoulder's breadth. Another potential pitfall peculiar to trail skiing is an abrupt change in snow temperatures because some areas are in shade and some exposed to the sun, yielding areas of melting slow snow alternating with patches of sheer ice. On these days, the development of a photographer's eye for sun and shadow may assist you immensely in anticipating conditions ahead.

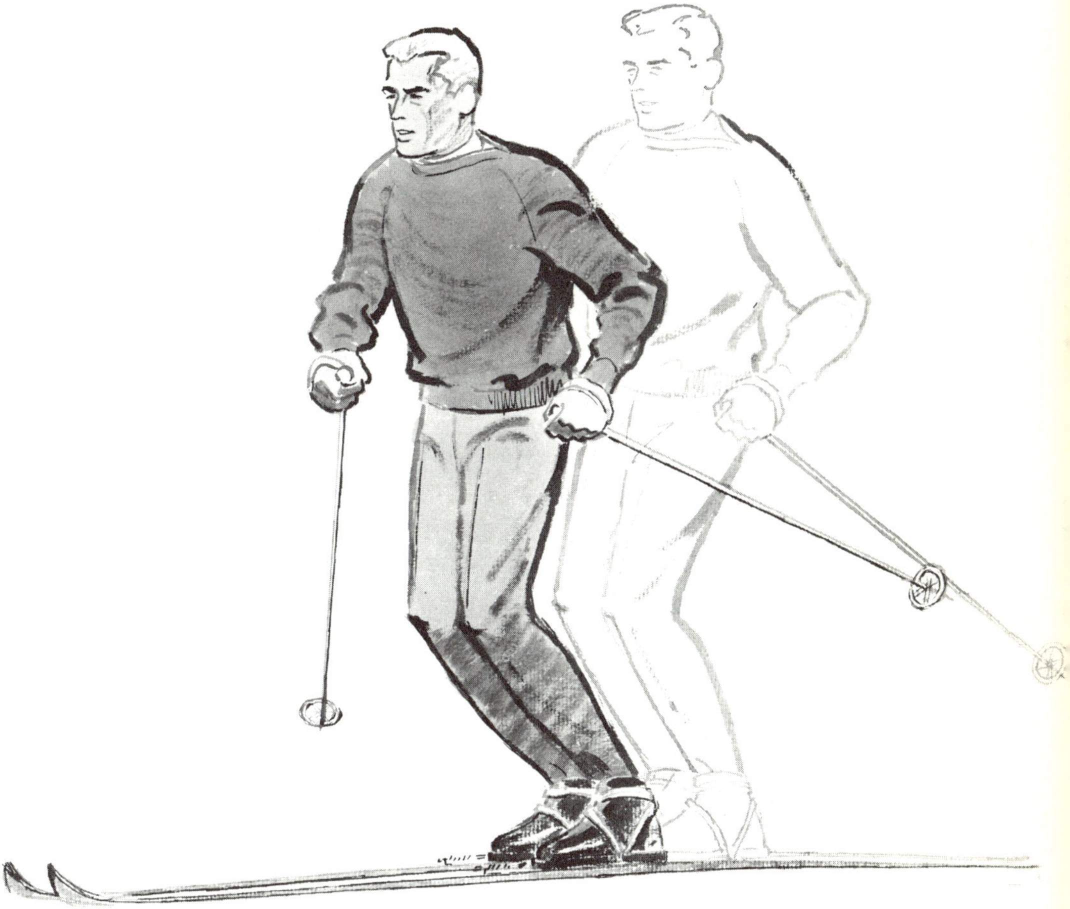

Handling Spring Conditions

by Rick Shambroom, Certified Instructor, CSIA

In springtime, you're apt to run into snow conditions that vary from ice and hard-frozen granular to light corn and wet, heavy mush. These hints apply to skiing the wet corn snow you find mid-day, after the sun has been on the slope a couple of hours. They will help you ski it more smoothly.

First, *ski closer to the fall line* than you might ordinarily ski. This will help you maintain speed and your turns will be of shorter radius, requiring less turning effort. *Your running position should be a little further back* than the position you use on packed or light powder. That is, hips lower and back. You should feel more compact. This will prevent dissipation of turning power and, at the same time, keep you from burying your tips.

Run on flatter skis. Excess edging will cut your speed too much. Be careful not to overdo your comma position. *Exaggerate your turning effort* (foot steering or heel push) and your lift. It *does* take more power to displace your skis in wet snow than in poof powder.

Your skis must be well waxed so that they'll slide easily. If you have wooden skis, be sure the bottoms are completely lacquered and no bare wood is exposed. In terms of enjoyment, it will pay you to have a good wet-snow wax combination applied with a hot iron. What it amounts to is this: in good powder you can get away with sloppy movements but in bad snow your technique *must* be good.

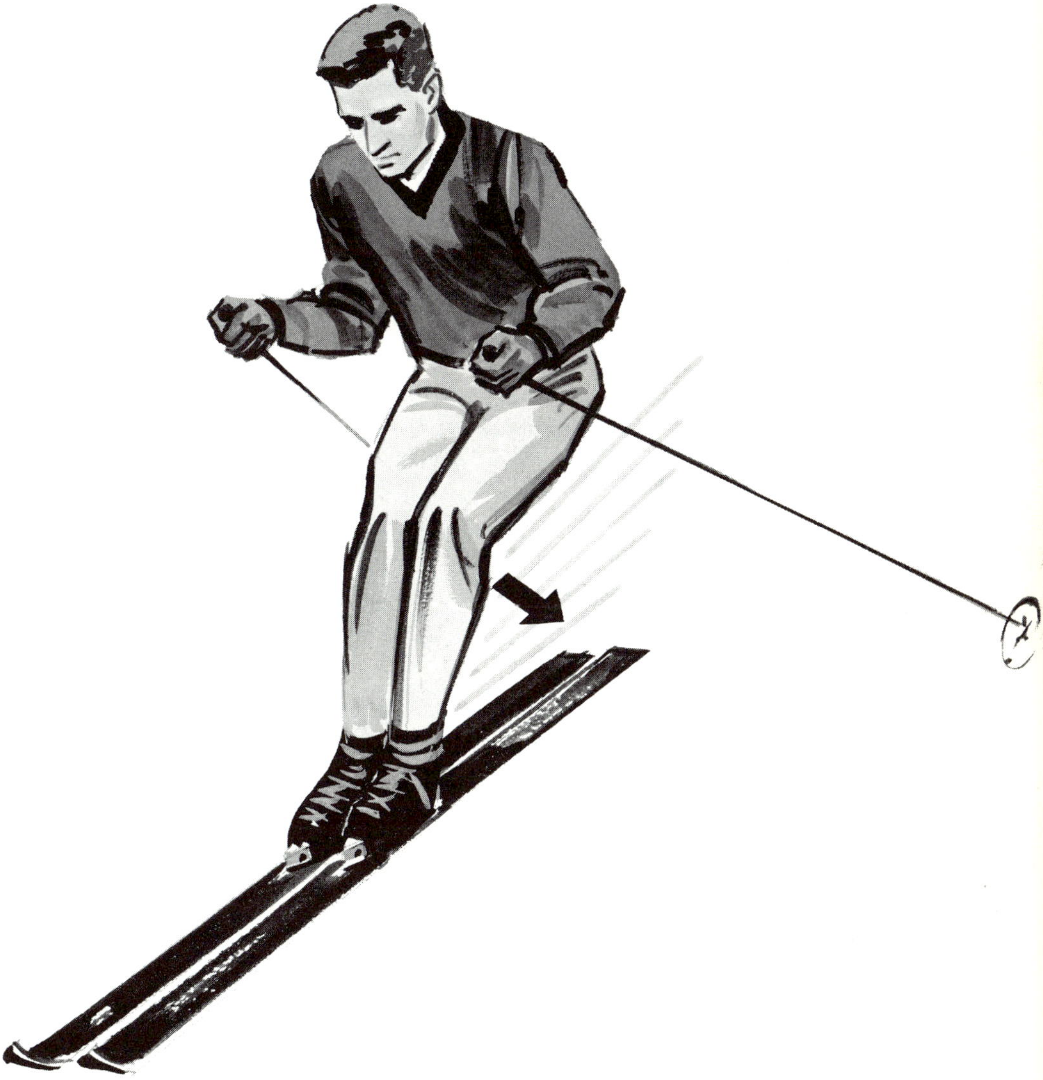

Downhill Running on Rutted Tracks

by Lee Quinn, Certified Instructor, FWSIA, Squaw Valley Ski School, Tahoe City, Calif.

The hardest, most jarring falls of the ski season usually occur in the spring when the runout section of the trails thaw and then freeze into icy rutted tracks. Everyone knows that these falls are caused by catching an outside edge, but few skiers utilize the simple remedy.

When running straight downhill on rutted tracks, you should separate your skis (about four to six inches apart) and weight the inside edges of both skis. This is *not* a snow plow. The skis remain parallel and your downhill position remains unchanged except for a slightly wider stance and the tilting of the skis to the inside edges. If you tilt the skis, the outside edges will ride up and over the converging ruts and keep from catching in them.

Only the outside edges cause such falls. If the inside edges do catch when running straight, it merely separates the skis. You can correct this, without causing a fall, by flattening the skis and sliding them together again.

Usually, sufficient edging is obtained by use of the ankles alone, but on long, fast runouts, deep icy ruts, or especially if you are tired after a hard day, don't hesitate to assume a knock-kneed position in order to keep the inside edges weighted and to take pressure off your ankles.

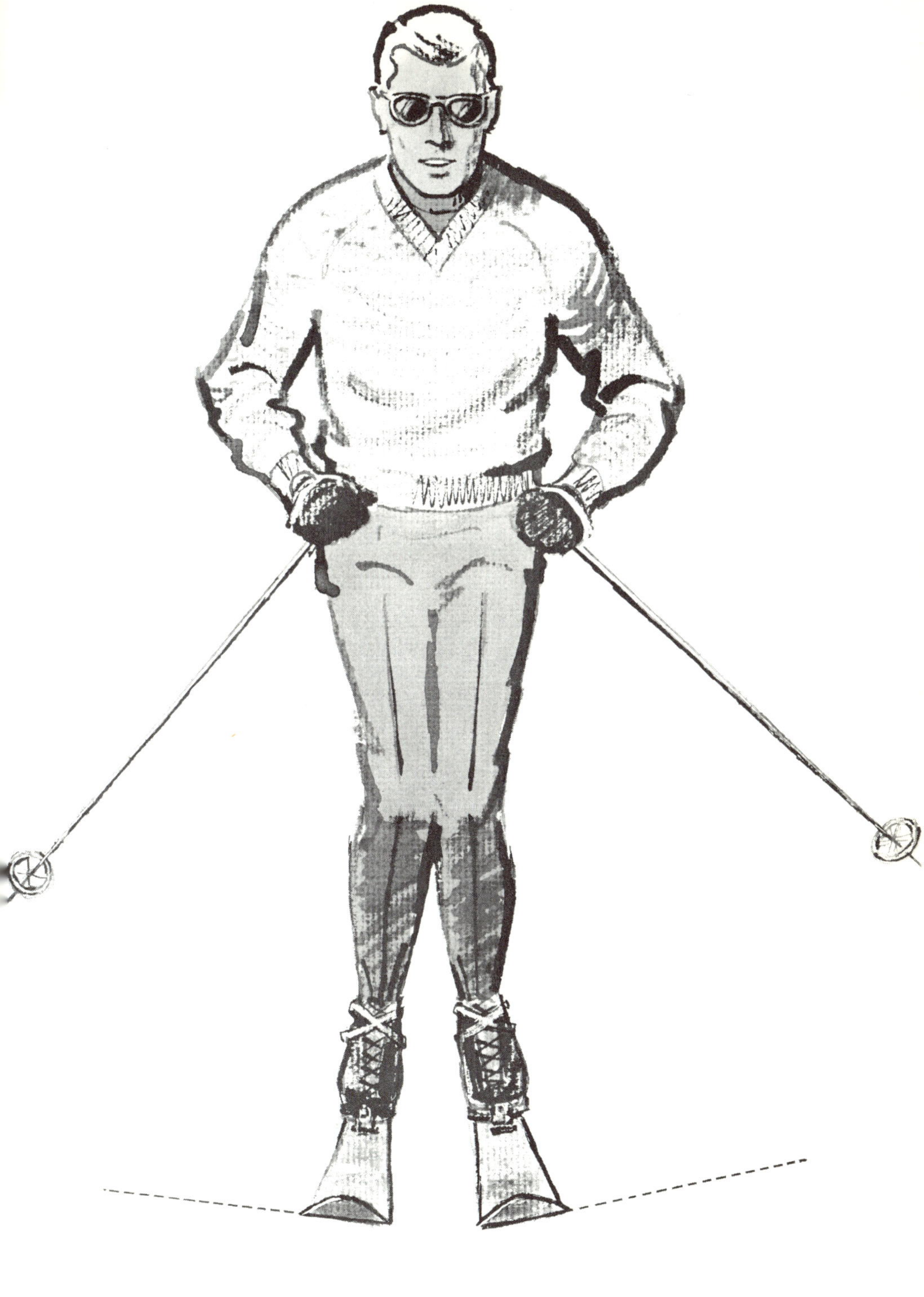

Traversing Moguls

by Duncan Grandin, Certified Instructor, SRMSIA, Winter Park Ski School, Winter Park, Colo.

Handling moguls creates an interesting problem for all skiers. It requires good balance, timing and control to traverse them. *Traversing on one foot is a safe, secure way to handle them. It is almost impossible to catch an edge or to cross skis when on one foot.* Also, one-footed skiing prevents too much stiffening of the body, develops weight control, and makes it easier for the skier to turn quickly.

Start out on a bumpy intermediate slope, traversing on your lower ski. Keep the uphill ski a little forward and slightly up or "floating." Keep shifting a little weight to the raised uphill ski, or guiding it, for stability. If you should lose your balance when approaching the crest, or on the crest of a mogul, immediately step onto the uphill ski to regain your balance. Then continue traversing on the lower ski, keeping your knees as bent and relaxed as possible to maintain control. To keep your traverse smooth and even, steer your lower ski with your weight and foot through the moguls, rather than trying to pick a direct line over them. Keep your upper body erect and relaxed, giving your legs as much freedom of motion as possible. Check your balance when necessary by touching your poles in the snow.

This method of "walking" over moguls reduces the jarring, stiffening effect produced by bouncing over them on two feet and gives you a more complete command of your turns. At the end of each turn, resume your one-footed traverse in the new direction.

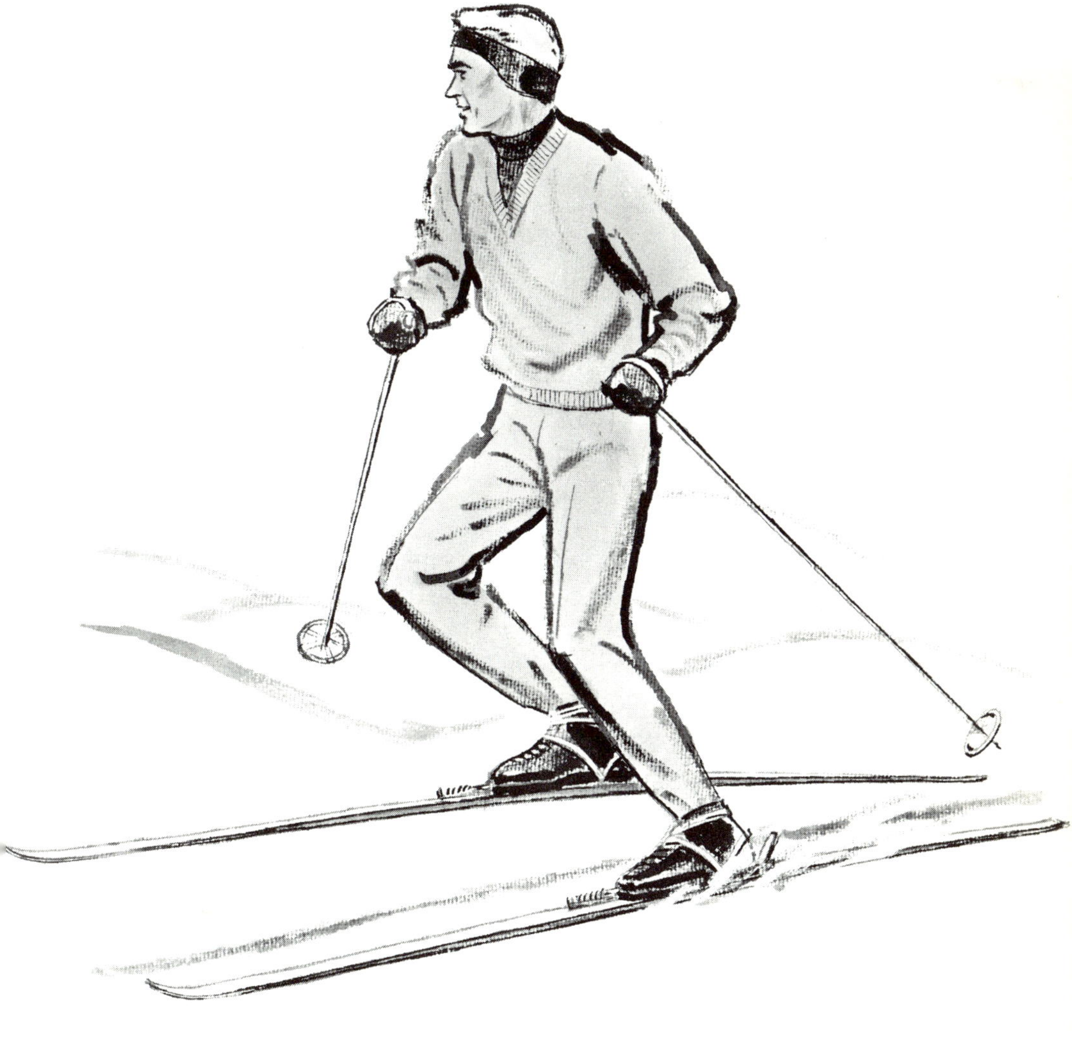

Picking Your Turns on Moguls

by Jacques Legras, Certified Instructor, FWSIA, Squaw Valley Ski School, Tahoe City, Calif.

With the modernization and popularity of skiing today, a skier rarely gets to enjoy a smooth, perfect snow surface. Most slopes are made up of bumps, grooves, and holes. The choice of terrain and the exact place to make a turn is therefore very important in order to maintain smoothness of rhythm, speed control, and balance throughout the run.

You may have noticed that, regardless of the technique used, *it is much easier to start a turn on the top of a mogul than above or below it.* The chances are that above or below the hump there will be deep grooves, tracks, or loose snow to interfere with the beginning of the turn. The convex shape at the top of a bump will allow your skis to sideslip more easily than the concave surface of a groove. At the precise moment your skis reach the top of the bump, the tips and tails meet practically no snow resistance; therefore, it is easier to start sideslipping into the turn. The rest of the turn (stem christie or parallel) depends upon your ability and style of skiing.

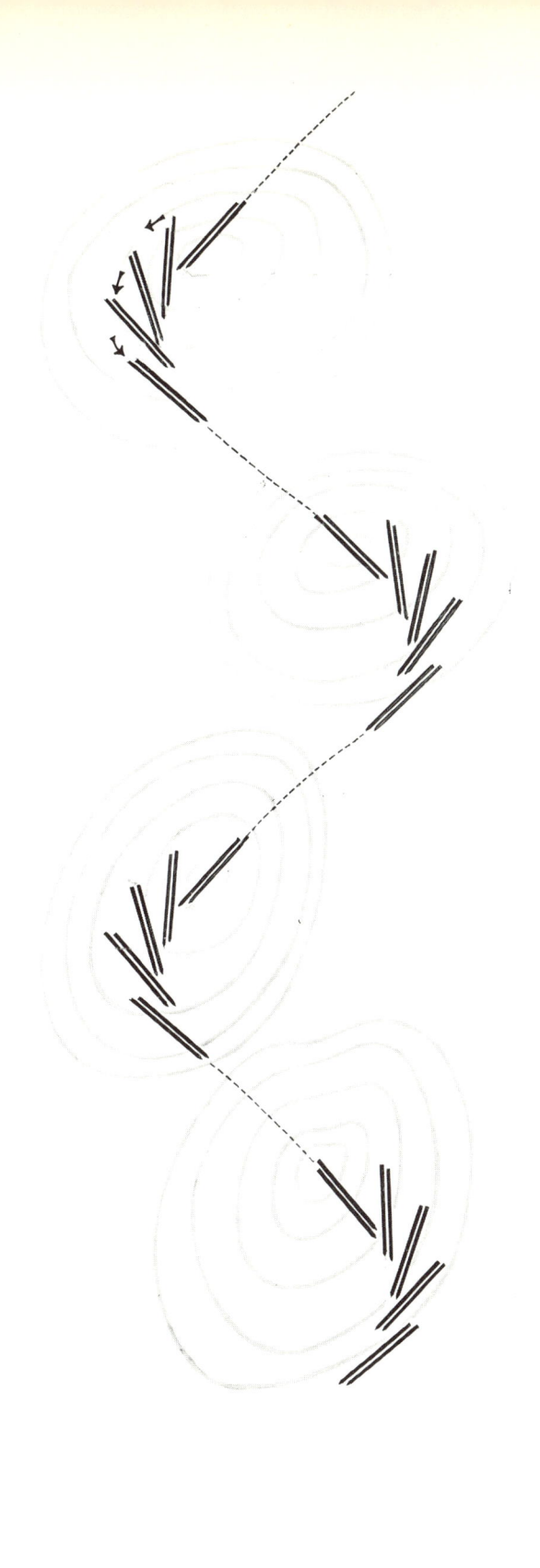

Hopping Moguls

by Paul Brown, Director, Big Tupper Ski School, Tupper Lake, N.Y.

Quite often, trails become bumpy and present problems for most skiers since they dare not attain sufficient speed nor have they the ability to try "double bumping" to get a smooth ride. Hence, they find themselves going "cross bumps" and, without being able to turn quickly enough, are forced to take a severe jarring each time they hit a bump. Because of this, most skiers travel at moderate speed through bumpy sections. The maneuver I am going to suggest can best be utilized at this moderate speed. It can be described as a combination pre-jump and airplane turn.

When the tips of your skis approach the crown of the bump, *you simply hop the tails of the skis in the air and turn them over the crown of the bump* so that you come down in the trough between moguls or on the downhill side of the first bump. In this way, by using a pre-jump, the abrupt bump will not throw you in the air. By turning your skis in the air, you avoid running head on into the uphill side of the next bump. *The tips of your skis should remain on the ground throughout this maneuver. Merely draw your heels up under your body rather than launching your entire body in the air* (which would be unsettling and apt to cause a fall).

Any bump or mogul that has a sharp uphill side and/or a sharp drop on the downhill side can be easily negotiated using this maneuver.

With a little practice, you'll soon be able to approach mogul patches with more confidence and less difficulty.

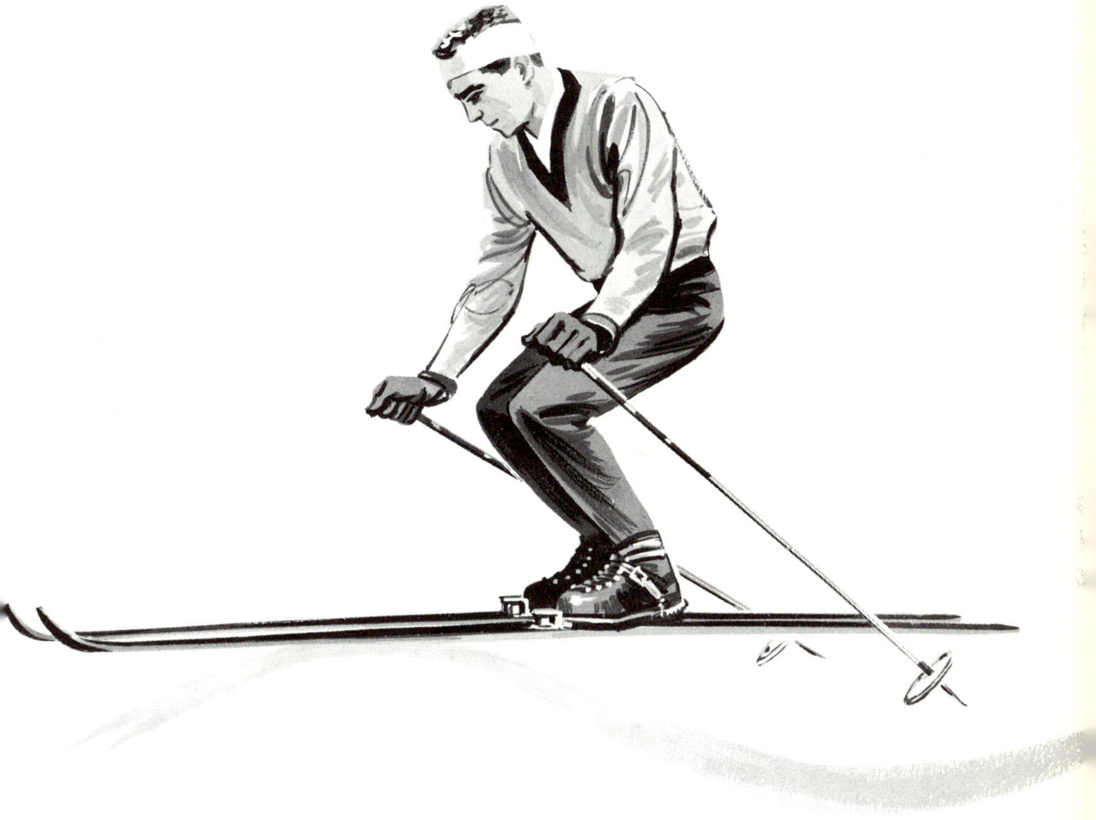

VII. *Choosing Proper Equipment*

Read this before you go shopping. New skier or expert, you'll be better prepared to know what to look for and which of the many excellent skis, boots, bindings, and poles are best for you.

How to Select Boots

A good boot is the most important item in a skier's knapsack. Its function is to transmit the force or strength needed to turn, slow down or stop, from the body to the ski. Just as a slipping clutch does not produce efficiency in driving a car, neither does a loose-fitting boot produce better skiing. A good boot is designed to give maximum support to your foot and ankle. It is built to keep out moisture and cold. It is made specifically for skiing, not for long walks or dancing. And while it is made to last and give good service, even the best boot will not last forever because it is made of leather and, in time, the leather will stretch. The amount of stretch and wear depends upon what kind of skier you are, how much skiing you do, and how well you care for your equipment.

The answer to a proper fit in ski boots is found by trial and error. Give the salesman your regular shoe size or let him measure your feet. If you know that one of your feet is larger, mention this to the salesman. Then try on the boot of your choice over one medium-weight pair of ski socks. The boot should feel snug, but not tight or painful. If your toe touches the front of the boot before lacing, this is not a disqualifying sign. Lacing the inner boot will push your foot back into the heel of the boot, relieving the pressure on the front part of your foot. If the pressure persists, however, try the next larger size. When completely laced, the boot should not feel too tight or it will cut off circulation. However, it is better to choose a boot that seems just a bit snug rather than one that is too loose, because the leather will stretch slightly while you ski. The heel of your foot should be firmly anchored in the boot with the upper part of the boot reaching well above the ankle. You can test the fit of your heel by holding down the heel of the boot against the floor with your hands, while you try to raise the heel of your foot inside the boot. Your heel should fit snugly inside the boot and the amount of give should be almost negligible.

Before you invest, place the boot on the floor or counter and make sure that the heel and sole are flat against the flat surface. You'll want your boot to sit flat on your ski, and if it rocks back and forth in the store, it will rock and roll on your ski, too. Be sure to try on both boots before buying, and if in doubt about the correctness of the fit, wait and try again.

Always bear in mind that not every boot will fit every foot. This is why most shops carry at least three or more different makes of ski boots. Try to be patient with the salesman: he cannot feel your comfort or discomfort when your foot is laced into the boot. He may have to fit you with several pairs of boots before finding the right one. For really difficult feet to fit, it may be advisable to have the boots made to measure. Most good ski shops have such a service available, and the better ski boots can be ordered from abroad at a slightly higher cost (most shops charge from $10 to $15 extra for this service). Proper fit is then guaranteed by both the manufacturer and the ski shop. Allow sixty to ninety days for making and delivering made-to-measure boots and do your ordering early in the season, so you won't spoil your winter vacation schedule.

What kind of boots will your money buy? Except for children's and junior boots, shoes selling for less than $30 are apt to be disappointing in terms of quality and durability, not to mention the all-important fit. If you plan to ski a good deal, it pays to get one of the better models in the $40 to $60 price range. Such a boot should feature double-boot construction (boot within a boot), have higher uppers for ankle support, a hinged back for better forward flexing of the ankle, and a sturdy sole covered with a thin non-skid rubber sole. The heels must have a groove large enough to accommodate the binding cable. The inside of the boot should be padded with soft sponge rubber lining to minimize the effects of the stiff outer leather. Naturally, boots may be purchased at prices considerably higher than $60. Such boots are mostly hand-stitched, imported models. They are usually rather stiff and are built for competitive skiing, although some models are designed for the average skier.

As far as children's boots are concerned, here are a few general suggestions. Look for simplicity of design to reduce the time needed for lacing. A double boot is fine for the teenager, but smaller children will do equally well with a simple model. It is also wise to buy the boots slightly larger than actually needed and let the youngster wear an extra pair of socks and a sponge rubber insole. You are dealing here with growing feet and this growth period should be anticipated by the parents.

After a year or so, the boots should fit well without the need for extra socks.

Finally, a *must* for all boots, whether children's or adult's is a tree or press to keep the boots in good shape, and some form of wax or preserver.

How to Select Skis

Owning a good pair of skis will free you from the chore of having to rent skis every time you decide to head for the snow country, or skiing on boards so warped and scratched as to make every movement a chore.

There are so many excellent skis being made, from so many different materials, that selecting a good pair can often be a bewildering experience. The skis are all shiny, colorful and professional looking. Their prices will run from about $35 to $195 and their characteristics will change with every model.

Basically, skis are made of wood, or a combination of plastic, metal and wood. The wood ski, too, makes extensive use of plastic materials such as a protective covering on the top and sides. The running surfaces on most better skis are made of a tough plastic designed to give speed, keep out moisture, and resist scratching and gouging due to wear. The plastic running surface does not eliminate the need for waxing—it merely reduces it.

Most wood skis are of laminated construction, which means that strips of wood, usually hickory, or a mixture of ash and hickory, are bonded into a billett which is then shaped to the proper dimensions. A ski without metal edges would be difficult to control on steep terrain or under icy snow conditions. Therefore, steel edges are a must on all skis, including children's as soon as they reach the stage of lift riding and downhill skiing. To offset an edge means that it has been attached in such a manner that the cutting edge protrudes slightly beyond the actual width of the ski. This affords the ski a better bite on packed snow or ice. Offset edges are recommended not only for the expert, but for the average skier as well.

The metal-plastic ski has been in use for about ten years and its popularity has grown tremendously. Metal skis are easy to maintain during the non-skiing months, but above all they are easy to ski on. In fact, until recently, they have appealed more to the recreational skier than to the competitor. However, new models, now available of both domestic and foreign manufacture, are suitable for all types of racing, and even jumping.

In selecting the proper skis, look for camber and flexibility. Here are some simple tests which will help you to choose the skis that are right for you.

Test for Camber. The camber is the amount of bow or arch built into your ski. You can see it by putting the ski bottoms together: they will touch at a point where the tips begin to curve up. They also touch where the tail ends meet. In the middle, or waist, however, the skis should measure one-and-a-half inches to two inches apart. This is the camber, and too much of it will make turning difficult. Too little camber, on the other hand, will make the skis wander and hard to control. To check your skis for equal camber, lay them down on a perfectly flat surface. The tips should have an equal amount of up-bend and the height of both skis at the middle section must be identical.

Test for Flexibility. The flexibility of your skis is extremely important. Too many skiers are using skis that are entirely too stiff. Generally speaking, your weight and skiing ability should determine the amount of flexibility in your skis. To check flexibility, grasp the ski tip with one hand, with running surface up, and place the other hand at the waist of the ski. Flex lightly. Then turn the ski upside down and grasp it by the tail end. Flex it again. Examine at least two or more models of the same ski in this manner and by process of elimination select the ski most suitable for you.

Test for Straightness. Holding the ski by its tip, sight down the running surface. Imagine a line drawn across the ski at the point where the tip begins to turn up, and another line as close to the tail as possible. If these imaginary lines are parallel, the ski is free of lateral warpage. To check for longitudinal twisting or warpage, place the running surfaces of the skis together, carefully matching the sides at the points of contact. Squeeze the skis until they are absolutely flat against each other. Warpage will show if the sides of the skis along the waist fail to match.

Test for Proper Length. To test a ski for proper length, stand and hold one ski up vertically beside you, its tail resting on the floor. Now stretch one arm straight up in the air. The ski should reach your wrist, or a little below your wrist, if it is the proper length for you.

Children's skis should be short. Until the age of ten, the ski length should more or less equal the child's height. Light, flexible skis are preferable, for your youngster will get more fun out of skiing with them.

Last but not least, skis do age over the years. To start out with grandfather's old slats that have been standing in the barn or attic for years is a mistake. Wood deteriorates just by standing around. Skiing itself has changed so much during the past few years that ancient equipment is not only inadequate but sometimes even dangerous. To fully enjoy the sport of skiing, you must have adequate and modern equipment.

How to Select Bindings

The next important item of equipment is the binding. Basically, there are three main types of bindings: the standard cable binding, the release binding, and the long thong.

The standard cable binding consists simply of a toeplate and a heel cable. The toe of the boot slides into the toeplate and the steel cable is sprung around the heel of the boot with just enough tension to permit you to raise your heel slightly.

The release binding is recommended to nearly all skiers, and most certainly to all recreational skiers. When you fall, the sudden jolt which your boot will exert against the binding will cause the binding to release the boot. Many different types of mechanisms have been designed to allow separation of boot from ski at a given point. The two main types are the cable-type release and the bootlock release.

The cable-type release has two safety factors: a front throw that will release when the pressure of tension becomes too great during a straight forward fall, and a toe piece that will release when lateral pressure becomes too great during a twisting fall.

The bootlock (or non-cable binding) relies solely on pressure supplied by steel springs to hold the boot in place. The bootlock will release in almost any direction, such as straight forward, backward, sideways, or any combination of these.

Both systems of release bindings are effective—when the bindings are properly adjusted. The ski shop will mount bindings for you. They will give them an arbitrary setting for release under normal, average conditions. You, the skier, must make the final adjustments yourself when actually skiing.

The third type of binding is the long thong, mostly used by racers and too often used by skiers who definitely should not be using it. Consisting of a toeplate and a long leather strap which binds the heel and ankle to the ski, the long thong provides the extra support required by racers traveling at very high speeds on chattering skis. However, it is interesting to note that more and more racers are now combining the long thong heel with the release-type toeplate.

In budgeting for your new equipment, you should allow at least $5 to $10 for standard cable-type bindings, and $15 to $25 for release bindings (which includes the fee for attaching them).

How to Select Poles

Ski poles should be selected with greater care than the average skier ordinarily gives them, since they are an integral part of equipment and absolutely necessary to ski technique.

A pole consists of a shaft which is usually made of steel, alloys of steel, aluminum, fiberglass, tonkin or other types of cane. Most skiers prefer aluminum or steel poles as opposed to bamboo or split cane since they are considerably more durable. Bamboo and cane poles are lighter and easier to handle, but they tend to break or shatter.

On top of the shaft there should be a comfortable handle and wrist strap designed to fit your hand. This wrist strap should be wide enough so as not to cut, and long enough to permit solid grasping of the grip when you are wearing bulky gloves. About three inches from the bottom of the pole, an aluminum, plastic, or rubber ring is attached to the shaft by means of a cotter pin or similar device, to prevent the pole from sinking into deep snow. The diameter of this ring should be sufficiently large to permit extensive weighting of it. At the same time, however, too large a ring will make the pole unnecessarily bulky and difficult to use in certain advanced techniques. A fairly sharp point at the bottom end of the pole will prevent undue slipping while negotiating ice.

The proper height of the ski pole depends upon your own height. In the ski shop or department store, your ski pole, with its point resting on the floor, should reach your armpit. It will not seem that high out in the snow, of course, since the point will be thrust down into the snow with the basket resting on the surface. The proper height of ski poles is extremely important in today's modern techniques, as well as in the more basic movements.

What should you spend for ski poles? Prices generally range from about $10 to $25 depending upon the material the pole is made of, and the workmanship involved.

Children's poles should be light and proportionately short. Seen all too frequently on the slopes are youngsters struggling with ski poles about a foot too long for them. Any ski shop will shorten them to proper length in a few minutes. At the same time, however, a pole too short will also hinder a child in learning how to ski. Since ski poles play such an important part in balance and ski technique, it is unfair to expect a youngster to learn with improper equipment.

SKI POINTERS ON EQUIPMENT

Proper Way to Lace Boots

by Neil Jacobs, Certified Instructor, CUSSA, Mount Christie Ski School, Oxford, Mich.

Good boots are the foundation in learning how to ski. And proper fit is just as important as proper lacing.

When fitting new boots, be sure to wear the stockings you will use for skiing. Place your foot in the unlaced boot and push it forward until your toes touch the front end of the boot. You should have approximately one-half inch space behind the heel of your foot to the back of the boot. Now press your heel back. The foot should feel snug in the boot, but *not* wedged in. Again, a loose boot is just as wrong as one that is too tight or too small.

The same is true when lacing a boot. If you lace it too tightly, you can cut off circulation and cause muscle cramping by forcing the muscles to function improperly. To lace a double boot properly, begin by placing your foot comfortably in the boot. Be sure that your foot is all the way back in the boot and that there are no wrinkles in the stocking.

Now start at the inner bottom laces and draw them up firmly, but not too tightly. There is a definite difference between firmness and tightness. Continue up to the middle of the boot. Keep the same tension here on the outer eyelets, but slacken slightly on the pull over the arch. Vital muscles that support the ankles and direct action through the feet attach to the arch. *Do not use an arch support of any nature,* for it will cause muscle cramping.

Continue the firmness of both laces in front of the ankles, or leg bones, and add more tension to the remainder of the lacing. This added tension will lock the ankles and insure maximum support. Tie the laces to the outside ankle bone so that the knot will not rest on a large artery and cut off circulation. It is even more important that the knot be on the outside when the outer boot covers the inner boot completely.

Lacing the outer boot, regardless of its material, follows the same procedure. When fabric laces become wet and loose, stop skiing and adjust them properly before the next run. There is no "next time" for an accident that results from a poorly-laced boot. I use a little trick in lacing that you might find valuable. To hold fabric laces in place, especially on open eyes in outer boots, carry the laces over the top, come around the eye and back over the same lace.

Remember that a well-fitting and well-laced boot will give you many added hours of skiing pleasure.

Proper Care of Boots

by John H. Henderson, Certified Instructor, Killington Basin Ski School, Sherburne, Vt.

The evolution of ski equipment that has brought us to our present degree of excellence has been no accident. If you have ever visited a ski or boot maker, you know that the skills and materials that go into the fashioning of equipment are of the best.

The better the equipment, the better should be its care. There is a right way to treat a pair of ski boots. When in use, the boots should be polished frequently with a good wax-base shoe polish. This will preserve the leather and, at the same time, prevent the boot from getting too hard or too soft. Never use any type of oil or softener on your boots because you will oversoften them and so lose the natural support of the leather.

The seams of your boots should be waterproofed—either with a commercial waterproof sealer, ski lacquer or any melted cold-snow wax. Boots should be kept in a press—both after a day's skiing and at the end of the season. If dampness occurs in your inner boots, don't put them near a fire or a radiator to dry. Rather, stuff them full of newspapers, which act as blotters and soak up the moisture. At the end of the season, store your boots in a dry closet. *Put them away clean and polished, stuffed with newspapers, in a press.* The little extra time and effort you spend will be repaid by extra seasons of use.

Ski Care Between Trips

by Hans Garger, Certified Instructor, SRMSIA, Loveland Basin Ski School, Georgetown, Colo.

Simple maintenance of your skis will pay off in the long run—in safety, performance, appearance and endurance. A little care can keep your skis in much better shape for seasons to come.

First, after a day's skiing, don't drag your skis across the driveway and carelessly throw them down. Clean them off first, if necessary, and put them in a safe place. *If you have enough room, mount two brackets on the wall and stand the skis up with the running surfaces toward you. If the skis will be standing on a cement floor, put a wooden board under the ski ends.* And never store your skis for any period of time near heating installations.

Check your skis frequently for loose screws on the bindings and steel edges, and keep them tight. File the edges to enjoy better and safer skiing, and protect the running surfaces with a good coat of lacquer.

At the end of the season, you should clean your skis, put a light coat of oil or grease over the steel edges and strap the skis together. Placing the skis face to face, with running surfaces together, strap them at the tip and tail, where the skis touch each other. Then put a square wooden block between them at the point where the toeplate of your binding is mounted. The wooden block should be just wide enough to stay in place by itself, without increasing the normal distance between the skis. If there is no distance at all between the skis without the block, they need no further maintenance. It's time then to buy a new pair.

Sharpening Edges

by Bob Bourdon, Sepp Ruschp Ski School, Stowe, Vt.

If you skied until the end of the season last year, you probably dulled your ski edges to some extent on thin snow cover. Now is the time to sharpen them for the coming season. Though sharp edges are unnecessary in soft snow, undamaged and perfect edges are absolutely vital for control in icy conditions. Edges that have been damaged should be replaced with new sections.

Even the edges on most new skis must be sharpened. Good edges are tough and hard, yet soft enough to be filed. Edges can be sharpened on a grinding wheel, a sanding belt, or with a butcher's steel, but I believe that using a file is best, and usually much kinder to your skis. Edges on metal skis can be hand-sharpened, but it is better to have the job done by a ski shop equipped for this purpose.

To sharpen edges, all you need is a good ten-inch file. *If possible, place the ski in a vise with the edge up and the running surface of the ski away from you. File diagonally across the steel edge, cutting only on the forward stroke.* Use the top edge of the ski as a guide to keep the file level. Test for sharpness by drawing your finger across the edge, not down its length. If the edge tends to scrape your finger, it is sharp. A slight hook can be rolled on an edge for use on real ice, but it makes the ski tricky to control. When conditions are that bad, don't ski unless you have to.

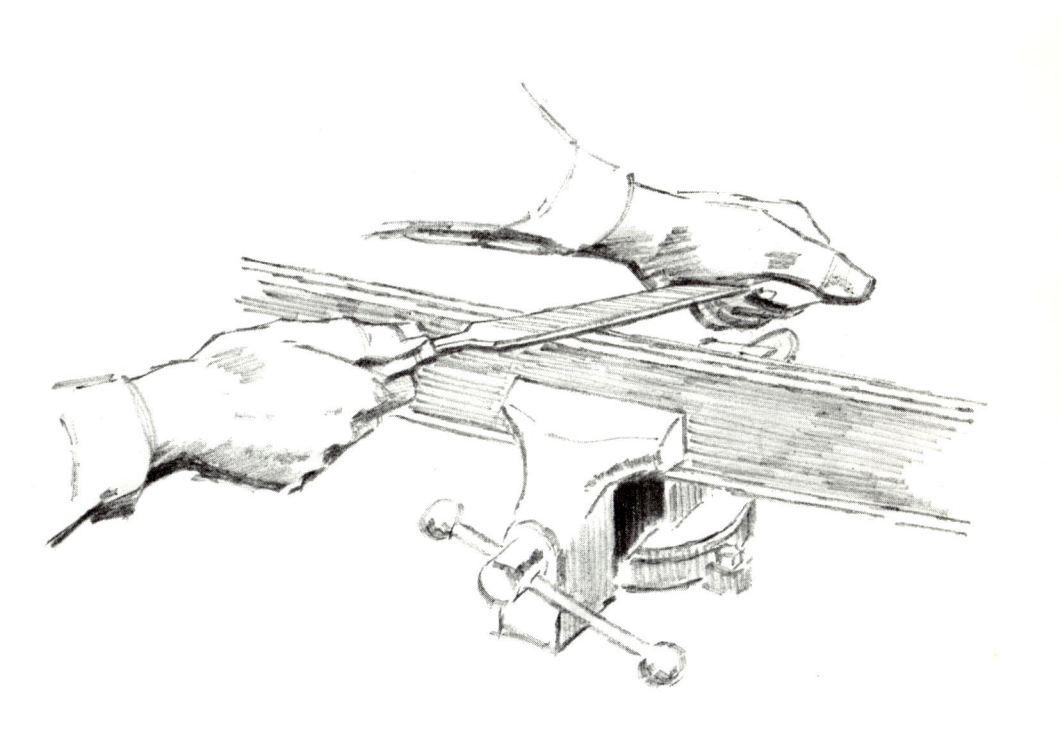

Conditioning Skis to Temperature

by Walt Haefli, Director, Dryden Ski School, Dryden, Mich.

During my racing years in Switzerland, I always made a habit of keeping my skis buried in the snow the night before race day. The reason: to get the skis accustomed to the outside temperature.

As a ski school director in recent years, I have noticed that many skiers take their skis out of warm cars, heated lodges, or rental shops, and lay them directly on the snow. The result is that the snow, contacting the warm skis, melts into water or moisture, which then freezes again to ice on the running surfaces of the skis.

This condensation and freezing process will occur even if your skis are lacquered and waxed. Then you will have the hard task of scraping ice from the bottoms of the skis. Beginners, especially, are never aware of this condition and it makes their first try on skis almost impossible. The skis will not move since the ice under the skis acts as a brake.

To remedy this condition, it is not necessary to bury your skis in the snow overnight. *If you stand the skis up against an outside ski rack or wall for at least 15 minutes before putting them on in the morning, you will condition the running surfaces of the skis to the outside temperature and keep them from icing up.*

Applying the Proper Wax

by Otto Ost, Certified Instructor, ISIA, Belmont Ski School, Helena, Mont.

One of the most controversial of all subjects in skiing is the proper method of waxing. No two skiers will agree on the kind of wax to use under every condition; however, there are some pointers that I consider basic.

First of all, no matter how well the wax has been applied, it will wear off in the process of skiing and the bottom of the ski will be exposed to the snow. For this reason, before you use your skis, put some type of base lacquer on the bottoms. (Of course, I am speaking here of skis that do not have a factory base on them.) When applying the base lacquer, make certain that the bottom of the ski is free from all old wax, old lacquer, etc. Use fine sandpaper and steel wool, along with plenty of elbow grease. Then, when the bottom is clean, apply the lacquer evenly (preferably with a brush), allowing it to dry sufficiently between applications. My advice is to buy a good known brand of base lacquer and use according to the directions on the container. One word of caution: Don't wait until the night before you go skiing to refinish and lacquer your ski bottoms.

If you were to wax your skis accurately for the ultimate in speed, you would have to rewax for about every five degrees of change in temperature. Therefore, my advice would be for waxing under general conditions. The rule I follow can be simply stated: *the colder the snow, the harder the wax; the warmer the snow, the softer the wax.* You will find that in warmer weather the need for wax becomes greater as the snow gets wetter. As a matter of fact, on some types of cold snow, the base lacquer on your ski bottoms is all that is necessary.

The most difficult conditions for which to wax properly, of course, are extreme conditions. At 15 to 20 degrees below zero, for instance, the grains of snow are very fine and granular and, for this reason, appear to form somewhat of a suction against the smooth surface of the ski bottom. Wax for these conditions with a very hard wax which is applied roughly and left rough. Spring snow, on the other extreme, must be treated with a soft wax, applied heavily and smoothly with a waxing cork. As a matter of fact, it is better to melt the soft wax and paint it on with a brush. *Begin painting the wax at the heel of the ski and proceed toward the tip.* This painting method uses a good deal of wax in a hurry, but on the other hand you will have a better wax job when you finish.

Every skier should include a wax kit as part of his equipment. This kit should contain at least three kinds of wax for the two extremes in temperature and one average wax for more normal snow conditions.

Where to Mount Bindings

by Ernie McCulloch, Director, Mont Tremblant Ski School, Mont Tremblant, Quebec, Canada

If bindings are placed correctly on your skis, the sport becomes a good deal easier. Many skiers mount the bindings either too far forward or too far to the rear of the skis. Consequently, the ball of the foot fails to rest on the balance point of the ski, where it belongs. To correct this common mistake, I use a simple system of measurement which the average skier can also employ for everyday recreational skiing.

With the ski lying flat on the floor, measure it from tip to tail in a straight line. By that I mean do *not* measure the curve of the shovel or the camber of the bottoms. At a point half this measured distance, draw a line across the width of the ski. Place the toe of your boot one-quarter inch behind this line, providing your boot size is less than size nine. If your boot size is nine, place the toe right on the line. If you wear a size ten, it should be one-half inch in front of the center line; size 11 would go three quarters of an inch in front; and size 12 would go one inch in front of the line.

For ordinary skiing, this method is the best I have found. It works for ordinary slalom racing, too, unless your feet are unusually large. On giant slalom skis, however, I place the toe of my boot a full half inch behind the mid-length line. And on my downhill skis I move it back anywhere from an inch to an inch and a half.

Proper Weight of Poles

by Bob Bourdon, Sepp Ruschp Ski School, Stowe, Vt.

The purpose of ski poles is to make skiing easier for traveling, both uphill and downhill. Offhand, many beginners may not agree with this idea. It usually takes beginners some time before they learn to use their poles effectively for climbing and even longer for downhill skiing. Thanks to modern-day lifts, however, skiers no longer need do much climbing. But modern-day techniques place increasing emphasis on the use of poles in downhill skiing. In either case—climbing or skiing—there is little sense in laboring with overly heavy poles. The rule of thumb: *Use the lightest poles you can get.*

The average skier uses heavier poles than he ought to. This excess weight impedes his dexterity with them. The next time you watch a really good racer, notice how he uses his poles on every turn. The ease with which he uses them is due in large part to their lack of weight. He uses the lightest, strongest poles he can. When you are shopping for a new pair of ski poles, therefore, spend as much time checking their weight as you do their length.

A good way to test the weight of a pole, after deciding on the proper length, is to grip it in the normal manner. Then, raise the tip until the pole is horizontal with the ground. Holding it in this position, shake the pole until you begin to get the "feel" of it. Compare several sets of poles in this manner. Your choice should be that set which feels lightest, particularly at the tip. In addition, check the size of the basket. Find out what material it is made of. Often, an otherwise good pole may have a too heavy or too clumsy basket, in which case the basket can be changed.

The best basket material is cane, laced with leather strips. It is light and surprisingly long-lasting. Combined with a tonkin cane pole of quality, it offers the best ski pole money can buy. Sure, you can break a cane pole by sitting on it. But until a more rugged material of equal weight is developed, it will remain the top choice with most racers.

Metal poles are your next best choice. Some of these are reasonably light and strong. They will generally outlast cane poles, but they are also more expensive. By way of experiment, use a pair of cane poles one day, then switch to a pair of metal poles the next day. Notice how much heavier the metal ones seem.

Choose the lightest poles you can get, and learn to use them properly. It's a sure way to improve your technique and your enjoyment.

Strengthening Ski Poles

by Graham White, Certified Instructor, USEASA, Manager, Elk Mountain Ski Center, Uniondale, Pa.

In the conventional-type ski pole, where the ring is fastened to the shaft with a cotter pin and a leather strap, the part of the pole which usually breaks first, and annoyingly soon, is the area right around the cotter pin fastening. *It is possible to get much longer life from this fastening simply by removing the ring and replacing it in an inverted position on the pole.* In this way, the cotter pin will be above the ring. And with the ring in this position, the fragile part of the fastening will not receive wear and tear since the ring itself contacts the snow first, and the ring is obviously better suited to stand the abuse.

The above method of attaching pole rings not only makes them last longer, but has the desirable effect of adding length to the pole, since the point of the pole will not penetrate so deeply into the snow. Thus, an inch or two of height is added to the pole without adding any weight.

There is another advantage to be gained by reducing the length of the pole below the ring. It greatly reduces the strain on the pole shaft, which occurs when the pole is thrust into hard-packed snow as you walk and the handle of the pole is moved forward before the point is withdrawn. It also helps to end those annoying jerks which occur when you push off to ski and the pole fails to come clear of the snow immediately.

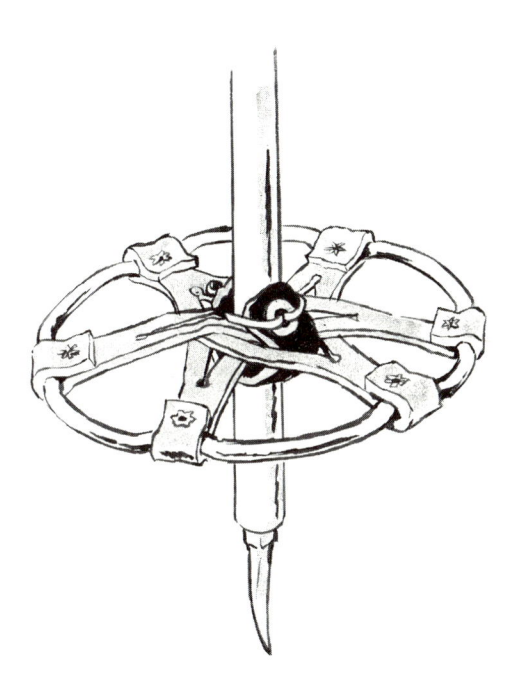

Repairing Broken Poles

by Jerry Mikacich, Certified Instructor, FWSIA, Edelweiss Ski School, Twin Bridges, Calif.

Two of the most common mishaps to ski poles are the breaking of the pole shaft and the loosening of the point. In many cases, you can make the repairs yourself.

There are two types of broken shafts. In the straight break, the broken ends of the pole can be joined together evenly at the point of the break. In the explosion break, the point of the break may be several inches long and the broken ends will not join evenly.

To repair a straight break, place a wooden dowel in the broken ski pole and glue the pole back together (Step 1). The dowel should fit snugly in place. Use wood glue for bamboo and cane poles, and liquid solder for metal poles. Now tape or wrap the break in the bamboo or cane pole with nylon thread (fishline). In metal poles, the break should be riveted (Step 2).

To repair an explosion break, place your good pole alongside the shattered one and cut out the shattered section of the broken pole. Angle the ends of the break (Step 1). Take a metal or bamboo insert from a discarded pole and angle the ends of the insert so that they match up with the broken ends of the pole. Place the glued wooden dowel through the insert and slip the dowel into the angle ends of the broken shaft (Step 2). Push the ends to meet the inserts and match the poles together. Dowel is glued in the same manner as the straight break repair. The pole can now be wrapped or riveted, making sure that two of the rivets are placed right through the angle of insert and the pole shaft (Step 3).

A lost pole point can be easily replaced. Plug the end of the pole (Step 1) and drill a small hole in the plug. Then screw in a wooden screw (Step 2) and grind the screw head to look like the point on your good pole (Step 3).

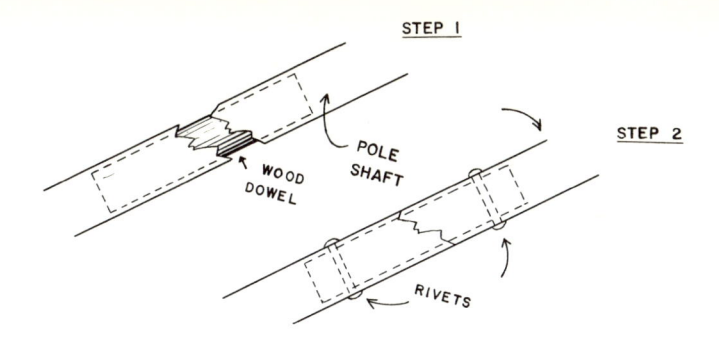

STEP 1

WOOD DOWEL
POLE SHAFT

STEP 2

RIVETS

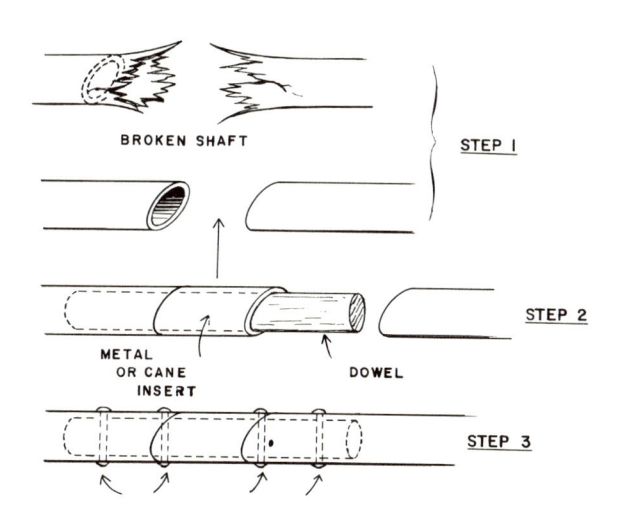

BROKEN SHAFT

STEP 1

METAL OR CANE INSERT
DOWEL

STEP 2

STEP 3

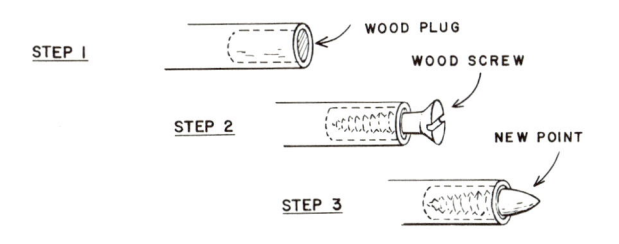

STEP 1
WOOD PLUG

STEP 2
WOOD SCREW
NEW POINT

STEP 3

Quick Tips for Comfort

by George Burgess, Certified Instructor, USEASA, Hannes Schneider Ski School, North Conway, N.H.

On snowy or rainy days, wet gloves can become a real problem to skiers. Here's a simple way to treat your gloves or mitts to prevent them from becoming sopping wet.

First, buy a cake of paraffin in your ski shop or grocery store. Then, making sure that your gloves or mitts are absolutely dry, slip on a glove and hold that hand over a stove or unit of your electric range. When the glove warms up (and this takes just a few moments, which is why you should not put the glove in the oven), start rubbing the cake of paraffin all over the glove. Work it in thoroughly, rewarming the glove from time to time. Don't be afraid to put on enough paraffin to have a really waxy surface, and keep renewing it from time to time throughout the season. This takes only a few moments and pays off in comfort.

Here is another tip for comfort. On very cold days, it is wiser to lace your ski boots looser than usual to prevent cold feet. If the boots are left loose enough to really do any good against the cold, however, the heel of you foot will slide up and down in the boot. To prevent this: use a heel lift. You can easily cut one out for yourself from a piece of sponge rubber. The lift, inserted under the heel of your foot, will raise your foot high enough in the boot to keep it snug and give you proper support, even when the boot is laced quite loosely. It is not necessary to glue this lift into the boot, since the pressure of your foot will hold the lift securely and comfortably in place.

How to Keep Goggles from Fogging

by Addison Augusta, Certified Ski Coach, USEASA, Hebron Academy, Maine

One of the quickest ways to ruin a good run down the mountain (and make yourself a candidate for an accident) is to have your goggles steam up like the inside of a Turkish bath. Fortunately, there is no need to put up with this irritation. The conventional-type flying goggle which most skiers now wear can be made virtually fog-proof.

The first step is to enlarge the vent holes in the sides of the goggle frames. Cut out the small pieces of rubber between the holes to make one long narrow opening instead of several small ones. This will increase air circulation inside the goggles.

The second step, and the real solution to the problem, is to take the clear plastic lens which comes with your lens set and insert it into the frame right along with the colored lens you are probably now using. (If you've thrown your clear plastic lens away, one can be purchased separately in any ski shop.) *The principle applied in using two lenses is exactly the same as that used in making Thermopane window glass.* A small insulating air space is trapped between the two layers of glass (or plastic) and this air space acts as a buffer between the temperature extremes. Slip both clear and colored lenses into the groove around the inside of the frames. If you have trouble fitting in both lenses, you can tape one lens onto the front of the goggle, making sure that there is no air leakage around the edges. If the holes for the snap fasteners that secure the lenses to the goggles should not line up exactly, new holes can be made by drilling with the point of a sharp penknife.

The color of your lenses is not directly connected with their tendency to fog, but color must be considered when two lenses are used. To keep visibility bright, my own preference is to use one clear lens and one amber or yellow. It should be obvious that those who combine two dark lenses may find that fogging was almost preferable to semidarkness.

SKI LIFE EXTRA

Getting Your Equipment in Shape
by Bill Beck, Former Olympic Racer and Coach

The foliage season has always been like a signal flare; it heralds the approach of another exciting winter of skiing. All too often, however, when the snowflakes actually arrive, they catch most skiers totally unprepared to face the first day on the slopes. Anticipation may be great, and ski talk fills many idle hours, but in the November rush of football games, a few last rounds of golf, or the coming holiday season, preparation for skiing is sadly lacking. A few more ambitious persons indulge in strenuous exercise programs, and the majority of skiers attempt conditioning knee bends to whip themselves quickly into shape. But what about equipment? The chances are that it has not been given a thought since the dust started collecting on it the previous spring.

The winter weekends ahead can be considerably more pleasurable if they are prepared for properly. Not only must the skier be in reasonably good physical condition to overcome early season fatigue, but equipment must also be at its best to deliver the utmost in enjoyment and to provide the maximum in safety precautions. A few well-spent hours working on your equipment now can mean untold satisfaction and safety later on, when you are hurrying off to your favorite ski area.

Although skis no longer need the maintenance they did in years gone by, they nevertheless require a quick inspection and minor check-up to assure perfect performance and to protect them from deterioration in the face of winter elements. Generally speaking, the more you paid for your skis initially, the less amount of work you will be compelled to do on them now. The fortunate owners of metal skis can expect to expend the least amount of energy on their equipment. Bottoms should be checked for noticeable gouges, which can be filled by plastic repair kits, available at any good ski shop. Undoubtedly the edges have picked up rust during summer storage; these should be cleaned with an oily cloth or steel wool. While working on edges, it is always advisable to square them up and sharpen them. Sharpening is achieved most easily by the use of an eight or ten-inch mill file. Work first along the surface of the edge and then at a 90-degree angle to the edge surface. Sharp edges are essential to controlled skiing, as is the elimination of the burrs on edges caused by hitting occasional rocks during the previous season. The chances are that there are no visible edge screws on your metal skis, but if there are, it is advisable to check their firmness with a suitable screw driver, possibly saving yourself lost edge sections later on.

The tops of metal skis usually need no vital attention. However, if you are concerned with their appearance, you may wish to take advantage of some of the ski polishes that are available for just this purpose, or you can use a more general-purpose wax to shine them up. For metal skis that have really been through the mill, many manufacturers offer factory refinishing or rebuilding services.

Enthusiasts of the wooden ski should expect to perform all the foregoing maintenance as well as a few additional checks. Most of the more costly models have plastic top edges which occasionally require sectional repairs. This can be achieved by the use of tube plastics, obtainable in assorted colors. Some manufacturers even offer the top plastic in strips which can be glued into place. This is particularly useful when the top edge strip is composed of more than one color.

The tops and sides of your skis should be adequately protected to prevent excessive moisture from penetrating the ski. If the tops are inadequately finished, or if you feel they need a face lifting, there are rugged plastic-based finishes now available which do an admirable job with a minimum of effort on both tops and sides.

Above all, don't neglect the running surface of your skis if you expect to get the greatest satisfaction and service from them. Generally, the more costly models will have a lifetime plastic sole which requires only occasional repairing of scratches or gouges. Some of the less expensive models, however, have thinner and less-permanent plastic coatings on the bottoms, which can literally wear out. These may require replacing if exceptional service is expected of them. Varying types of plastic bases are available which can be painted on as a replacement. Although not as durable and lasting as the better factory jobs, they are nevertheless quite satisfactory.

If your skis come with a plain wooden or lacquered bottom, as only the most economical skis do now, you might wish to try one of the packaged plastic bases on them. If you want the simplest application, regular ski lacquer is acceptable, but it should be applied in several coats for adequate protection.

Although ski warpage is considerably less of a problem now than it used to be, thanks to superior laminated wood and metal construction, it is still an item that should be checked. Sometimes only a slight warp can make skiing difficult, and any significant warpage can render a ski practically uncontrollable.

Since nearly all skiers now use some form of release binding, it is imperative that these be checked, if for no other reason than safety alone. Many of the release-type bindings have moving parts which should be inspected for corrosion and wear, and which should be cleaned and properly greased or oiled periodically. If you are contemplating buying new boots this winter, don't forget that your bindings will probably need readjusting to accommodate the new boots. Even if you are resigned to your old boots for another year, it is a good idea to check the binding adjustment. The top of a lonely mountain on a sub-zero December day can be a highly frustrating place to readjust a release binding!

Boots should get a going-over along with your other equipment. Check for mildew caused by dampness, and treat the boots to several layers of good shoe polish. An application of sole and seam sealer will also keep destructive moisture out. Repair of severed stitching can prolong the life of a ski boot considerably, and the insertion of new laces will prevent a struggle with knots later on.

Even ski poles should get consideration in a preseason equipment check. Are the wrist straps secure? Are the grips, if they have stitching, in condition to last another season? The loss of a pole ring can be most annoying, yet can easily happen if it is worn out or inadequately attached. A tight cotter pin will prevent this.

Perhaps one of the most neglected pieces of equipment in a skier's possession is his automobile rack, and yet it takes only a few minutes to make it as good as new. Many racks come with rubber attachment devices or suction cups. Since rubber deteriorates, it is always wise to replace these parts every few years, if necessary, to provide trouble-free service. Another cause for irritation can be the sponge rubber used for padding on many racks, which often has a habit of coming unglued.

To be completely prepared for the first snowfall, with proper equipment as well as physical conditioning, it is necessary to spend a little get-ready time right *now*. If you don't have the do-it-yourself aptitude, or cannot spare the necessary time, an experienced ski shop can accommodate your needs. But regardless of who does the work, make sure that all your equipment is in first-class shape—ready for the season ahead.

Check List for Equipment

SKIS:
Repair plastic bottoms
Replace edge sections
Clean edges
File edges
Polish tops of skis
Replace top strips
Check for warpage

BINDINGS:
Oil moving parts
Check release adjustment

BOOTS:
Apply shoe polish
Apply sole-and-seam sealer
Replace laces

POLES:
Secure wrist straps
Check stitching on grips
Secure pole rings

AUTOMOBILE RACKS:
Check rubber suction cups
Reglue sponge rubber padding

VIII. *Pre-season Conditioning*

Proper conditioning is one of the most important and most neglected aspects of skiing. The exercises that follow were chosen by top coaches and experts for their special emphasis on strengthening muscles most subject to the rigors of the sport.

Coach Yourself into Shape

by Tap Goodenough

Throughout the United States, hundreds of college racers train for the coming season by sprinting, running up and down hills, working on trampolines, lifting weights, and doing calisthenics. By contrast, millions of recreational skiers, eagerly awaiting the first snowfall, do relatively little to get into shape.

To emulate, in moderation, what the collegians do each year, *Ski Life* contacted ski coaches in various sections of the country—Ed Blood, of the University of New Hampshire, a former Olympic jumper; Sven Wiik, coach at Western State College in Colorado, who prepped our Olympic cross-country racers; Fred Lonsdorf, ski coach at Michigan College of Mining and Technology; and Chelton Leonard, of the University of New Hampshire—for their favorite warmup exercises.

In addition, here is helpful advice from Allison Merrill, of Dartmouth College. "While recreational skiers don't need to train as hard as racers, for those of all ages I advocate as much walking as possible. Don't ride in elevators before or during the ski season." Middlebury College coach Robert "Bobo" Sheehan agrees. "Even if you ski for fun only, a little jogging is a fine way to limber up." Robert Beck, coach at Montana State College, advocates rapid sequences of squat bends for everyone, in addition to plenty of bending exercises and use of the trampoline.

And here is one universal exercise for both competitive and recreational skiers: "When faced with starchy foods at meals, don't push up, don't push down; push *AWAY* from the table!"

Coach Ed Blood, of the University of New Hampshire, recommends:

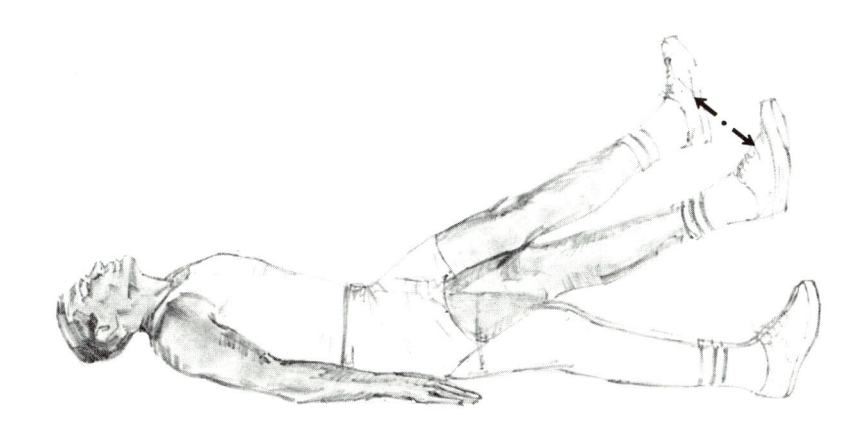

Strengthen abdomen: Lie flat on your back and raise your legs up about two feet off the floor. Spread them slowly apart, bring them slowly back together, then slowly down again. Repeat exercise ten to twenty times.

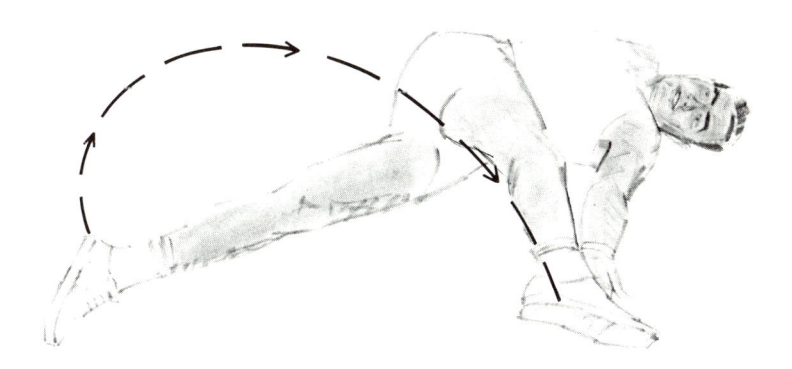

Hip limbering: Stretch out on your back, flat on the floor, arms out at sides. Alternating, cross one leg over the other, then try to touch your left hand with right foot, and your right hand with left foot. Increase to ten to fifteen times.

Coach Sven Wiik, of Western State College, recommends:

Strengthen legs: Stand with feet six inches apart, arms forward. Bend knees so that seat touches heels. Bob once, then jump up. Repeat five to ten times.

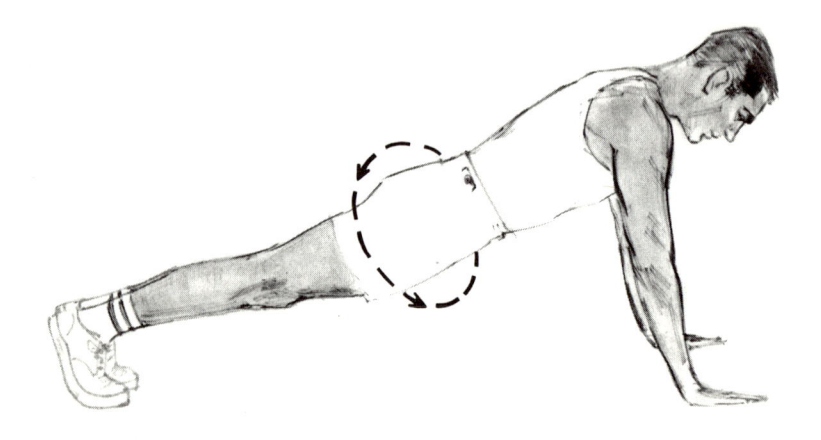

Pushups: Do ten pushups in a fast tempo. Keep moving your hands closer to each other. In the same position, roll your hips.

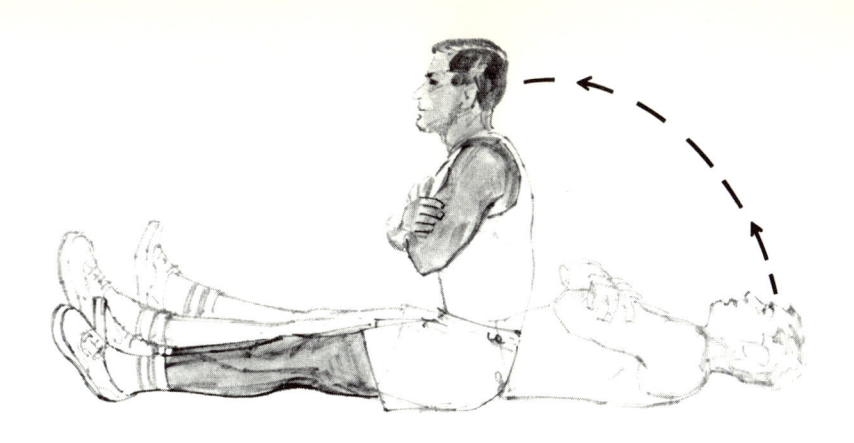

Front roll to sitting stance: Lie flat and quickly lift legs fifteen inches to a V position. Sit up without touching floor with hands. Lower body back to floor. Repeat this five to ten times.

Coach Chelton Leonard, of the University of Nevada, recommends:

Knee pushups: With aid of wall, stand on ball of one foot, leaning forward. Keep heel on floor and push knee forward. Slowly rise on toe until knee is straight. Knee should describe imaginary circle. Now repeat pushup with the other foot.

Coach Fred Lonsdorf, of Michigan Tech, recommends:

Strengthen tendons: Standing with your feet together, bounce on ankles turned far left and then far right. Then alternate by turning your ankles in and out. Now, with heels flat, bend your knees in an extreme forward position and bounce up and down keeping hand pressure on the knees. (This latter position should resemble a squat.) Repeat whole series.

SKI POINTERS ON CONDITIONING

Warm-up Exercises

by Rudy Kuersteiner, Director, Snow Ridge Ski School, Turin, N.Y.

Year after year a great number of skiers get hurt at the tops of trails and slopes. The reason: stiff bones and cold muscles from the long ride up the lift do not respond quickly. This can be easily counteracted, and your skiing made safer, by doing some rigorous exercising before starting on any descent. Here are a few simple exercises to benefit all skiers.

For the *novice*—assume a wide snow-plow position on flat ground and plant the poles near the ski tips. Keeping the ski tips on the snow, move the heels of the skis together and apart again with quick successive lifting motions. It is important that arms and poles be kept in one straight line, so that the maximum support from the poles will prevent sliding forward. Open and close the skis from five to ten times at short intervals.

For *intermediates*—stand in a traverse position on a moderately steep slope. Drop into a crouch with knees forward and into the hill. Unweight the skis completely with a strong lifting motion and, simultaneously, hop both skis downhill about five to ten inches, landing well on the edges to prevent sliding. Repeat several hops in quick succession, keeping skis pointed across the slope. Practice in both directions.

For *advanced skiers*—successive one-pole jump turns are muscle-warming. Landing should be low, with knees pressed into hill to prevent sliding. Each turn should be followed immediately by another. Do five to ten of these at short intervals. Relaxing the body and continuous motion are essential to achieve best warm-up results. These exercises will not only safeguard against injury but will permit greater enjoyment out of each and every run.

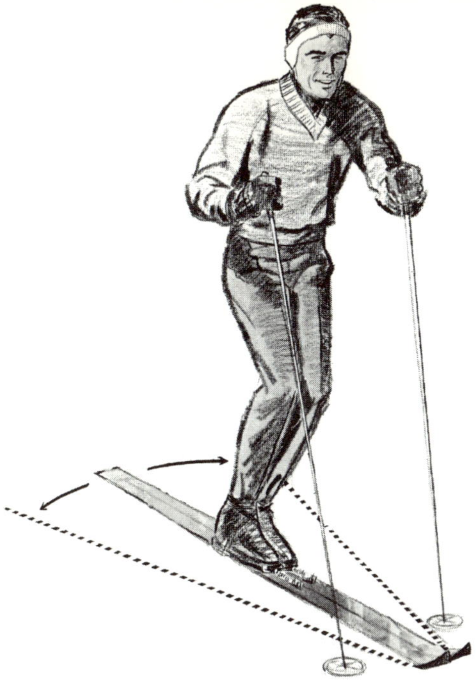

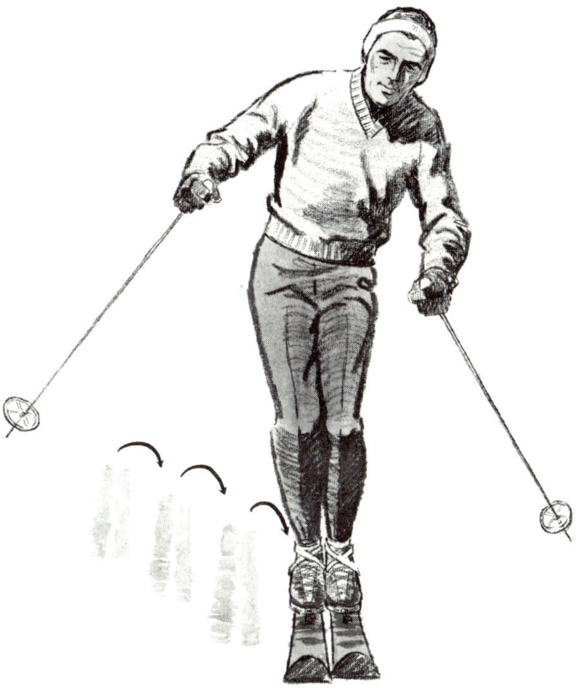

First Run of the Day

by Rick Shambroom, Certified Instructor, CSIA

You can make your entire day's skiing more enjoyable by using a few simple tricks on your first run. The idea is this: make a conscious effort to get the feel of the snow and your skis, warm up your muscles, and boost your confidence.

Before you start your first run of the day, try some warm-up exercises. Skiing is one of the few sports in which the participants use practically every muscle in the body without first warming up. Winter temperatures don't help to loosen up your muscles, either. Even two or three minutes of exercise will be worth your time in added enjoyment. Try a few deep knee bends with heels flat on your skis, or touching your toes with knees straight, or twisting the upper body to the right and left. Better still, ski down fifteen or twenty yards and climb back up.

Pick a trail or slope that you can handle without pushing your ability. Resist the temptation to take one of the tough runs on the mountain, even though your friends implore you to join them. You'll feel better if you are not "challenged" on your first run.

As you start down the slope, make a series of rapid turns close to the fall line. *Pick an imaginary point part way down the slope and see how many turns you can make between your starting spot and that imaginary point.* This will have the effect of forcing you into a rhythm, certainly one of the keys to graceful skiing.

Try skating on your skis. Besides being a wonderful exercise in balance, skating is a good means of getting the feel of your skis. Make a few hop christies, if they are part of your repertoire. Or stop at the side of the slope out of the way of other skiers, and jump as high as you can, landing as gently as you can. The emphasis here is on easy landing. This will give your knees a more flexible feeling.

Confidence is an integral part of the novice and intermediate skiers' ability. You will find it worth while to make your first run of the day on one of the easier slopes where you can warm up properly. Experts, even at their high level of ability, take warm-up runs.

SKI LIFE EXTRA

Confessions of an October Backslider
by Merrill Pollack

Until recently it had never occurred to me that escalators in railroad stations had any significant relationship to skiing. Child of our technology that I am, I'd always assumed that escalators were the best invention since stairs. It seems now that I've built my life on an untenable premise. While my proposition holds true for ordinary mortals, I've been put on notice that this attitude is disgraceful for anyone who thinks of himself as a skier.

My enlightenment came one evening after work when I was strolling to the suburban station with a fellow named George. Our conversation dwelt on the approach of October, that dreadfully frustrating month when summer is finally over and winter hasn't yet begun. We agreed that October was the limbo month, when, statistically speaking, more skiers are likely to go out of their minds than at any other time of the year.

This heady intellectual exchange had us in excellent spirits by the time we reached the railroad station. But, once inside the doors of the station, it disappeared abruptly. George automatically headed for the long flight of stairs up to the trains—at least three stories high—while I, just as automatically, headed for the adjacent escalator. He looked at me in surprise as he trotted upward, keeping pace with the escalator. I looked at him with incredulity.

"Why are you riding?" he demanded.

"Why are you walking?" I demanded.

We were moving upward about three miles per hour, George beginning to go red in the face and blowing a little, I poised, unruffled, the picture of a true man of the world, master of my fate.

"How . . . in . . . hell . . . do . . . you . . . expect . . . to . . . get . . . your . . . ski . . . legs . . . in . . . shape . . . if . . . you . . . don't . . . climb . . . stairs?" George asked, getting his words out in a series of little puffs.

"Good Lord, man," I replied, "how do *you* expect to have any legs left for skiing if you abuse them climbing stairs so recklessly?"

"Don't give me that," George panted. "Good exercise. Running up stairs . . . running up hills . . . best thing skier . . . can do before the snow actually . . . comes."

He fell behind a bit at this point and had to put on a burst of speed in order to come alongside so he could hear my answer.

"Listen, son," I informed him. "A couple of years back, when I was working on the fourteenth floor of an office building, the elevator operators went on strike. I had to hike up and down those stairs twice a day for a week. By my calculations, my legs got enough conditioning during that strike to last me for the next twenty years."

"Helluva . . . skier . . . you . . . are . . . with that . . . attitude," George sneered. "You're . . . lazy . . . you'll never . . . amount . . . to . . . any . . . thing."

I had to turn at this point because George was losing ground again. "I'll bet you do deep knee bends and pushups, too," I flung down the stairwell. "And ride bicycles and run in place, and—" At this point I subsided; the people near me on the escalator were eying me nervously and George was too far behind to hear, anyway.

I waited for him at the top of the escalator. When he came heaving up to join me, his face was the color of Wonder Red wax—whether from annoyance or exertion I could not decide.

"Of . . . course . . . I exercise . . . regularly," George snarled. "Don't . . . you?"

"Certainly not. What a ridiculous idea!"

He shook his head despairingly. "You're a disgrace . . . to skiing. If you don't . . . spend . . . all of . . . October . . . exercising . . . like crazy . . . I guarantee . . . you'll make . . . yourself . . . the laughingstock . . . of the slopes."

"Tut, my boy," I answered nonchalantly. "I can demonstrate beyond the shadow of a doubt that the absolute contrary is true, that situps do not skiers make, that—"

George never did stay to hear my learned dissertation. He glanced at his watch, gasped that he had a minute left to catch his train, and took off in a staggering, lurching sprint that left me filled with admiration.

After dinner that night, still reflecting on George's admirable physical condition and his dire prophecies, I began feeling guilty. Was he right? Was I going to waste October and end up a blob of jelly, a comic spectacle in the snow? An abominable snowman?

"No!" I cried. And, summoning my four children—three girls and a boy, ranging in age from seven and a half down to 11 months—I lined us all up for a session of pre-skiing exercises. Pushups first. "Hup, hup, hup," I chanted in cadence, pumping up and down to show them how easy it was.

After I'd done two pushups the floor seemed to turn red and the carpet leaped up and hit me in the face. "Beer!" I groaned and my eldest, always clear-headed in emergencies, dashed off and returned in a moment with the life-saving brew. I quaffed it and soon felt marvelously well, tingling with life, glowing with a sudden insight.

George was right and so was I. George is militant; I am not. Live and let live. George and all the other dedicated skiers of this earth can go right ahead and spend October in violent exercise. I give them my blessing. Being just as dedicated to skiing but of a more mental turn of mind, I shall spend October *thinking* about my muscles and form. After all, skiing is not accomplished by brute strength. Skiing is control, skiing is grace. My mind controls my body, does it not? How many people run up snow-covered hills, anyway? Who wants to do pushups while wearing skis?

So, having solved in my own fashion the problem of exercises, I feel spiritually ready to cope with some of the other aggravations that face all skiers in the grim, bleak month of October.

Part of my time shall be spent contemplating the bottoms of all the skis in the house. October is the time to remove all traces of old wax, examine the lacquer or plastic base, check the condition of edges, tighten screws. If the bottoms are sufficiently battered, one should scrape the skis down to the bare wood, sand the surface to a glassy sheen, then apply a new base. I know all about these niceties; many winters ago I worked in a ski shop and did these things day after day. During that one season I serviced something like three hundred pairs of skis and got out skiing about three times. That kind of experience leaves permanent scars on the soul.

So I shall spend some hours thinking about the millions of skiers industriously working on their skis and I shall smile, Buddha-like, at those belonging to me and mine. One mustn't be carried away in matters of this sort. Six years ago I applied a plastic base to all our skis. That original base still remains, dented and scraped and, here and there, gouged and chipped. One of my skis has a six-inch longitudinal split up near the toe; it's held together by a few small pieces of edging; it makes a lovely chattering sound whenever I go downhill. I wouldn't give it up for anything, and I won't repair or modify the other skis, either. This is not because of perversity. I simply refuse to offend the gods again. This requires explanation.

There's an old Japanese legend to the effect that some craftsmen used to do such superb work that the gods became jealous and heaped all manner of punishments on their heads; ever since, the craftsmen have been careful to leave one obvious flaw in every piece of work they do. Now, as I have indicated, I'm something of a craftsman in the ski renovation line. That longitudinal split I mentioned a moment ago occurred *after* the last refurbishing job I did on my skis. The lesson is clear to me, even if it baffles my skiing friends. Clearly, that last work I did on the skis was too good. My attitude now is one of caution; don't stir up those thin-skinned gods. It's all right to fill a nick here, a gouge there and tighten screws and the like. I may even go so far as to run a dust-cloth over the boards and sandpaper the rust off the edges, but beyond that I dare not go. I don't want invisible and jealous Furies tossing me into wild eggbeaters when I'm up on the slopes.

Late fall is the time, of course, when department stores and ski shops put all the new equipment on display. October Saturdays are excellent for touring the shops, with or without *famille*. Year after year I've done the rounds, a connoisseur of the beautiful, an eager seeker after the new and sometimes goofy gear. Because I feel obligated to keep up with new developments, it behooves me to test each unfamiliar item I see. Sometimes this is dangerous. One year I nearly threw a hip out of joint while trying out a gadget that enables one to practice ski turns indoors. Another time I mashed a thumb while checking the tension of a rear-throw cable binding. Once I pulled a tendon trying to pull a ski boot out of a sample safety binding that had been adjusted too tightly. One must be philosophical.

Whenever I see a new brand of ski I feel compelled to check its springy qualities. This is easily done if you wedge the heel of the ski into a corner, grasp it by its middle and tip and wiggle it back and forth. This is legitimate research, but some ski salesmen don't seem to understand. In fact, there's one shop I won't go to any more because they don't have the right attitude about such investigations. It's not that I'm any more thin-skinned than the next fellow, but my skier's integrity was challenged there. I had been testing skis contentedly for an hour or so when a salesman hove into view, eyed the clutter of skis around me and watched anxiously as I whipped a metal job back and forth.

"You plannin' to buy somethin' or are you just exercising?" he asked nastily.

I fingered the money in my pocket—about a dollar and a half, as I recall—and informed him that I might or might not buy, depending.

"What'd you have in mind, bub?" he demanded.

"A perfect ski," I retorted.

He said something that sounded like "Arrgghh," and began picking up skis and returning them to the racks. He was muttering as he worked and I leaned close to listen in: "For eight years this clown has been coming in here," he mumbled, "tryin' out every blankety-blank thing in the place, an' I've yet to see him shell out more than a buck . . ."

"Sirrah!" I barked.

"Listen, Mac," he barked back, *"All* of these skis is perfect! Don't 'sirrah' me!"

"Not one of them comes close in quality to the ones I have home," I shot back. "Sirrah!" And, with that, I stalked out, having put the cur in his place.

I tell this little tale not to parade my *savoir-faire* in awkward situations, but merely because it may serve as a guide of sorts to skiers who share my passion for studying the new merchandise and who, like myself, can't be bothered with carrying large sums on their persons.

Once the October skier has checked the new equipment, he owes it to himself to study the new clothing styles, too. After-ski wear is more gorgeous than ever before, I see. And the skiing outfits are now so beautifully tailored that a skier standing still gives the illusion of hurtling downhill at terrific speed. Admirable. Dramatic. Stretch pants are part of the secret. They're comfortable and rugged. But, alas, they're not able to cope with every bulge and blob of time. The saddest story I've heard recently concerns a man whose hips and tummy stretched farther and faster than the capacity of last year's stretch pants. The poor fellow got absolutely nowhere trying to use the pants as a down-payment on a new model.

As for myself, I'm all set. I see no reason to give up my twelve-year-old woolen navy blue trousers, venerable but still elegant; my ten-year-old plaid shirt, and, newer, my navy blue nylon parka and my flaming red sweater. These garments, along with my ankle-length 10th Mountain Division camouflage coat and my Canadian tam-o-shanter (a lovely creation of green, blue, purple, orange, red and yellow) will see me through rain or sleet or snow or hail. And, I have a new sartorial triumph, knitted for me by my affectionate wife. It's a scarf made of multicolored wool—red, orange, yellow, green, blue and violet—and it looks like a rainbow having a case of hiccups. Eye-catching. I guarantee there won't be anything like it on the slopes.

Now it seems to me I've outlined a fairly stimulating program for the month of October. If you pace yourself correctly you can so clutter up your mind that November—and the first snowfall—seems but a moment away. I know very well that some skiers champ at the bit and at the first report of snow, however light, jump into their cars and speed far to the north just for a look at the wonderful stuff. They see one snowflake and jump up and down, babbling excitedly. Not me. My standards are more exacting; I never go north to look at the stuff until I can wallow in it.

Awaiting that moment, I spend my evenings pursuing civilized recreations. Wearing my ski clothing, I settle in before a roaring log fire, surrounded by back issues of skiing magazines. It's always intellectually stimulating to browse through them. When that pales, I always turn to the family photo album to look at snapshots taken on previous ski trips. Before the children are sent to bed we all enjoy a hearty session singing ski songs. It's fun to reread my collection of old snow reports. At least once each night I telephone the weather bureau to ask what the chances are for snow. If one of the ski clubs is putting on an evening of ski movies, or a fashion show, I'll always venture out. It's pleasant to memorize all the words on all the brochures I've saved from ski resorts and lodges I've visited over the last eighteen years. I keep abreast of snow reports from ski areas in the Alps, in Chile and the Himalayas, promising myself that someday, when I'm a bit ahead financially, I'll dash over for a quick weekend, just to get my legs in shape. Until then, I can always use my time profitably, studying road maps and planning routes to every area within a 3,000-mile radius of my home. It keeps my spirits up, too, to telephone my skiing friends often and ask them what they think the chances are of snow . . .

Really, it's all very simple, this business of surviving the month of October. I can't imagine why skiers make such a foofooraw about it. After all, November is one of the shorter months; it lasts only thirty years.

GLOSSARY OF SKIING TERMS

Abstem   An opening of the tail of the downhill ski away from the parallel position.

Arlberg   Mountain region of Austria which fathered the classic Arlberg and the modern Austrian techniques. The former stresses rotation, the latter reverse shoulder.

Arlberg strap   A strap attached to the ski or binding which, when wrapped around the boot and ankle, furnishes support and keeps a loose ski from running away.

Base   A firm layer of hard-packed snow immediately covering frozen ground, necessary to prevent skis from cutting through to bare ground. Also, a protective layer of lacquer or plastic covering the running surface of the ski.

Boiler plate   A hard sheet of ice that results when a deep freeze sets in after a warming period.

Camber   The upward arch or bow in a ski that provides flexibility and carries the skier's weight.

Chairlift   A means of uphill transportation consisting of a series of moving chairs suspended from a cable. A chair accommodates one or two skiers.

Check   Any maneuver used to slow down the movement of skis.

Christie   Short for "Christiania," the basic turning maneuver in modern intermediate or advanced skiing. In any form of christie, the skis must be in a parallel position as the turn is completed.

Comma   The angulated body position used in modern reverse shoulder skiing. In the traverse position, knees are pressed into the hill, upper body is centered over the downhill ski, with downhill shoulder drawn back, giving appearance of a comma.

Corn   A snow type, found in spring or warm weather, formed by alternate freezing and thawing. Its honey-combed structure permits easy turning.

CSIA   Canadian Ski Instructors Alliance, the association of ski instructors which sets standards of instruction and certifies professional ski teachers in Canada.

CUSSA   Central United States Ski Association.

Downhill   In racing, one of the three basic forms of Alpine competition in which skiers compete against time on a downhill run, following the natural terrain of the trail, restricted only by occasional control gates.

Downhill ski   In any ski maneuver, the lower ski or the one which will become the lower ski upon completion of the maneuver.

Edging   A control method to prevent or arrest the slipping action of the skis by application of steel edges into the snow.

Fall line   The imaginary line marking the shortest route down a slope.

FIS   Fédération Internationale de Ski, the international ski federation that supervises organized skiing and regulates international competition.

Flush   An arrangement of slalom gates containing three or more closed gates in a tight series.

Frozen granular   A snow type composed of tiny crystals of frozen snow, often confused with ice.

FWSA   Far West Ski Association.

Garland   An exercise in which skis are alternately slipped downhill and traversed across hill. Variations are stem garlands, sideslip garlands, etc.

Gate   An arrangement of two flags or markers through which a skier must pass in a race. Gates are usually set in various combinations or figures to comprise a slalom course and are also used as controls in downhill and giant slalom racing. Various figures include single gates (open or closed), hairpins, flushes, and H-gates.

Geländesprung   An airborne maneuver used to clear obstacles or bumps, performed by springing into the air, using both poles for support.

Giant slalom   A basic form of Alpine racing which combines the elements of downhill and slalom competition. Usually a controlled downhill race into which several series of gates have been set.

Glühwein   A hot spiced wine drink, popular after skiing.

Gondola   A means of uphill transportation consisting of a moving enclosed car suspended from a cable.

Heel thrust   The act of releasing edges and pushing the tails of skis down the hill before, during, or after a maneuver.

Herringbone   A basic method of climbing on skis, performed by placing each ski up the hill in alternate steps, maintaining an inverted V position and using poles for support.

ISA   Intermountain Ski Association.

J-bar   A ski lift for uphill transportation consisting of a series of J- or L-shaped bars attached to a moving overhead cable. The skier leans against the bar and is pulled uphill.

Kandahar   Famous Austrian ski trail after which several international racing events are named.

Kick turn   A method of reversing direction while standing on skis. Performed only from a stationary position.

Leash   A strap, cord, or Arlberg strap used to retain skis after they have been released by a release binding.

Lift line   A queue of skiers waiting to load onto a ski lift. Also, a common designation for a trail descending directly under a ski lift.

Long thong   A long leather strap-type binding that winds around the boot, which provides support and holds the skier firmly to his skis.

Mambo   An exaggerated style of skiing with flattened skis, utilizing a hip-wiggling, rhythmic motion and delayed countermovement.

Mashed potatoes   Heavy, wet snow resulting from the melting action of warm weather. Usually sticky and hard to ski.

Mogul   A mound of snow created by the displacement of snow as one skier after another follows a track and turns in the same spot. Usually occurs on steeper slopes after a heavy snowfall.

NRMSA   Northern Rocky Mountain Ski Association.

NSA   National Ski Association, the parent organization of organized skiing in America. A member of the FIS, it has seven regional divisions throughout the country.

NSPS   National Ski Patrol System, a nationwide organization of volunteer skiers, trained in first aid and winter rescue procedures. Associated with NSA, it promotes ski safety and administers aid to disabled skiers on the slopes.

Parallel christie   An advanced turn in which both skis remain together throughout the entire execution of the turn.

Piste   A ski trail.

PNSA   Pacific Northwest Ski Association.

Pomalift   A means of uphill transportation consisting of a disc affixed to a long steel bar. The skier straddles the disc and is pulled up the hill. Poma bars are not attached to the overhead cable until the skier is loaded.

Powder   A snow type, usually found in cold weather after a fresh snowfall, composed of light, dry flakes.

Pre-jump   A maneuver, similar to a geländesprung, in which the skis are lifted into the air on the uphill side of a bump or mogul, before the crest is reached. Permits the skier to land on the smooth, downhill side of the bump.

Release binding   A modern mechanism for affixing the ski boot to the ski, designed to permit the boot to be thrown free of the ski when a desired degree of stress, tension, or twist is exceeded.

Reverse shoulder   A style of skiing in which the upper body faces down the slope or, therefore, to the outside of a turn, as opposed to the older style of rotation. The lower body twists in opposition to the upper body, giving a "reverse shoulder" appearance.

Rope tow   A means of uphill transportation consisting of a moving rope. The skier grasps the rope and is pulled up the hill.

Rotation   Usually connotes the classic, Arlberg style of skiing in which a turn is initiated by a rotating motion of the shoulders and upper body in the direction of the turn. The lower body follows the action of the upper body toward the inside of the turn.

Royal christie   An advanced maneuver in which the outside ski is lifted high off the snow as the turn is executed on the inside ski.

Ruade   A turning maneuver performed by retracting the ski tails off the snow and pivoting around on the tips, especially useful in deep snow or on steep slopes.

Rücklage   Literally a "backward leaning" or shifting of the weight.

Safety binding   A misnomer. See "Release binding."

Schmieren   A style of skiing keeping skis flattened while turning. Edges are not used.

Schrittbogen   A style of skiing in which the tail of the inside ski is lifted off the snow during a turn, permitting a complete shift of weight to it when it is replaced on the snow during the succeeding turn. Literally, a "step turn," which it resembles.

Schuss   Skiing straight down the fall line, without turns or checks.

Short swing   The basic appearance of modern wedeln, so called because of the short, swinging motion of ski tails from side to side during the maneuver. (See Wedeln.) Also known as *Kurzschwingen*.

Sideslip   A slipping of the skis sideways down a slope by flattening the skis.

Sitzmark   The impression made in the snow by a fallen skier.

"Ski!"   A warning cry, indicating that a loose ski is coming down the hill.

Slalom   A basic form of Alpine competition in which a racer must descend a course designated by a series of slalom gates, set singly or in combinations, passing through each gate successively.

Snow bunny   A new or beginning skier.

Snow plow   A fundamental maneuver for controlling speed or stopping at slow speeds, in which the heels are pushed out, bringing the skis to a V position.

Snow-plow turn   A fundamental maneuver for turning at slow speeds, performed in a snow-plow position with the weight shifted to one ski.

Spring conditions   A snow reporting term used to designate a condition in which, due to temperature variations, surface characteristics change continually. Usually found in warm or spring weather when surfaces change from ice or frozen granular in the early morning to granular, corn, or mashed potatoes at midday, then back to frozen granular or ice as the temperature drops again.

SRMSA   Southern Rocky Mountain Ski Association.

Stem   An opening of the tail of the uphill ski away from the parallel position.

Stem christie   An intermediate turn in which one ski is stemmed to facilitate weight shift. At the start and completion of the turn, the skis are parallel.

Stem turn   A basic turn in which both skis are stemmed into a snow-plow position during the turn. It is started and ended from a traverse position with skis parallel. Also known as an Advanced Snowplow Turn or a Double Stem Turn.

T-bar   A ski lift for uphill transportation consisting of a series of T-shaped bars attached to a moving overhead cable. The skier leans against the cross bar and is pulled up the hill.

Traverse   Travel across a slope.

Turntable   A swiveling plate incorporated into a binding, usually under the boot heel, to facilitate the release of the boot in a fall.

Ullr   The ancient Norse god of winter.

Unweighting   The momentary removal of weight from the tail of the skis to permit the execution of a maneuver.

Uphill ski   In any ski maneuver, the ski which is on or will end up on the uphill side of the skier.

USEASA   United States Eastern Amateur Ski Association.

Vorlage   A forward leaning or shifting of the weight.

Warp   A lateral twist in a ski.

Wax   A preparation applied to the running surface of a ski to facilitate its movement and to reduce friction with the snow.

Wedeln   An advanced skiing style utilizing a continuous series of short parallel turns down the fall line unbroken by traversing.

Weighting   The act of applying weight to the skis.